THE EXPERIMENT AS A SOCIAL OCCASION

Paul L. Wuebben
University of Tennessee

Bruce C. Straits
University of California, Santa Barbara

Gary I. Schulman
University of California, Santa Barbara

⊂⊃The Glendessary Press, Inc.
Berkeley, California

ISBN Number 0-87709-220-6 paper
0-87709-720-8 cloth
Library of Congress Number 73-88641

Printed in the United States of America.
First printing January 1974

Table of Contents

Preface

While the title of this book is *The Experiment as a Social Occasion,* it might also have been called "The Social Psychology of Experimental Research with Human Subjects," or "The Sociology and Psychology of Experiments." As each of these designations implies, the theme of the book is the social interaction which accompanies, and takes place during, the execution of an experiment in the social sciences. Interest in this area of study has been given impetus both by the substance of the field per se—social psychologists and others are interested in social interaction processes whatever the occasion of their occurrence—and by a growing concern about the effects social interaction may have on experimental findings.

The social psychology of experimental situations, broadly defined, has a long history. However, the explicit recognition and active study of social factors in experimentation is a relatively recent phenomenon. This book brings together a set of reprinted articles which, we believe, represent the major perspectives within this field. In the original essays which precede the reprinted articles we have attempted to structure work in the social psychology of the experiment in terms of its relationship to the fundamental logic of the experimental method of research. Thus, the first two of our essays provide a brief statement about the nature of experimentation in the social sciences and our third essay discusses the relevance of social features of the experiment to basic assumptions of the experimental method. Our concluding essay critically examines a number of the strategies which have been proposed as solutions to the problems raised by social factors in experiments.

We wish to thank the authors and the publishers of the articles reprinted. We wish also to thank, and absolve from any responsibility for our errors, Professors John Baldwin, Douglas A. Bernstein, John W. Cotton, Donald A. Hansen, Rae R. Newton, Thomas P. Wilson, and Don Zimmerman, all of whom read earlier drafts of this book.

The order of authorship of this book was determined by a random selection device; the product represents truly equal contributions by each of the authors.

Part One
INTRODUCTION

1
The Logic
Of Experimentation*

In this chapter we will examine the logic of the experimental method. We will not be concerned with different types of experimental designs nor with the kinds of statistical procedures used in analyzing data from experiments. Rather we will discuss the *basic* assumptions common to all experimental designs. We hope to make clear to the reader the reasons why most scientists believe that experimentation is a primary method of testing causal relationships.

CAUSAL THINKING IN SCIENCE

Most scholars would agree that the most general goal of any science is the discovery or invention of "order" in the phenomena with which it deals. At the most elementary level, a science seeks to order its phenomena by developing schemes of classification which reliably distinguish one thing or event from another; biologists, for example, have schemes which classify forms of life. Other, more complex, kinds of order are exemplified in the various sciences (Cohen and Nagel, 1934, ch. 13). But the kind of order most commonly

*References cited in this chapter may be found in the bibliography.

thought of as distinctively the product of a scientific enterprise is "causal" order.

Most people would probably agree that what they have in mind when they say "x causes y" is that a change in x "produces" a change in y. That is, there exists in the real world some process or mechanism by which a change in x *necessarily forces* a change in y. But even though the notion of "cause" is intuitively clear, scientists and others have experienced great difficulty in precisely explicating just what is meant when we say "x is a cause of y." It would be inappropriate to engage in any extended discussion of the complicated concept of "cause" in this book. However, as we shall see, experiments make their major contribution to scientific knowledge by virtue of their providing "best" evidence for causal relationships. A brief discussion is therefore in order.

It has been known ever since Hume's famous treatise *An Inquiry Concerning Human Understanding* that the "common sense" notion of cause cannot be maintained in simple form. For when we look closely at what scientists *observe* when they do empirical research, we see that they never achieve direct evidence relevant to the *production* of a change in y by x. What they *can* observe is that in the "real world" a change in y *is associated with* a change in x under specified conditions. That is, they can observe the temporal relationship between two variables (for example, x always occurs before y); they can observe the form of the relationship between two variables (when x is made to be relatively high in value, y is found to be relatively low in value); and they can make these observations any number of times under various conditions and note the results (the relationship between x and y is invariant—it turns out to be the same each time we look at it). Note what is missing: it is not possible for the scientist to observe x "producing" a change in y. The scientist can never make empirical observations that reveal that a change in x "must," either logically or metaphysically, "produce" a change in y.[1]

[1] For a more complete discussion of these points, see Blalock (1961).

This seems to leave us in what appears to be an intellectually uncomfortable position. For if all we can observe are empirical relationships between variables, must we not admit to the class of relationships we call "causal" a number of relationships which do not seem to belong there? For example, winter and spring have always been observed to stand in a particular relationship to each other: winter always precedes spring. Must we not say winter "causes" spring? Fortunately, upon reflection, we can answer in the negative. We "know" that winter does not cause spring because the science of astronomy has constructed a *theory* which tells us, among other things, that winter does not cause spring but rather something else—planetary movement—causes both. A person who would maintain that winter causes spring can agree with the astronomer that the empirical fact is that spring is invariably preceded by winter. Where they differ is in their *theory* of why the fact is so. One says winter "causes" spring. The other says that both winter and spring are "caused" by another variable.

The notion of causation as production is best regarded as a *theoretical* notion (or, more precisely, as a meta-theoretical notion). We can never directly observe cause as production. Nevertheless, we can and do talk about causation when discussing our theories, because employing such terms has been found to be useful in achieving organized knowledge of phenomena and in making successful predictions about the relationships we *do* observe in the real world. Simon (1957, pp. 10–12) states the point succinctly and well.

> Observation reveals only recurring associations. The proposition that it is possible to discover associations among events that are, in fact, invariable ceases to be a provable statement about the natural world and becomes instead a working rule to guide the activity of the scientist. He says, "I will seek for relationships among events that seem always to hold in fact, and when it occurs that they do not hold, I will search for additional conditions and a broader model that will (until new exceptions are discovered) restore my power of prediction." The only "necessary" relationships among variables are the relationships of logical necessity that hold in the scientist's model of the world, and there is no guarantee that this model will continue to describe the world that is perceived.

Statements about causal relationships (in the sense of production), then, are best regarded as theoretical, or metatheoretical statments, rather than empirical, statements. We think in terms of cause-effect relationships and we make scientific statements in that form because we find that it is a useful way to describe order in the phenomena with which we deal. As scientists, we are always in the position of saying, "As of now, the best way to make sense of the world is as follows." As of now, that "best way" involves thinking in terms of causal relationships.

But to make causal statements it is necessary that we have certain kinds of empirical evidence. In the next section we shall see why experiments are uniquely suited to provide us that evidence.

THE POWER OF EXPERIMENTS
IN TESTING CAUSAL RELATIONS[2]

Although there are many reasons for doing experiments, it is undoubtedly true that the most common reason is to acquire information relevant to a hypothesis that one variable is causally related to another. As it was contended in the last section, statements about causes are essentially theoretical statements. Observations made in the real world can never be *sufficient* conditions for saying that x and y are causally related. Yet it is also true that certain kinds of empirical evidence are *necessary preconditions* for the making of causal statements. It is in producing that kind of empirical evidence (of necessary preconditions) that experiments are particularly useful.

We have already alluded to the kind of empirical evidence which is needed if one is to assert with scientific confidence that x is a cause of y. Let us be explicit at this point. Three

---

[2] It should be noted that in the following discussion we will ignore problems met in executing experiments. Indeed we will be describing a very simple, "ideal" experiment in terms of the *logic* involved. The remainder of this book deals with problems with experiments.

kinds of empirical evidence are essential if a scientist wishes to make statements of causal relationships. First, he needs evidence that two or more variables co-vary, i.e., that changes in the value of x are observed to be associated with changes in the value of y. Second, he needs evidence that one variable, the independent variable (x), is temporally antecedent to the other variable, the dependent variable (y). Finally, the scientist needs evidence that other variables are not responsible for the observed relationship between the independent and dependent variables.

Evidence that two or more variables co-vary is typically provided by applying standard statistical tests of significance and association to the data generated in an experiment. Since the experimental situation is *created* by the scientist for the sole purpose of testing a causal relationship, the scientist has relatively great control of the sources of variation operating in the experimental situation (see discussion below). Because of this control, the scientist can make legitimate use of sophisticated statistical models in determining the manner in which his variables co-vary.

Evidence that the independent variable is temporally antecedent to the dependent variable is particularly unambiguous in experimental research. Again, since the experimenter creates and controls the experiment, he simply must make certain that he first manipulates the independent variable and then measures changes in the dependent variable. Thus, as compared to other research strategies in which the problem of temporal ordering is often very thorny (Rosenberg, 1968), in experimental research it is (usually) inconsequential.

In some senses, it is in providing the third kind of evidence needed to establish causal relationships—evidence that other variables have not confounded the relationship—that experiments have the greatest advantage over other kinds of research. Experiments are situations *created* by the scientist and therefore, within the limits of his knowledge and technology, the scientist can determine in advance which variables in which form will be present in the situation. In particular the scientist can attempt to eliminate from the situation or to control at known levels those variables which may be confounded with the variables of interest.

As the dictionary defines it, to confound is to "mix up or lump together indiscriminately; confuse." If some variable, z, is confounded with an investigator's independent variable, x, there is no way of determining if x is causing variation in the dependent variable or if z is the effective causal agent.

For example, suppose a researcher is interested in testing the hypothesis that small groups with a certain pattern of communication will solve problems faster than will groups with another pattern. If the groups with the first kind of pattern also have the most intelligent leaders, differences in leader intelligence rather than differences in patterns of communication may be responsible for any problem-solving differences between the two sets of groups. It is the purpose of most experimental designs, therefore, either to eliminate confounding factors from the study or to control them at known levels.

The virtues of controlling as many potentially confounding variables as possible are clear. First, if a variable is controlled at known levels, it can neither confound the findings nor contribute to random error. Second, it is scientifically important to know how the relationships between the variables which we are studying is affected by *known* levels of other variables (e.g., it is important to know that the relationship between temperature and the freezing point of water changes with altitude). Although scientists attempt to control as many potentially confounding variables as possible, it must be emphasized that knowing which sources of variation to control is not intuitively obvious. To know what to control requires firm scientific understanding of the phenomena under investigation, a condition which does not often obtain in the social sciences. Further, we may "know" some variables are confounding but the nature of those variables may be such that they are difficult or impossible to control. In any case, the scientist can never be certain that he knows and has controlled *all* potentially confounding variables. It is at this juncture that another great advantage of experimentation comes into play.

Since the experimenter controls the situation he has created, he can *assign* his experimental units (individuals, dyads, groups, etc.) to the experimental conditions by a random method. In this way the effects of potentially confounding variables which are unknown or which cannot be controlled are "neutralized" in the sense that they should not produce systematic differences between experimental conditions.

The importance of random assignment of subjects to experimental conditions may be better appreciated through the following example. Suppose a researcher wants to study the effects on their strategies of the amount of money players can win in a competitive game. The investigator decides to have one experimental condition in which subjects can win $15, one in which they can win $5, and one in which they can win $1. Suppose the hypothesis is that as the amount of money they can win increases, players will be more likely to violate certain rules in an attempt to win the money. Now, we can easily imagine any number of factors other than amount of money that may be related to willingness to violate the rules—for example, subjects' "need" for money, their general honesty, their mood at the moment, and so forth. It would be impossible or impractical to attempt to control all of these potentially confounding variables. However, if we assign subjects to the experimental conditions by a random method (e.g., by flipping a coin), then potentially confounding variables should not affect our dependent variable in a *systematic* way. Rather, chance alone will determine how those variables are distributed over our three experimental conditions. By applying a statistical test to our data, we can determine what the probability is that any observed differences among our dependent variables are due to chance variation in confounding variables. If that probability is low, we have evidence that is consistent with the hypothesis that the independent variable *did* causally affect the dependent variable.

It is clear that the experiment is suited particularly well to the testing of causal relationships. Still, as Blalock (1961, p. 21) points out, "In practice, even the most carefully designed experiment falls short of the ideal." For example, in manipulating our independent variable we may inadvertently have manipulated another variable which may be "really" responsible for any effects on our dependent variable.

These and innumerable other problems are met in efforts to successfully implement the logic of experimentation when human beings are the object of study. The remainder of this reader deals directly with those problems.

THE ORGANIZATION OF THE BOOK

While the basic assumptions of the experimental method have informed innumerable studies in the social sciences, the applicability of experimental methodology to human behavior has not been unquestioned.

The articles that are reprinted in the following pages and our original essays that accompany them are organized around two critical themes.

The first theme in large part deals with limitations on the *utility* of the experimental method in studying some kinds of human behavior. Some of the traditional kinds of criticism which have been leveled at experimental methodology are that experimental situations tend to be "artificial" or "trivial" when compared to situations in the "real world." Therefore, it has been argued, successfully executing an experiment on, for example, the relationship between level of anxiety and the desire to interact with others tells us very little about how these variables are related in the real world. Questions of generalizing experimental findings to other settings are questions of "external validity." Part 2 of this book deals with questions of external validity and related criticisms.

The second critical theme has to do with questions about experimental methodology that are relevant to "internal validity." When one asks questions about internal validity one is essentially asking if, within a given experiment, a causal relationship between two variables has in fact been established. The bulk of the book is concerned with such questions in terms of the theoretical perspective of the social psychology of the experiment. Within this perspective, the experiment itself is seen as a social situation. It is maintained that what goes on in an experiment involves social interaction between subject and experimenter, interaction in which the motivations of both subject and experimenter and the manner in which each defines the situation may influence the outcome, i.e., the experimental data. For example, it has been shown that under certain conditions an experimenter may be unconsciously communicating to subjects his expectations about how they should behave. In such a case the value of the dependent variable may be a function not of the independent variable that the experimenter thought he manipulated but rather of the experimenter's own unintended behavior. It is to variables such as these that the social psychology of the experiment points in looking for extraneous variables which may affect internal validity.

In the book's final essay, we critically review suggestions for handling some of the problems of extraneous variation associated with the social psychology of the experiment. Further, we explore the methodological implications of the contention that any experiment is, in part, a social system consisting of at least (a) an experimenter, (b) a subject, and (c) the relationship between them. Finally, we consider the possibility that because experiments are social systems, nontraditional ways of dealing with extraneous variation may be necessary.

Part Two
EXTERNAL
VALIDITY

2
Traditional Objections
To Experimentation

Social scientists and others have not been sparing in pointing out both real and imagined limitations on experimentation with human subjects. In this section we shall briefly consider some of the more "traditional" criticisms of experimentation.

No serious social scientist would deny that there are both moral and practical limitations to experimental research with human subjects.[1] To take an extreme but unambiguous example, no one would propose inflicting varying degrees and kinds of brain damage on human infants in an effort to discover how brain damage affects maturation, even though such an experiment might be scientifically important. It is

[1] An extensive debate about the appropriate ethical standards for research involving human subjects has recently been taking place among psychologists. The scope of the present book does not permit adequate exploration of these important issues. The interested reader is referred to recent issues of the *American Psychologist* in which references to works which we feel to be particularly relevant to this debate may be obtained.

also undoubtedly correct that sheerly practical concerns inhibit certain kinds of experimentation. For example, very
long-term experimentation with small groups in a completely
controlled environment is economically infeasible at the present time, since no experimenter has sufficient funds at his
disposal to pay subjects to participate in such a project.

Limitations to experimentation because of moral and practical reasons, then, are real but hardly surprising; similar
limitations apply to *any* research strategy (see Mills, 1969,
for a more extended discussion). However, there have been
other criticisms which have been traditionally aimed primarily, if not exclusively, at experimentation. Perhaps the
charge that has been most frequently made is that experiments are "artificial" or "contrived." It is hard to know
exactly what is meant by such a criticism, but several interpretations are possible. If to say that experiments are artificial or contrived is to say that the events of an experiment
wouldn't take place unless the experimenter set up the situation in the first place, the charge is certainly accurate. As we
have already stated, ideally everything that takes place in an
experiment is controlled by the experimenter who sets up the
situation in such a way that the results of the study will be
maximally useful in testing causal relationships among the
variables of interest. Thus from the scientist's point of view
the experiment is particularly attractive *because* it is contrived, *because* it is artificial and *because* it is therefore
devoid of all the confounding variables that exist in the real
world.

Another interpretation of the contention that experiments
are contrived and artificial is that experimental situations and
events do not look like non-experimental situations and
events. For example, it may be correctly contended that a
study of the relationship between social power and degree of
satisfaction in a small group may involve experimental tasks
and events which cannot be observed in naturally occurring
small groups outside of the laboratory. As Aronson and Carlsmith (1968) put it, events in the laboratory may lack "mundane realism," i.e., they may not "look like" events in every-

day life which presumably are controlled by the same variables as those which are being investigated in the laboratory. But that is precisely the point. Events may, on the surface, appear to be different and still be controlled by the same variables. The familiar distinction between genotype and phenotype is applicable at this point. For example, individual members of a species may look different in terms of outer physical appearance (phenotype) and yet they may still be subject to the fundamental genetic variables that define all members of their species. In other words, to criticize experiments because they lack "mundane realism" is to misunderstand the purpose of experimentation in *any* science. Variables to be investigated are selected because of their presumed *theoretical* significance. Once the scientist decides, for reasons of theory, which variables he wishes to investigate, he must then decide how best to carry on the investigation, how to "operationalize" his variables, e.g., he must decide what kinds of experimental tasks to use. He will make that decision, in large part, on the basis of the degree of experimental control and precision of measurement afforded by various means of operationalization. Questions of mundane realism are not paramount, nor is there any reason for them to be of concern. (This is not to suggest that real problems of operationalization do not exist in experimentation. See the discussion in the next essay.)

Finally, a third kind of charge might be implied by the assertion that experiments are contrived and artificial. That is, because experiments frequently lack mundane realism, it may be hard or impossible to generalize from findings in experiments to events in other settings, e.g., the "real world." Questions about generalizing from experimental settings to other settings, the reader will recall, are known as questions about "external validity." That one can never be "certain" that findings from *any* kind of research will hold true in other research settings is unquestionably correct. However, when questions are raised about the external validity of *experimental* findings, it is often implied that there is something peculiar to experimental research, something that makes it particularly open to questions of external validity. Now what that something might be, aside from the kinds of considerations which have already been discussed (and dismissed) above, is not specified. It is entirely possible, however, that critics are disturbed that experiments do not contain the myriad variables, confounded with each other, that are found in everyday life. While true, scientists view this as an advantage, for the experimental method has proven successful in many sciences as the means by which complex sets of causal relationships may eventually be unraveled. In any case, if any investigator feels an important variable or set of variables has been excluded from any given experiment, he is not prevented from designing—indeed he is encouraged to design—another experiment or study which does include the neglected variables. That is the way in which scientific disputes are resolved and scientific progress made.

Before concluding our discussion of traditional criticisms of experimentation, we must mention one other criticism which is relevant, not to the *logic* of social scientific experimentation, but to the way in which that logic is put into practice. It is often pointed out that most experimental subjects are college students, not because the logic of experimentation demands it, but because college students are easily available for service as subjects. The contention is frequently made, then, that studies using college students as subjects cannot produce findings which are generalizable to other populations which might be quite different from students. Now it *may* be true that any given set of findings will not hold in populations different from those involved in the original research. Whether that is so is an empirical matter, i.e., a question of fact. If any scientist believes he has identified a population-related variable which may affect any set of findings, he should, as a scientist, conduct a study to test his theory. But to suggest, as some have, that the problem might be solved by representative sampling from the universe of theoretical relevance—mankind?—is not helpful. In response to the misunderstanding of the practice of "science" involved in such a recommendation, we can do no better than to quote Campbell (1969, pp. 360-61).

> ... More typical of science is the case of Nicholson and Carlisle. Taking in May, 1800, a very parochial and idiochronic sample of Soho water, inserting into it a very biased sample of copper wire, into which flowed a very local electrical current, they obtained hydrogen gas at one electrode, oxygen at the other, and uninhibitedly generalized to all the water in the world for all eternity ... (The limitations to the generalization have emerged from checking in nonrepresentative ways on an initial bold generalization.) ... In this light, had we achieved one, there would be no need to apologize for a successful psychology of college sophomores ... Exciting and powerful laws would then be presumed to hold for all men or all vertebrates at all times, until *specific* applications of that presumption proved wrong. (Emphasis and parentheses added.)

INTRODUCTION TO REPRINTED ARTICLES

Reprinted on the pages immediately following, the reader will find two articles that deal with more or less "traditional" limitations to experimentation with human subjects. Both articles focus on experimentation dealing with attitude change, but many of the points they make are applicable to experimentation on a wide variety of topics. Hovland, in what has come to be regarded as a "classic" article, discusses some of the reasons for differing results from experimental, as opposed to survey, studies of attitude change. Hovland contends that such differences are due to "accidental" factors, historical precedents, and differences in research design. (It is unclear whether he regards design differences as intrinsic to the two types of studies.) Weick, in the following article, sees no limitations to experiments; in his opinion, only *experimenters* have been limited. He contends that many problems in experiments have been the result both of researchers' limited conceptions of experimentation and of the sometimes contradictory goals involved in any experiment. Both articles offer valuable suggestions for improving experimental research.

3
Reconciling Conflicting Results Derived From Experimental And Survey Studies Of Attitude Change

Carl I. Hovland

Two quite different types of research design are characteristically used to study the modification of attitudes through communication. In the first type, the *experiment,* individuals are given a controlled exposure to a communication and the effects evaluated in terms of the amount of change in attitude or opinion produced. A base line is provided by means of a control group not exposed to the communication. The study of Gosnell (1927) on the influence of leaflets designed to get voters to the polls is a classic example of the controlled experiment.

In the alternative research design, the *sample survey,* information is secured through interviews or questionnaires both concerning the respondent's exposure to various communications and his attitudes and opinions on various issues. Generalizations are then derived from the correlations obtained between reports of exposure and measurements of attitude. In a variant of this method, measurements of attitude and of exposure to communication are obtained during repeated interviews with the same individual over a period of weeks or months. This is the "panel method" extensively utilized in studying the impact of various

Reprinted with permission of the publisher from *The American Psychologist,* 1959, 14, pp. 8-17.

mass media on political attitudes and on voting behavior (cf., e.g., Kendall & Lazarsfeld, 1950).

Generalizations derived from experimental and from correlational studies of communication effects are usually both reported in chapters on the effects of mass media and in other summaries of research on attitude, typically without much stress on the type of study from which the conclusion was derived. Close scrutiny of the results obtained from the two methods, however, suggests a marked difference in the picture of communication effects obtained from each. The object of my paper is to consider the conclusions derived from these two types of design, to suggest some of the factors responsible for the frequent divergence in results, and then to formulate principles aimed at reconciling some of the apparent conflicts.

DIVERGENCE

The picture of mass communication effects which emerges from correlational studies is one in which few individuals are seen as being affected by communications. One of the most thorough correlational studies of the effects of mass media on attitudes is that of Lazarsfeld, Berelson, and Gaudet published in *The People's Choice* (1948). In this report there is an extensive chapter devoted to the effects of various media, particularly radio, newspapers, and magazines. The authors conclude that few changes in attitudes were produced. They estimate that the political positions of only about 5 percent of their respondents were changed by the election campaign, and they are inclined to attribute even this small amount of change more to personal influence than to the mass media. A similar evaluation of mass media is made in the recent chapter in the *Handbook of Social Psychology* by Lipset and his collaborators (1954).

Research using experimental procedures, on the other hand, indicates the possibility of considerable modifiability of attitudes through exposure to communication. In both Klapper's survey (1949) and in my chapter in the *Handbook of Social Psychology* (Hovland, 1954) a number of experimental studies are discussed in which the opinions of a third to a half or more of the audience are changed.

The discrepancy between the results derived from these two methodologies raises some fascinating problems for analysis. This divergence in outcome appears to me to be largely attributable to two kinds of factors: one, the difference in research design itself; and, two, the historical and traditional differences in general approach to evaluation characteristic of researchers using the experimental as contrasted with the correlational or survey method. I would like to discuss, first, the influence these factors have on the estimation of overall effects of communications and, then, turn to other divergences in outcome characteristically found by the use of the experimental and survey methodology.

Undoubtedly the most critical and interesting variation in the research *design* involved in the two procedures is that resulting from differences in definition of exposure. In an experiment the audience on whom the effects are being evaluated is one which is fully exposed to the communication. On the other hand, in naturalistic situations with which surveys are typically concerned, the outstanding phenomenon is the limitation of the audience to those who *expose themselves* to the communication. Some of the individuals in a captive audience experiment would, of course, expose themselves in the course of natural events to a communication of the type studied; but many others would not. The group which does expose itself is usually a highly biased one, since most individuals "expose themselves most of the time to the kind of material with which they agree to begin with" (Lipset et al., 1954, p. 1158). Thus one reason for the difference in results between experiments and correlational studies is that experiments describe the effects of exposure on the whole range of individuals studied, some of whom are initially in favor of the position being advocated and some who are opposed, whereas surveys primarily describe the effects produced on those already in favor of the point of view advocated in the communication. The amount of change is thus, of course, much smaller in surveys. Lipset and his collaborators make this same evaluation, stating that:

> As long as we test a program in the laboratory we always find that it has great effect on the attitudes and interests of the experimental subjects. But when we put the program on as a regular broadcast, we then note that the people who are most influenced in the laboratory tests are those who, in a realistic situation, do not listen to the program. The controlled experiment always greatly overrates effects, as compared with those that really occur, because of the self-selection of audiences (Lipset et al., 1954, p. 1158).

Differences in the second category are not inherent in the design of the two alternatives, but are characteristic of the way researchers using the two methods typically proceed.

The first difference within this class is in the size of the communication unit typically studied. In the majority of survey studies the unit evaluated is an entire program of communication. For example, in studies of political behavior an attempt is made to assess the effects of all newspaper reading and television viewing on attitudes toward the major parties. In the typical experiment, on the other hand, the interest is usually in some particular variation in the content of the communications, and experimental evaluations much more frequently involve single communications. On this point results are thus not directly comparable.

Another characteristic difference between the two methods is in the time interval used in evaluation. In the typical experiment the time at which the effect is observed is usually rather soon after exposure to the communication. In the survey study, on the other hand, the time perspective is such that much more remote effects are usually evaluated. When effects decline with the passage of time, the net outcome will, of course, be that of accentuating the effect obtained in experimental studies as compared with those obtained in survey researches. Again it must be stressed that the difference is not inherent in the designs as such. Several experiments, including our own on the effects of motion pictures (Hovland, Lumsdaine, & Sheffield, 1949) and later studies on the "sleeper effect" (Hovland & Weiss, 1951; Kelman & Hovland, 1953), have studied retention over considerable periods of time.

Some of the difference in outcome may be attributable to the types of communicators characteristically used and to the motive-incentive conditions operative in the two situations. In experimental studies communications are frequently presented in a classroom situation. This may involve quite different types of factors from those operative in the more naturalistic communication situation with which the survey researchers are concerned. In the classroom there may be some implicit sponsorship of the communication by the teacher and the school administration. In the survey studies the communicators may often be remote individuals either unfamiliar to the recipients, or outgroupers clearly known to espouse a point of view opposed to that held by many members of the audience. Thus there may be real differences in communicator credibility in laboratory and survey researches. The net effect of the differences will typically be in the direction of increasing the likelihood of change in the experimental as compared with the survey study.

There is sometimes an additional situational difference. Communications of the type studied by survey researchers usually involve reaching the individual in his natural habitat, with consequent supplementary effects produced by discussion with friends and family. In the laboratory studies a classroom situation with low postcommunication interaction is more typically involved. Several studies, including one by Harold Kelly reported in our volume on *Communication and Persuasion* (Hovland, Janis, & Kelley, 1953), indicate that, when a communication is presented in a situation which makes group membership salient, the individual is typically more resistant to counternorm influence than when the communication is presented under conditions of low salience of group membership (cf. also, Katz & Lazarsfeld, 1955, pp. 48-133).

A difference which is almost wholly adventitious is in the types of populations utilized. In the survey design there is, typically, considerable emphasis on a random sample of the entire population. In the typical experiment, on the other hand, there is a consistent overrepresentation of high school students and college sophomores, primarily on the basis of their greater accessibility. But as Tolman has said: "college sophomores may not be people." Whether differences in the type of audience studied contribute to the differences in effect obtained with the two methods is not known.

Finally, there is an extremely important difference in the studies of the experimental and correlational variety with respect to the type of issue discussed in the communications. In the typical experiment we are interested in studying a set of factors or conditions which are expected on the basis of theory to influence the extent of effect of the communication. We usually deliberately try to find types of issues involving attitudes which are susceptible to modification through communication. Otherwise, we run the risk of no measurable effects, particularly with small-scale experiments. In the survey procedures, on the other hand, socially significant attitudes which are deeply rooted in prior experience and involve much personal commitment are typically involved. This is especially true in voting studies which have provided us with so many of our present results on social influence. I shall have considerably more to say about this problem a little later.

The differences so far discussed have primarily concerned the extent of overall effectiveness indicated by the two methods: why survey results typically show little modification of attitudes by communication while experiments indicate marked changes. Let me now turn to some of the other differences in generalizations derived from the two alternative designs. Let me take as the second main area of disparate results the research on the effect of varying distances between the position taken by the communicator and that held by the recipient of the communication. Here it is a matter of comparing changes for persons who at the outset closely agree with the communicator with those for others who are mildly or strongly in disagreement with him. In the naturalistic situation studied in surveys the typical procedure is to determine changes in opinion following reported exposure to communication for individuals differing from the communicator by varying amounts. This gives rise to two possible artifacts. When the communication is at one end of a continuum, there is little room for improvement for those who differ from the communication by small amounts, but a great deal of room for movement among those with large discrepancies. This gives rise to a spurious degree of positive relationship between the degree of discrepancy and the amount of change. Regression effects will also operate in the direction of increasing the correlation. What is needed is a situation in which the distance factor can be manipulated independently of the subject's initial position. An attempt to set up these conditions experimentally was made in a study by Pritzker and the writer (1957). The method involved preparing individual communications presented in booklet form so that the position of the communicator could be set at any desired distance from the subject's initial position. Communicators highly acceptable to the subjects were used. A

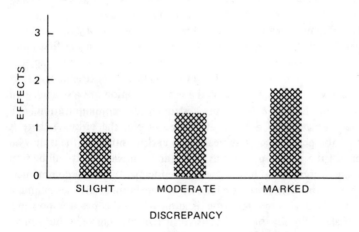

FIG. 1. Mean opinion change score with three degrees of discrepancy (deviation between subject's position and position advocated in communication). [From Hovland & Pritzker, 1957]

number of different topics were employed, including the likelihood of a cure for cancer within five years, the desirability of compulsory voting, and the adequacy of five hours of sleep per night.

The amount of change for each degree of advocated change is shown in Figure 1. It will be seen that there is a fairly clear progression, such that the greater amount of change advocated the greater the average amount of opinion change produced. Similar results have been reported by Goldberg (1954) and by French (1956).

But these results are not in line with our hunches as to what would happen in a naturalistic situation with important social issues. We felt that here other types of responses than change in attitude would occur. So Muzafer Sherif, O. J. Harvey, and the writer (1957) set up a situation to simulate as closely as possible the conditions typically involved when individuals are exposed to major social issue communications at differing distances from their own position. The issue used was the desirability of prohibition. The study was done in two states (Oklahoma and Texas) where there is prohibition or local option, so that the wet-dry issue is hotly debated. We concentrated on three aspects of the problem: How favorably will the communicator be received when his position is at varying distances from that of the recipient? How will what the communicator says be perceived and interpreted by individuals at varying distances from his position? What will be the amount of opinion change produced when small and large deviations in position of communication and recipient are involved?

Three communications, one strongly wet, one strongly dry, and one moderately wet, were employed. The results bearing on the first problem, of *reception*, are presented in Figure 2. The positions of the subjects are indicated on the abscissa in letters from A (extreme dry) to H (strongly wet). The positions of the communication are also indicated in the same letters, *B* indicating a strongly dry communication, *H* a strongly wet, and *F* a moderately wet. Along the ordinate there is plotted the percentage of subjects with each position on the issue who described the communication as "fair" and "unbiased." It will be seen that the degree of distance between the recipient and the communicator greatly influences the evaluation of the fairness of the communication. When a communication is directed at the pro-dry position, nearly all of the dry subjects consider it fair and impartial, but only a few percent of the wet subjects consider the identical communication fair. The reverse is true at the other end of the scale. When an intermediate position is adopted, the percentages fall off sharply on each side. Thus under the present conditions with a relatively ambiguous communicator one of the ways of dealing with strongly discrepant positions is to *discredit* the communicator, considering him unfair and biased.

A second way in which an individual can deal with discrepancy is by distortion of what is said by the communicator. This is a phenomenon extensively studied by Cooper and Jahoda (1947). In the present study, subjects were asked to state what position they thought was taken by the communicator on the prohibition question. Their evaluation of his position could then be analyzed in relation to their own position. These results are shown in Figure 3 for the moderately wet communication. It will be observed that there is a tendency for individuals whose position is close to that of the communicator to report on the communicator's position quite accurately, for individuals a little bit removed to report his position to be substantially more like their own (which we call an "assimilation effect"), and for those with more discrepant positions to

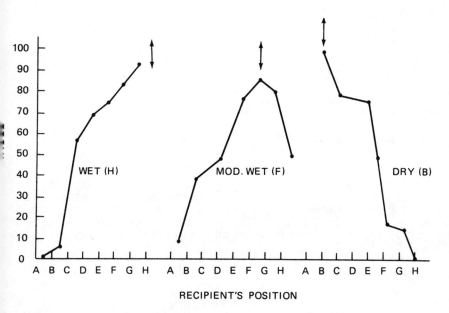

FIG. 2. Percentage of favorable evaluations ("fair," "unbiased," etc.) of wet (*H*), moderately wet (*F*), and dry (*B*) communications for subjects holding various positions on prohibition. Recipients positions range from *A* (very dry) to *H* (very wet). Position of communications indicated by arrow. [From Hovland, Harvey, & Sherif, 1957]

report the communicator's position as more extreme than it really was. This we refer to as a "contrast effect."

Now to our primary results on opinion change. It was found that individuals whose position was only slightly discrepant from the communicator's were influenced to a greater extent than those whose positions deviated to a larger extent. When a wet position was espoused, 28% of the middle-of-the-road subjects were changed in the direction of the communicator, as compared with only 4% of the drys. With the dry communication 14% of the middle-of-the-roaders were changed, while only 4% of the wets were changed. Thus, more of the subjects with small discrepancies were changed than were those with large discrepancies.

These results appear to indicate that, under conditions when there is some ambiguity about the credibility of the communicator and when

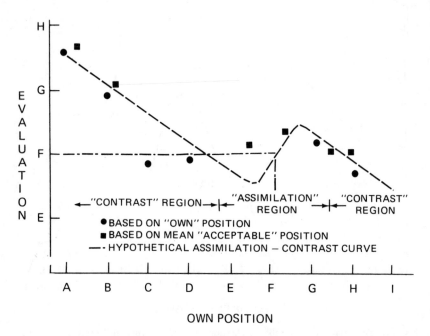

FIG. 3. Average placement of position of moderately wet communication (*F*) by subjects holding various positions on the issue, plotted against hypothetical assimilation-contrast curve. [From Hovland, Harvey, & Sherif, 1957]

the subject is deeply involved with the issue, the greater the attempt at change the higher the resistance. On the other hand, with highly respected communicators, as in the previous study with Pritzker using issues of lower involvement, the greater the discrepancy the greater the effect. A study related to ours has just been completed by Zimbardo (1959) which indicates that, when an influence attempt is made by a strongly positive communicator (i.e., a close personal friend), the greater the discrepancy the greater the opinion change, even when the experimenter made a point of stressing the great importance of the subject's opinion.

The implication of these results for our primary problem of conflicting results is clear. The types of issues with which most experiments deal are relatively uninvolving and are often of the variety where expert opinion is highly relevant, as for example, on topics of health, science, and the like. Here we should expect that opinion would be considerably affected by communications and furthermore that advocacy of positions quite discrepant from the individual's own position would have a marked effect. On the other hand, the types of issues most often utilized in survey studies are ones which are very basic and involve deep commitment. As a consequence small changes in opinion due to communication would be expected. Here communication may have little effect on those who disagree at the outset and function merely to strengthen the position already held, in line with survey findings.

A third area of research in which somewhat discrepant results are obtained by the experimental and survey methods is in the role of order of presentation. From naturalistic studies the generalization has been widely adopted that primacy is an extremely important factor in persuasion. Numerous writers have reported that what we experience first has a critical role in what we believe. This is particularly stressed in studies of propaganda effects in various countries when the nation getting across its message first is alleged to have a great advantage and in commercial advertising where "getting a beat on the field" is stressed. The importance of primacy in political propaganda is indicated in the following quotation from Doob:

> The propagandist scores an initial advantage whenever his propaganda reaches people before that of his rivals. Readers or listeners are then biased to comprehend, forever after, the event as it has been initially portrayed to them. If they are told in a headline or a flash that the battle has been won, the criminal has been caught, or the bill is certain to pass the legislature, they will usually expect sub-

sequent information to substantiate this first impression. When later facts prove otherwise, they may be loath to abandon what they believe to be true until perhaps the evidence becomes overwhelming (Doob, 1948, pp. 421-422).

A recent study by Katz and Lazarsfeld (1955) utilizing the survey method compares the extent to which respondents attribute major impact on their decisions about fashions and movie attendance to the presentations to which they were first exposed. Strong primacy effects are shown in their analyses of the data.

We have ourselves recently completed a series of experiments oriented toward this problem. These are reported in our new monograph on *Order of Presentation in Persuasion* (Hovland, Mandell, Campbell, Brock, Luchins, Cohen, McGuire, Janis, Feierabend, & Anderson, 1957). We find that primacy is often *not* a very significant factor when the relative effectiveness of the first side of an issue is compared experimentally with that of the second. The research suggests that differences in design may account for much of the discrepancy. A key variable is whether there is exposure to both sides or whether only one side is actually received. In naturalistic studies the advantage of the first side is often not only that it is first but that it is often then the only side of the issue to which the individual is exposed. Having once been influenced, many individuals make up their mind and are no longer interested in other communications on the issue. In most experiments on order of presentation, on the other hand, the audience is systematically exposed to both sides. Thus under survey conditions, self-exposure tends to increase the impact of primacy.

Two other factors to which I have already alluded appear significant in determining the amount of primacy effect. One is the nature of the communicator, the other the setting in which the communication is received. In our volume Luchins presents results indicating that, when the same communicator presents contradictory material, the point of view read first has more influence. On the other hand, Mandell and I show that, when two different communicators present opposing views successively, little primacy effect is obtained. The communications setting factor operates similarily. When the issue and the conditions of presentation make clear that the points of view are controversial, little primacy is obtained.

Thus in many of the situations with which there had been great concern as to undesirable effects of primacy, such as in legal trials, election campaigns, and political debate, the role of primacy appears to have been exaggerated, since the conditions there are those least conducive to primacy effects: the issue is clearly defined as controversial, the partisanship of the communicator is usually established, and different communicators present the opposing sides.

Time does not permit me to discuss other divergences in results obtained in survey and experimental studies, such as those concerned with the effects of repetition of presentation, the relationship between level of intelligence and susceptibility to attitude change, or the relative impact of mass media and personal influence. Again, however, I am sure that detailed analysis will reveal differential factors at work which can account for the apparent disparity in the generalizations derived.

INTEGRATION

On the basis of the foregoing survey of results I reach the conclusion that no contradiction has been established between the data provided by experimental and correlational studies. Instead it appears that the seeming divergence can be satisfactorily accounted for on the basis of a different definition of the communication situation (including the phenomonon of self-selection) and differences in the type of communicator, audience, and kind of issue utilized.

But there remains the task of better integrating the findings associated with the two methodologies. This is a problem closely akin to that considered by the members of the recent Social Science Research Council summer seminar on *Narrowing the Gap Between Field Studies and Laboratory Studies in Social Psychology* (Riecken, 1954). Many of their recommendations are pertinent to our present problem.

What seems to me quite apparent is that a genuine understanding of the effects of communications on attitudes requires both the survey and the experimental methodologies. At the same time there appear to be certain inherent limitations of each method which must be understood by the researcher if he is not to be blinded by his preoccupation with one or the other type of design. Integration of the two methodologies will require on the part of the experimentalist an awareness of the narrowness of the laboratory in interpreting the larger and more comprehensive effects of communication. It will require on the part of the survey researcher a greater awareness of the limitations of the correlational method as a basis for establishing causal relationships.

The framework within which survey research operates is most adequately and explicitly dealt with by Berelson, Lazarsfeld, and McPhee in their book on *Voting* (1954). The model which they use, taken over by them from the economist Tinbergen, is reproduced in top half of Figure 4. For comparison, the model used by experimentalists is presented in the lower half of the figure. It will be seen that the model used by the survey researcher, particularly when he employs the "panel" method, stresses the large number of simultaneous and interacting influences affecting attitudes and opinions. Even more significant is its provision for a variety of "feedback" phenomena in which consequences wrought by previous influences affect processes normally considered as occurring earlier in the sequence. The various types of inter-

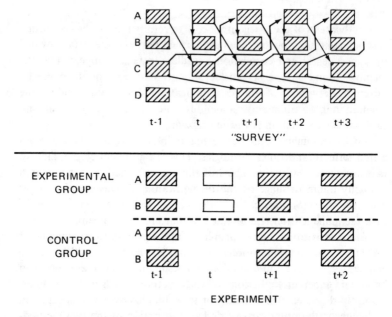

FIG. 4. TOP HALF: "Process Analysis" schema used in panel research. (Successive time intervals are indicated along abscissa. Letters indicate the variables under observation. Arrows represent relations between the variables.) [From Berelson, Lazarsfeld, & McPhee, 1954]   BOTTOM HALF: Design of experimental research. (Letters on vertical axis again indicate variables being measured. Unshaded box indicates experimentally manipulated treatment and blank absence of such treatment. Time periods indicated as in top half of chart.)

action are indicated by the placement of arrows showing direction of effect. In contrast the experimentalist frequently tends to view the communication process as one in which some single manipulative variable is the primary determinant of the subsequent attitude change. He is, of course, aware in a general way of the importance of context, and he frequently studies interaction effects as well as main effects; but he still is less attentive than he might be to the complexity of the influence situation and the numerous possibilities for feedback loops. Undoubtedly the real life communication situation is better described in terms of the survey type of model. We are all familiar, for example, with the interactions in which attitudes predispose one to acquire certain types of information, that this often leads to changes in attitude which may result in further acquisition of knowledge, which in turn produces more attitude change, and so on. Certainly the narrow question sometimes posed by experiments as to the effect of knowledge on attitudes greatly underestimates these interactive effects.

But while the conceptualization of the survey researcher is often very valuable, his correlational research design leaves much to be desired. Advocates of correlational analysis often cite the example of a science built on observation exclusively without experiment: astronomy. But here a very limited number of space-time concepts are involved and the number of competing theoretical formulations is relatively small so that it is possible to limit alternative theories rather drastically through correlational evidence. But in the area of communication effects and social psychology generally the variables are so numerous and so intertwined that the correlational methodology is primarily useful to suggest hypotheses and not to establish causal relationships (Hovland et al., 1949, pp. 329-340; Maccoby, 1956). Even with the much simpler relationships involved in biological systems there are grave difficulties of which we are all aware these days when we realize how difficult it is to establish through correlation whether eating of fats is or is not a cause of heart disease or whether or not smoking is a cause of lung cancer. In communications research the complexity of the problem makes it inherently difficult to derive causal relationships from correlational analysis where experimental control of exposure is not possible. And I do not agree with my friends the Lazarsfelds (Kendall & Lazarsfeld, 1950) concerning the effectiveness of the panel method in circumventing this problem since parallel difficulties are raised when the relationships occur over a time span.

These difficulties constitute a challenge to the experimentalist in this area of research to utilize the broad framework for studying communication effects suggested by the survey researcher, but to employ well controlled experimental design to work on those aspects of the field which are amenable to experimental manipulation and control. It is, of course, apparent that there are important communication problems which cannot be attacked directly by experimental methods. It is not, for example, feasible to modify voting behavior by manipulation of the issues discussed by the opposed parties during a particular campaign. It is not feasible to assess the effects of communications over a very long span of time. For example, one cannot visualize experimental procedures for answering the question of what has been the impact of the reading of *Das Kapital* or *Uncle Tom's Cabin.* These are questions which can be illuminated by historical and sociological study but cannot be evaluated in any rigorous experimental fashion.

But the scope of problems which do lend themselves to experimental attack is very broad. Even complex interactions can be fruitfully attacked by experiment. The possibilities are clearly shown in studies like that of Sherif and Sherif (1953) on factors influencing cooperative and competitive behavior in a camp for adolescent boys. They were able to bring under manipulative control many of the types of interpersonal relationships ordinarily considered impossible to modify experimentally, and to develop motivations of an intensity characteristic of real-life situations. It should be possible to do similar studies in the communication area with a number of the variables heretofore only investigated in uncontrolled naturalistic settings by survey procedures.

In any case it appears eminently practical to minimize many of the differences which were discussed above as being not inherent in design but more or less adventitiously linked with one or the other method. Thus there is no reason why more complex and deeply-involving social issues cannot be employed in experiments rather than the more superficial ones more commonly used. The resistance to change of socially important issues may be a handicap in studying certain types of attitude change; but on the other hand, it is important to understand the lack of modifiability of opinion with highly-involving issues. Greater representation of the diverse types of communicators found in naturalistic situations can also be achieved. In addition, it should be possible to do experiments with a wider range of populations to reduce the possibility that many of our present generalizations from experiments are unduly affected by their heavy weighting of college student characteristics, including high literacy, alertness, and rationality.

A more difficult task is that of experimentally evaluating communications under conditions of self-selection of exposure. But this is not at all impossible in theory. It should be possible to assess what demographic and personality factors predispose one to expose oneself to particular communications and then to utilize experimental and control groups having these characteristics. Under some circumstances the evaluation could be made on only those who select themselves, with both experimental and control groups coming from the self-selected audience.

Undoubtedly many of the types of experiments which could be set up involving or simulating naturalistic conditions will be too ambitious and costly to be feasible even if possible in principle. This suggests the continued use of small-scale experiments which seek to isolate some of the key variables operative in complex situations. From synthesis of component factors, prediction of complex outcomes may be practicable. It is to this analytic procedure for narrowing the gap between laboratory and field research that we have devoted major attention in our research program. I will merely indicate briefly here some of the ties between our past work and the present problem.

We have attempted to assess the influence of the communicator by varying his expertness and attractiveness, as in the studies by Kelman, Weiss, and the writer (Hovland & Weiss, 1951; Kelman & Hovland, 1953). Further data on this topic were presented earlier in this paper.

We have also been concerned with evaluating social interaction effects. Some of the experiments on group affiliation as a factor affecting resistance to counternorm communication and the role of salience of group membership by Hal Kelley and others are reported in *Communication and Persuasion* (Hovland et al., 1953).

Starting with the studies carried out during the war on orientation films by Art Lumsdaine, Fred Sheffield, and the writer (1949), we have had a strong interest in the duration of communication effects. Investigation of effects at various time intervals has helped to bridge the gap between assessment of immediate changes with those of longer duration like those involved in survey studies. More recent extensions of this work have indicated the close relationship between the credibility of the communicator and the extent of postcommunication increments, or "sleeper effects" (Hovland & Weiss, 1951; Kelman & Hovland, 1953).

The nature of individual differences in susceptibility to persuasion via communication has been the subject of a number of our recent studies. The generality of persuasibility has been investigated by Janis and collaborators and the development of persuasibility in children has been studied by Abelson and Lesser. A volume concerned with these audience factors to which Janis, Abelson, Lesser, Field, Rife, King, Cohen, Linton, Graham, and the writer have contributed will appear under the title *Personality and Persuasibility* (1959).

Lastly, there remains the question on how the nature of the issues used in the communication affects the extent of change in attitude. We have only made a small beginning on these problems. In the research reported in *Experiments on Mass Communication,* we showed that the magnitude of effects was directly related to the type of attitude involved: film communications had a significant effect on opinions related to straightforward interpretations of policies and events, but had little or no effect on more deeply intrenched attitudes and motivations. Further work on the nature of issues is represented in the study by Sherif, Harvey, and the writer (1957) which was discussed above. There we found a marked contrast between susceptibility to influence and the amount of ego-involvement in the issue. But the whole concept of ego-involvement is a fuzzy one, and here is an excellent area for further work seeking to determine the theoretical factors involved in different types of issues.

With this brief survey of possible ways to bridge the gap between experiment and survey I must close. I should like to stress in summary the mutual importance of the two approaches to the problem of communication effectiveness. Neither is a royal road to wisdom, but each represents an important emphasis. The challenge of future work is one of fruitfully combining their virtues so that we may develop a social psychology of communication with the conceptual breadth provided by correlational study of process and with the rigorous but more delimited methodology of the experiment.

4
Promise
And Limitations
Of Laboratory Experiments
In The Development
Of Attitude Change Theory

Karl E. Weick

Trying to write on an overworked topic such as laboratory experiments can be a disquieting experience. In an effort to say something new, fantasy is often unloosed, and it sometimes leads to strange places. And so it was in the early stages of this chapter.

In thinking about laboratory experiments, my attention became fixated on the letter "D." For example, much of the focus in recent attitudinal research has been on *dissonance, discrepancy,* and *divergence.* Furthermore, if we look at the current batch of criticisms concerning the laboratory, a surprising number of them follow a patterr traced in "D's." For example, laboratory experimenters are now haunted by thoughts of *deception, debriefing, demands, disclosure, discretion, dishonesty, deutero-problems, discomfort,* and *dissembling.* If we go on to look closely at the *responses* to these criticisms, we find disillusionment, defection, dabbling, defiance, or defense. Unfortunately what we do not find is a healthy amount of determination, discipline, deliberation, digging, or daring.

Reprinted with permission of author and publisher from *Attitude, Ego-Involvement, and Change,* Carolyn W. Sherif and Mazafer Sherif, eds. (New York: John Wiley & Sons, 1967), pp. 51-75.

It is important to look closely at potential limitations of the laboratory because most investigators are eager to document, demonstrate, describe, delineate, detect, discover, duplicate, and disprove. For many of these activities the laboratory is essential. The purpose of this chapter is to suggest that some of the criticisms of the laboratory have been diversionary; they have centered on pseudo-issues. Once these issues are pinpointed, we can accurately dissect experiments and examine their place in the development of attitude change theory.

It is probably apparent by now how my discussion will end. Most discussions of the laboratory conclude by acknowledging that there are limitations to field research and limitations to laboratory research, and, therefore, science will progress if both methods are used. I take a somewhat more controversial position. My conclusion, stated in advance, is that there are *NO* limitations to experiments. The limitations instead involve laboratory *experimenters,* their decisions and their concerns. Laboratory experiments themselves are not inherently limiting. Instead the limitations arise from the ways in which experiments have been implemented and the conception of what a laboratory is. Given this perspective, it should be apparent that there is hope for change and improvement if we can just get to the experimenters.

The remainder of the chapter will be divided into two main sections. Since I have stated rather blatantly that there are no limitations to experiments, I shall first deal with several ways in which laboratory experiments do, in fact, limit and constrain attitude research. The second main section dwells on promises of laboratory experiments and suggests some solutions to the limitations that are uncovered.

LIMITATIONS OF THE LABORATORY

Fault can be found with laboratory experimenters at many points for their preoccupations, oversights, and naivete. It is not our intent to absolve them from responsibility for these errors. But, many criticisms of experiments have not been helpful because they have produced labels that are more evaluative than descriptive, more global than specific. As a result, the impression has emerged that several problems in the conduct of laboratory experiments are intractable. It is concluded that experiments are most useful for a selected and relatively narrow range of questions in attitude research. The latter conclusion seems both questionable and premature.

The following discussion enumerates seven properties of laboratory experiments that have blinded experimenters to crucial issues in attitude change. These properties, however, are not immutable. They can be modified by changes in research conceptions and procedure. There is the further possibility that those properties of the laboratory that resist changes can be exploited more fully to provide answers about significant issues in attitude change. The first property contains one example.

The Compliant Laboratory

One crucial drawback of the laboratory for attitude change research is that many laboratory settings produce acquiescence rather than independence (Orne, 1962). The phrase "obedient subject" used to refer to a person who was loyal to a ruler in some mythical kingdom. Lately the phrase has become an onerous threat to the experimenter who tries to demonstrate that he knows something about attitude change.

The aura of compliance in the laboratory stems from several sources: the presumed credibility of the experimenter, his role as an expert, the uncertainty with which subjects approach experiments, their desire to help science, the fact that experiments are tied closely to classroom work because of requirements for credit, and so forth. Because compliance is pervasive, a distorted view of attitude change often emerges from the laboratory.

The experimenter is salient as a powerful person who controls rewards and punishment. Therefore, he is apt to induce some change, but the change is usually fleeting. Even if the experimenter intends that manipulations in an experiment produce enduring change, it is probable that pressures toward compliance would swamp his manipulations. For example, if we adopt Kelman's (1958) terminology, it is conceivable that attitude change could be produced in the laboratory because the subject finds something attractive about the communicator that he would like to emulate (identification). The point is that the subject probably never gets the chance to entertain this possibility. Compliance is more salient, and any changes that are produced reflect the pressures of the immediate experimenter-subject relationship.

One solution to this problem is simply to turn a vice into a virtue. If compliance is a prominent component of the laboratory, if it is expected and therefore has high ecological validity in this setting, why not exploit the laboratory to learn more about compliance? Our knowledge concerning this topic is still scant.

This solution is not very elegant to researchers who are fascinated by other processes. Researchers are also unwilling to have their interests legislated by a shortcoming of laboratory procedures. To many, it seems important instead to discover ways in which pressures toward compliance can be reduced. This is a difficult problem to solve, but it clearly deserves attention.

Pressures toward compliance might be reduced by having accomplices of the experimenter who were noncompliant (accomplices who essentially show that noncompliance is acceptable); by disengaging experiments from classes; by greater usage of hired subjects or subjects in natural settings; by conveying the impression to students that science is fallible; or by using laymen to administer experimental treatments. Admittedly, these are weak suggestions that probably create more problems than they solve. The point is that careful attention directed toward this rather specific issue might go a long way toward increasing the relevance of laboratory experiments for attitude change research.

The Confrontive Laboratory

Numerous issues in attitude change research have been bypassed in the typical experiment simply because once the subject arrives at the laboratory, he is confronted by an attempt to persuade him and he must do something about the attempt before he leaves, even if this means ignoring it. Hovland (1959) noted that laboratory experiments are somewhat unique because subjects have little opportunity to expose themselves selectively to issues. Sherif, Sherif, and Nebergall (1965) make the important point that "the laboratory ... [omits] the first and crucial phase of most communication situations: the communicator must secure and hold an audience for his message" (p. 171).

The fact of confrontation has many drawbacks other than the omission of the first stage in communication. Dissonance theorists have studied largely postdecisional phenomena. Since their research situations confront subjects with decisions that *must* be made, they have essentially overlooked the fact that persons often *avoid* (e.g. Braden and Walster, 1964) or postpone decisions.

The confrontive nature of the laboratory probably may have persuaded researchers that persons hold beliefs that are highly interrelated. While it may be true that persons *do* strive to maximize consistent linkages among their beliefs, it is also true that the nature of most experimental situations makes it very difficult for a subject to compartmentalize his beliefs and to restrict their linkages. Furthermore, many measurement procedures used in the laboratory actually *suggest* linkages to the subject. Before experimenters conclude that persons try to maximize linkages in consistent directions, they would be wise to reexamine whether this impression might not be an artifact of laboratory procedures.

Still another problem posed by confrontation is that it is difficult for subjects to delay tension reduction. Most laboratory situations compel the subject to deal with discomfort immediately. There is little chance for the subject to maintain discomfort in order to gain more information about an issue. Yet there seem to be many occasions when persons will tolerate inconsistency in order to reexamine their beliefs and decisions and to profit from their mistakes. The impression that persons make immediate and large shifts in their beliefs merely to restore balance may be less a commentary on people than a commentary on the unique pressures that operate in the laboratory.

These problems are serious but not insolvable. Having pinpointed them, we are now in a better position to take corrective action. One implication is that a theory of attitude change built largely on laboratory experiments will have some obvious gaps. These gaps may center on issues of selective exposure, tolerance of momentary discomfort, and number of linkages. But one remedy is to study just these questions. Freedman and Sears (1965), for example, have recently shown that selective exposure can be studied in the laboratory.

Perhaps even more basic is a reconsideration of the issue of change. Hovland (1959) noted that change is demonstrated much more frequently in the laboratory than it is in the field. Presumably, this greater incidence of change is partly due to confrontations. The crucial question, however, seems to be not so much whether the *amount* of change differs in the two settings but whether the form and structure of change differ in the two settings. Latitudes of noncommitment (Sherif, Sherif, and Nebergall, 1965) may be more extensive in the laboratory than they are the field. If so, change may be demonstrated more readily in the laboratory. But does this mean that there is discontinuity between change processes observed in the laboratory and change processes observed in the field?

Problems of confrontation may also be minimized by embedding an attitude change manipulation in other events, permitting the subject some options concerning exposure. Relevant data would be provided both by those who choose to be exposed and those who do not.

Finally, it seems reasonable to suggest that the laboratory setting, in all its confrontiveness, may provide opportunities to study persuasible moments (Watson, 1966). There are occasions when persons are easily persuaded, for example, after a series of failures (Mausner, 1954). Although these moments may be fleeting, they are certainly not rare in everyday life. They may produce as much impact as more concentrated attempts at persuasion. If laboratory experiments were directed less at trying to simulate the impacts produced by mass media and more at trying to capture fleeting instances when confrontation is plausible and persons are susceptible, they might be better able to supplement existing knowledge.

The Rational Laboratory

Experiments seem to have an uncommonly rational and logical flavor. Literate, knowledgeable college students, whose classroom experience has probably alerted them to gaps in their thinking, are brought into a setting where they are on display before a presumably rational, incisive, sophisticated psychologist. Is it any wonder that these subjects feel some pressures to appear consistent?

The flavor of rationality is often enhanced because large amounts of information are presented that must be read and evaluated. Information is easy to manipulate in an experiment. But its presentation in a single concentrated message can easily prod persons to look for flaws, inconsistencies and gaps. Since there are few distractions in the laboratory while the information is being presented, these flaws may be especially visible. We should not overlook the additional fact that the typical attitude change experiment bears a marked resemblance to the classroom situation where pressures do indeed exist for coherence and consistency of thought.

Remedies for the rational flavor of experiments are difficult to suggest. Remedies may not be necessary if we consider the laboratory as a good setting in which to study the *rational* side of attitude change. Obvious as this point may be, experimenters seem to miss it on occasion. Many theories of attitude change turn out to be hypotheses that should be considered special cases within more general theories of cognition. Failure to grasp this point has meant that experimenters use more complex procedures than would otherwise be necessary. Their time might more profitably be spent examining conditions that cause attention to narrow, conditions that inhibit discrimination and selection, and conditions in which persons attain and revise concepts.

Problems created by rationality per se might yield to changes in procedure such as separating portions of the communique so that it is more difficult for the parts to be compared, or one might distract subjects so that their attention is divided between the communique and another task. Other possible procedures to minimize the rational set of the laboratory might be to sanction inconsistency by convincing subjects that open-mindedness is as much of a virtue as orderliness and consistency, to confront the subject with several issues so that it is more difficult for him to monitor the consistency of his responses, to make experiments less public so that subjects feel fewer pressures to appear consistent or to divorce attitude change experiments from educational settings.

In many ways, the fact that the laboratory is rational may not be too crucial for attitude change research. The principal effect of the rational flavor will be to magnify considerations of consistency. The laboratory may present an accurate portrait of the attitude change process when people are thoughtful, deliberate, and objective. It may provide less information about how persons process a communique when their capacities for critical thinking are subordinated to other interests such as affiliating with a reference group, seeing what a prominent communicator looks like, or "killing time" (see Festinger and Maccoby, 1964, for an example of nonrationality in the laboratory).

The Lonely Laboratory

Hovland (1959) and Sherif, Sherif, and Nebergall (1965) have made the important point that when subjects enter the laboratory they do not leave their reference groups at the door. It is one of the ironies of current social psychology that it has become a psychology of individuals and not of individuals in groups. This emphasis has serious consequences for attitude change research, for many important attitudes are formed and maintained in order to retain ties with persons whose evaluations count.

If a subject is isolated from reference persons in the laboratory, he may exhibit marked attitude change because he is unable to compare his attitudes with those of relevant peers or because he knows that peers are unlikely to find out what stand he took. On the other hand, he may try to act as if the reference group were present and respond to the message in terms of his best guess of how others would respond. Still another possibility is that the subject may convince himself that the reference group really is indifferent about the issue, in which case his concern with the issue would diminish also.

It is understandable that researchers have been reluctant to look at attitude change in anything but an individual setting. It is difficult to compose in the laboratory a set of persons that the subject will take seriously. If intact groups are brought into the laboratory, it is difficult to account for observed attitude change because the effects may be due to some moderating variable that the group members share in common.

There are numerous ways in which one might respond to the fact that the laboratory is a lonely setting. Reexamination of the concept of reference groups would seem to be part of the solution. It is true that social support is important in attitude change. It is also true that social support can originate in many places, whether it be with reference individuals or reference groups. It is commonly assumed that when a person is urged to adopt a discrepant position, he reinstates a prominent group in order to evaluate the consequences of shifting his belief. It would seem equally plausible that a person with several important groups might also search among these groups until he found one that would support the new position.

Most persons have assumed that the reference group is fixed and the attitude is free to vary. We are suggesting that when a subject receives a persuasive communique in a lonely setting, the reverse may occur, namely the attitude is fixed and the reference population is varied. Notice that in most discussions of reference groups there is the presumption that persons are highly dependent on a small number of groups. To phrase this in Thibaut and Kelley's (1959) language, it is presumed they have a low comparison level for alternatives. The effect of the comparison level for alternatives on persuasibility is relatively unknown, but it would seem important to learn the relationship in order to explain what happens when subjects are isolated from groups.

There is still some ambiguity about what role reference groups play when subjects arrive at the laboratory. However, there is no ambiguity concerning the fact that attitude change typically occurs in the company of other persons and that the evaluations of other persons are an important input. Recent concepts such as diffusion of responsibility (Wallach, Kogan and Bem, 1964) and social facilitation (Zajonc, 1965) have striking implications for attitude change. Researchers studying intra-individual processes have been slow to pick up these leads. It is as though researchers, ever since they started to simulate a group by means of a tape recording (Blake and Brehm, 1954), have believed that they were studying social interaction. More accurately, they are study-ing social *reaction,* not social *inter*action. For this reason they have bypassed one of the crucial ways in which a group can influence atti-tude change.

Social support implies an *exchange* of views, not merely a recitation of views. Discussions of attitudinal issues are admittedly difficult to control; but rather than ignore exchange because it presents stubborn methodological problems, researchers might more profitably spend time developing procedures to allow the lonely subject to have some com-pany. These procedural refinements could range from improved obser-vational categories to encode influence in ongoing groups (e.g., Hoff-man and Maier, 1964) to such devices as the use of multiple-track recorders to convey controlled, quasi-conversational inputs to the sub-jects (J. Darley private communication, 1966).

As a final point, it should be mentioned that the vice of the lonely laboratory can also be translated into a virtue for at least one important set of questions in attitude research. If a subject is removed from group ties and has few standards to use in evaluating a communication, then perhaps the standards which he adopts are especially sensitive to situa-tional conditions. Our knowledge about the effects of situational vari-ables on the establishment of anchors is quite incomplete. Research by Whittaker (1964) and Schachter and Singer (1962) suggests that sig-nificant relationships exist in this area. Uncertainty has high ecological validity in the laboratory, and uncertainty is not as rare in field settings as we might imagine. Ego-involvements may be potent in determining the placement of communications. Still, a person who ignores his sur-roundings is in for a great deal of trouble in trying to adapt to con-tingencies.

The Impatient Laboratory

A seemingly innocuous property of many laboratory experiments is that they last for one or two hours. This strict scheduling is often mandatory so that experiments can be coordinated with the class schedules of the subjects. Furthermore, experimenters are always wary that subjects will talk about experimental procedures, regardless of what they promise. One of the best ways to minimize this possibility is simply to run the experiment quickly "before the word gets around." The collapsing of significant persuasion events into one hour has the obvious consequence that we often have theories about immediate reac-tions to persuasion but know less about long-term effects. However, long-term change is being assessed with greater frequency (e.g., Freedman, 1965; Walster, 1964) so this is not quite the problem that it used to be.

There are other more subtle ways in which impatience has colored some of the conclusions about attitude change that have come from the laboratory. For one thing, most experimenters assume that experimental treatments are engaged immediately and that their effects are not delayed. They also presume that treatments operate simultaneously and throughout the exercise. If there is any lag in the impact of a treatment, it is assumed to be randomly distributed across subjects. Perhaps a more realistic picture of what occurs is that subjects initially are confused by laboratory procedures. Their attention is not focused wholly on the instructions because they are trying to figure out what the experimenter is up to. They are unfamiliar with the experimenter and are getting used to him.

The harassed experimenter who must get everything completed within the hour often does not have time to permit the subject to get acclimated. As a result the subject is often engaged in reading or listening to persuasive materials *before* all of the instructions sink in. Thus, *early* in the experiment his exposure to information is not affected by the manipulations; but in the latter stages his behavior may well be under the control of the manipulation. If a single score is used to measure the impact of the message, it is possible that the partial impact of the manipulation will be obscured, and no differences will emerge. The point is that the treatment may actually be potent, but what has happened is that the manipulation was not in effect the entire time. Closer attention to this phenomenon, and steps to study its effect, might go a long way toward separating stable from unstable laboratory phenomena.

Impatience may take quite a different form. Perhaps our experiments are too long; perhaps we are not impatient enough. A ten-second exposure to a sign in which the persuasive content is varied systematically might produce just as much change as a one-hour exposure. Webb et al. (1966) suggest, for example, that traffic signs on highways might be constructed with varying degrees of fearful messages, the behavior of drivers being observed from a helicopter once they pass the sign. Although it may seem ludicrous to compare the impact of a ten-second message with that of a ten-minute or a ten-hour message, there is no reason a priori to expect that one has any more impact than the other. Many of the problems of laboratory settings that we have discussed so far are absent in the ten-second exposure, and there is some evidence that brief events can produce irreversible change (e.g., Davis, 1930).

Attitude change, after all, often boils down to a process where some message initiates activity in the subject, activity which may continue long after he leaves the persuasion setting. There seems to be nothing magical about a one-hour exposure that promises more subsequent activity than a ten-second exposure. In fact, if one takes the Zeigarnik demonstration seriously (e.g., Cartwright, 1942), it is conceivable that a short cryptic communique might produce more deliberation than a self-contained, symmetrical, packaged communique.

Experimenters who believe that significant events occur in one-hour units also may be prone to make incomplete analyses of events that are short-lived. The richness of data obtained over a very short period of time has been dramatically demonstrated in an important book by Pittenger, Hockett, and Danehy (1960) entitled *The First Five Minutes*. These authors have made an exhaustive analysis of only the first five minutes of the first interview between one therapist and one patient. Trivial as this segment might seem when compared with information produced over several therapy sessions, the startling fact is that almost all of the significant themes that later emerged in more detail during the therapy were present in the first five minutes. Furthermore, these themes were *repeated* several times during the first five minutes.

The point seems clear that extending the duration of an attitude change experiment offers no assurance that significant content or attitudinal structure will emerge. A more intensive look at shorter segments of persuasion may produce just as much information as a more cursory look at longer segments. A close look at a short segment has the added advantage that a more restricted range of verbal prods from the communicator are present. Hence, it is easier for the investigator to see relationships between inputs from the communicator and responses by the audience.

Although it may seem that we are belaboring the issue of time, it does seem reasonable that the typical one-hour unit of time for exposing subjects to a communique need not be regarded as prescriptive. If experimenters reexamine their ideas about duration of exposure, they might be better able to devise more potent manipulations, gain a better understanding of the process of attitude change at a molecular level, and even propose some valuable concepts to help explain what occurs during attitude change.

The Sedentary Laboratory

Most subjects who participate in attitude change experiments lead an uncommonly passive life. They are seated, exposed to a communique, evaluate the message, and then are excused, very possibly to leave the laboratory and take some action that will either stabilize or undo the effects of the message which they just heard. Alas, the experimenter will never know, because he remains in the laboratory, comfortable that he has observed a significant portion of the attitude change process.

One of the most common discussions among researchers is that there seems to be a poor fit between attitudes and behavior. Perhaps their puzzlement is not so surprising when we consider that very seldom do they watch attitude change *and* behavior at one sitting in the laboratory. Seldom are subjects given the opportunity to *do* anything about their beliefs. Thus, it should not be surprising that attitudes change in the laboratory but that these changes are fleeting.

The changes might be more stable *IF* the subject could do something to validate or find support for them (e.g., Festinger, 1964). Hovland made a similar point in 1959 (p. 182), yet it has often been overlooked in favor of his more straightforward comparisons of the laboratory and the field. He noted that the field has numerous feedback loops that are absent in the laboratory. One consequence of these loops is that they affect influences that occurred earlier in the persuasion sequence.

Recent research on task enhancement (Weick, 1964, 1966b) shows that if persons agree to work on a task for insufficient reasons, they reevaluate the situation and find additional attractions. More important, when they are actually given the chance to take some action that would validate these revised beliefs, they engage in such behavior to a striking degree. It appears that persons are eager to find support for cognitive realignments, and intense behavioral involvement tends to generate such support. Furthermore, once the belief is validated, it becomes quite stable. It is *not* abandoned as soon as the subject leaves the laboratory.

Failure to provide opportunities for attitude-relevant actions has also meant that researchers have overlooked an especially engaging portrayal of the attitude change process, namely the self-fulfilling prophecy (Merton, 1968). Although there are certain ambiguities about this formulation, it does suggest some interesting questions. The notion here is, of course, that a person makes a false definition of a situation (for example, Negroes are inferior), and this definition evokes a behavior that makes the false conception come true (for example, funds for education are withheld, and Negroes turn out to be inferior and un-educated). Here is an excellent example where actions coupled with feedback loops affect prior beliefs.

Incidentally, one part of Merton's formulation that is generally over-looked is the interesting proposition that there is also a "suicidal proph-ecy." This is a prophecy that "so alters human behavior from what would have been its course had it not been made, that it *fails* to be borne out. The prophecy destroys itself" (p. 423). If greater attention were paid to actions subsequent to attitude change, it seems probable that researchers might also "discover" this effect. One can think of several instances where prophecies are self-destructive. A person, for example, believes that the skills of Negroes are vastly underrated. He assigns to a Negro employee a task that he is incapable of doing, and because of the erroneous initial definition of the situation, the proph-ecy fails.

Until researchers take more seriously the old bromide that "the belief fathers the reality" and until they provide subjects with more opportunities to do something about beliefs, they will have to be con-tent both with temporary changes in attitudes and with theories of attitude change that fail to specify mechanisms for stabilization.

The Petty Laboratory

Undoubtedly the most persistent objection to laboratory studies of attitude change is that subjects confront trivial issues, issues in which the latitude of noncommitment is extensive, issues that are not ego-involving. Some warrant is seen for this practice because if a researcher wants to study change, he must choose an issue on which change can occur. But warrant for this practice seems to vanish when theoretical positions differ on the relationship between discrepancy and attitude change. Because the issue of ego-involvement in attitude change has constructively been hounding the laboratory experimenter for some time, it should be examined closely.

At the outset it might be well to mention that ego-involvement can be a seductive label. It is a concept with many meanings, and until its recent operationalizing in the form of the own-categories procedure (Sherif, Sherif, and Nebergall, 1965) it was an elusive target. It was easy, for example, to argue that if social judgmental phenomena did not occur, the subjects were not involved, and if they did occur, that subjects were involved. However, convincing independent checks on involvement were difficult to obtain. Hopefully the recent advances in measurement of ego-involvement will arrest some of the data-free controversy about this variable and direct it toward more specific issues.

If ego-involvement is low in the laboratory, one obvious solution is to heighten it. Experimenters have often been lazy when it comes to choosing an issue and often adopt whatever is uppermost in *their own* minds at the moment. Carolyn Sherif (see Sherif, Sherif, and Nebergall, 1965, p. 184), however, more systematically canvassed students to find out what they were concerned about and found that public affairs were much less important than were issues involving interpersonal problems. Experimenters may be much more out of touch with student life than they realize. Acknowledgment of this fact coupled with greater attention to student concerns might improve the attitudinal content of laboratory studies using student subjects.

Aside from issue content, ego-involvement may be enhanced by pointing out to the subject that his beliefs are vulnerable (McGuire, 1964) or by pointing to inconsistent notions that he has about a topic (McGuire, 1960). One drawback of these procedures is that they could easily shake the confidence that a subject has in his beliefs and make him uncertain. Uncertainty heightens influenceability. The point is that the experimenter might have a difficult time knowing whether attitude change occurred because the subject was uncertain or because he was ego-involved or both.

Ego-involvement can also be enhanced if the subject makes a choice. And it is this issue around which some misunderstanding of dissonance theory has emerged. The misunderstanding has occurred because dissonance researchers have never been very explicit about this point. Temerlin (1963), a psychotherapist, has presented an incisive description of the relationship between choice and involvement. His main point is that a man is his choices or the techniques he uses to avoid making choices. Whenever a person makes a choice, he shows someone else what he is like, and there is always the danger that the impression conveyed will be negative. Temerlin also demonstrates that defense mechanisms can be viewed as ways to avoid choice and responsibility.

The relevant point of all this seems to be that the mere act of making a choice can heighten ego-involvement. A choice, after all, is a performance, and it is a performance that is open to inspection and evaluation. Thus, even though much dissonance research involves issues that seem trivial, the point is that these issues may become more involving for the subject because he has taken some stand relative to them. A portion of himself is on display that was not earlier. Since it is not immediately clear whether the choice conveys a favorable or unfavorable impression, the person should feel considerable pressure to convince himself, at least, that the choice was credible or to disengage himself from any responsibility for the choice. Thus, it seems that when dissonance research is criticized for using trivial issues the criticism may be misplaced. It is not the issue, it is the choice that produces involvement. Now, if the choice is such that the person is unlikely to see it as an extension of himself, then indeed low ego-involvement is present.

Let us suppose for the moment that it is difficult to get subjects ego-involved in the laboratory. Even if this is true, the situation is certainly not hopeless. Although latitudes of noncommitment may be extensive on issues studied in the laboratory, it would be absurd to presume that all issues have identical latitudes. At least it should be possible to order laboratory issues in terms of those which have greater and lesser latitudes of noncommitment. If this is done, then we have some gradations of ego-involvement, fine as they may be. If the predictions of judgmental theory are valid, differences in placement and attitude change should be evident even in this restricted range.

As a final point concerning the pettiness of the laboratory, it seems possible that "big" issues, significant topics, beliefs in which noncommitment is minimal, may be the exception rather than the rule. The fact that we often have to look so hard to find an ego-involving issue may be less of a commentary about our resourcefulness and more of a commentary on the way things are where we are looking. It is easy to be deceived that because we as experimenters dwell on a single issue and become absorbed in it while writing communiques and quizzing endless subjects that the issue really is prominent and that subjects single it out in real life for a great deal of attention. There is a certain routine about life, a *lack* of confrontation that we may overlook. The academic mind seeks controversy, delights in debate, and devours information. It may, after all, be a rather specific and narrow model on which to base our ideas about attitude change. When issues arise in everyday life, they do not always arise with forewarning and fanfare, nor do persons always see the relevance of an issue to their self-concept or to their group ties. They may have only the vaguest ideas about the implications of an issue. Thus, we might find large amounts of concern and interest without these necessarily being reflected in narrow latitudes of noncommitment.

Maybe all it boils down to is this: Although we may know something about how persons handle dramatic and prominent issues, we probably know very little about mundane attitude change, change on issues that involve the small, relatively insignificant topics which constitute the bulk of a person's daily interaction. There does seem to be a certain amount of drama associated with attitude research. Issues with high ego-involvement may be less prominent in daily interaction than we suppose. For some purposes, reactions to issues on which the person is noncommitted may be just as crucial as those on which he is highly committed.

PROMISES OF THE LABORATORY

Until now we have been discussing limitations of the laboratory with several suggestions about what could be done about the problems. This section describes a few more general solutions to some of the problems that have already been discussed.

Infiltrate Sensitivity Training Groups

A seemingly lucrative and insufficiently tapped source of data about attitude change would seem to exist in T-groups (e.g., Schein and Bennis, 1965). These are groups in which persons are together for an extended period of time and in which there is a "joint commitment among interdependent persons to 'process analysis' " (Shepard, 1964, p. 379). T-groups seem to contain most of the properties that we would deem important in the study of attitude change: The groups do become a reference group within a relatively short period of time; there is extended face-to-face contact; almost nothing *but* ego-involving topics emerge; throughout there is an emphasis on the *accurate* placement of communiques, but this emphasis is emergent and permits before and after comparisons; persons are pressed toward expanding their latitudes of acceptance and rejection and narrowing their latitutdes of non-commitment; selective exposure is identified and attacked; and there are attempts to help participants tolerate inconsistency and to accept paradox as a part of life.

It might be mentioned in addition that many of the problems associated with asymmetric interaction (Jones and Thibaut, 1958) between the experimenter and the subject in laboratories are absent in T-groups. There is a more equitable exchange, namely the participants provide observations and personal data in return for which they receive help with their concerns. Logically at least, the pressures for ego-involvement are high because the more honest the person is, the more relevant and valuable will be the feedback.

Technically, an investigation of T-groups may not qualify as a laboratory experiment in the usual sense. In this connection it seems important that we avoid being provincial about what a laboratory experiment is. One solution to many of the problems we have detailed is to maintain flexibility concerning *sites* for data collection, while retaining those properties of the laboratory that we have learned to value. Surely, there is no rule that a laboratory has to be in an academic setting.

Diversify Persuasion Tasks

There is considerable sterility among experimenters concerning the format of most persuasion tasks. Not only are these tasks quite transparent to an alert subject, but, as noted earlier, they are only crude analogues of persuasion settings in everyday life. They seldom permit the subject to engage in relevant actions.

A particularly interesting approach to attitude change is the research of Breer and Locke (1965). Basically their notion is that if some attitude (such as cooperation, individualism, or future orientation) is instrumental to task performance and if the task is successfully performed, then the attitude will be adopted more readily by the subject in later situations. Failure at the task will hinder adoption of the attitude. The importance of this work seems to lie not so much in the formulation itself as in the suggestion that crucial beliefs can be embedded in tasks and that, depending on their instrumentality for task accomplishment, beliefs will be adopted or rejected.

Dependent Variable Obsession

It seems ironic that even though persons who study attitude change repeatedly make pronouncements that attitudes are inferred from behavior, they have been negligent in detailing the behaviors from which attitudes are inferred. Instead, most researchers seem preoccupied with independent variables. For the dependent variable, they have settled for crude ratings as the basis to accept or reject hypotheses. It would seem crucial to look more closely for behavioral correlates of attitudes, behaviors such as posture (Scheflen, 1964), facial expression (e.g., Ekman,

1965), gestures (e.g., Krout, 1954), vocal inflections (e.g., Hargreaves and Starkweather, 1963), hesitations in speech (e.g., Goldman-Eisler, 1958), verbal slips (Mahl, 1956), and distances people stand from one another (e.g., Sommer and Ross, 1958).

For example, Hall (1966) presents considerable evidence suggesting that persons who are attracted to one another stand or sit closer together. Proximatic behavior has several implications for procedures in attitude change experiments. Suppose that a communicator tries to change the beliefs of several students. At the conclusion of his presentation, the experimenter tells the subjects and the communicator to fill out some forms in another room before they leave. When the subjects go to the adjacent room they find several folding chairs stacked against the wall. In order to answer the questionnaires they have to set up their own chairs. The dependent variable is simply how far each subject sits from the communicator. Presumably, those subjects who were more persuaded will like the communicator more and will sit closer to him than will those subjects who resisted the persuasion. Admittedly there are some problems with this measure. For example, a person who resists a communicator may feel uncomfortable and want to show the communicator that there was "nothing personal" about the fact that the message was unpersuasive. A subject who felt this way might sit close to the communicator.

Problematic as some of the proposed behavioral measures may be, it seems clear that they are not any more ambiguous than are several of the paper-and-pencil measures that investigators have labored over for years. Refinements of behavioral indices of attitude (e.g., Cook and Selltiz, 1964) coupled with more vigorous attempts to conceptualize linkages between attitudes and behavior (Weick, 1966b) should increase the relevance of attitude change experiments.

Many social psychologists erroneously assume that most of the significant interactions among persons are verbal. There is an ample, sophisticated, and relevant literature concerning nonverbal behavior, showing both that attitudinal content is encoded in body language and that these indices are much more difficult to falsify than are self-reports.

Aside from using nonverbal behaviors to assess attitude change, studies of attitude change would profit from greater use of unobtrusive measures, measures that do not alert the subject that his beliefs are being assessed. An elegant example of an unobtrusive attitude measure is the "lost letters" technique developed by Milgram, Mann, and Harter

(1965). The investigator essentially "loses" stamped letters in places such as telephone booths, store counters, and along sidewalks. The letters are addressed to persons with clearly differing beliefs (for example, N.A.A.C.P., White Citizens Council, Friends of the American Communist Party, Medical Research Associates, Mr. Walter Carnap). When a person finds one of these letters, he is free to mail it, destroy it, or ignore it. Presumably his beliefs will be an important determinant of his actions. Thus, with appropriate controls in the form of letters addressed to neutral persons, it is possible to assess for various areas within a city or state, the prevailing sentiment on important issues without the participant realizing that his response is part of an attitude survey.

Incidentally, the use of unobtrusive measures seems to be especially pertinent in testing a judgmental theory of attitude change, because placement of communiques is a crucial process and placement can be affected by measurement procedures. Sherif, Sherif, and Nebergall (1965, p. 228) note, however, that camouflaging an "exhortation to change" can reduce displacement. This would suggest that embedded manipulations and unobtrusive measures would be especially important in testing judgmental theory.

Temper Nature

Much of the folklore concerning experiments and field research suggests that investigators tighten controls in the laboratory, whereas in the field they abandon controls. Both sides of this folklore are clearly unrealistic. Laboratory experiments are frequently less controlled than persons thought, as is shown elegantly in Friedman's (1964) discussion of the "standardization myth." It is also clear now that field observers are *more* obtrusive than had been imagined. They often unwittingly divert and control supposedly natural events. In short, the two research strategies are becoming more alike.

The prospect of subtle manipulative controls in natural settings has some obvious attractions, as indeed the Sherifs (e.g., Sherif, Harvey, White, Hood, and Sherif, 1961) have demonstrated. Recently this strategy of research has been described in detail and has been termed "tempered naturalness." Essentially the idea is as follows:

> The trappings of the natural event are preserved, it unfolds in a conventional manner, but some of its peripheral qualities are qualified. . . . The most common means to accomplish such qualification is to put boundaries around some portion of the ongoing event. This

means essentially that participants are exposed to an input that has a beginning and an end, an input that fits into the setting in the sense that it is plausible and expected, an input that is nonreactive and does not arouse suspicion, and an input that permits greater precision in measurement. The input that is referred to is essentially modeled after a laboratory task that has been altered sufficiently in appearance so that it fits into the setting for observation. It is the task which elicits the behavior which the observer records. A directed setting consistent with this model can be created either when an intact task is plausibly "dropped into" the behavior stream (e.g., visitors to a health exposition see films about lung cancer that vary in vividness and their subsequent actions are watched, Leventhal and Niles, 1964) or when the stream of activities is altered so that it contains the essential properties of a task (e.g., the beliefs of a person in a shopping center are mildly or strongly attacked by a communique which she reads during a feigned "man on the street" radio interview, Miller, 1965)(Weick, 1966a).

The use of tempered naturalness seems to have the advantage that it lends coherence to the process of inquiry. When persons advocate that both the field and laboratory should be used as sites for data collection, they sometimes overlook the important point that alternating between the two strategies makes it more difficult to maintain similar or comparable definitions of a concept. When an investigator shifts from the field to the laboratory or vice versa, he typically makes sizeable changes in procedures and measures. When these changes are made, it becomes difficult to tell whether the same process is being studied or whether the potential explanations have multiplied.

One advantage of "tempered naturalness" is that the investigator does not start at one end of the continuum of internal-external validity (Campbell, 1957); instead he starts at a middle point. The advantage of starting at a middle point is that it is easier for the investigator to remove or add properties systematically and to keep track of the ways in which his procedures have been modified. In addition, he can move from the central position to either a field or laboratory setting with fewer changes in procedure. This means that definitions of variables remain essentially intact and there is greater likelihood that the investigator is studying the same process.

It would be incorrect to conclude that we are arguing against those persons who advocate that the field and laboratory be used as complementary sites for data collection. Quite to the contrary. The position maintained here is that both sites are necessary. If both are employed, concepts will become more robust. The point here is if a study originates in a relatively pure laboratory or field setting, the investigator typically must change several features of the basic procedure as he moves to the other setting. As these changes proliferate, there is more danger that a different process is being observed. It would seem that investigators who use both sites have not always been mindful of this possibility.

As a final point concerning tempered naturalness, it should be noted that, since this strategy shares many features found also in the laboratory, there may be the attendant temptation to use this strategy for one-shot investigations. One important advantage of field studies is that they can be extended over time, and, therefore, they often provide a more detailed picture of the process and stability of attitude change. There is a certain compactness about tempered naturalness that may lead the investigator to repeat the error of "impatience" discussed earlier and to look at only a short portion of the attitude change process. It would seem worthwhile in designing a procedure which is based on tempered naturalness to incorporate manipulations and measures that permit greater exploitation of the temporal dimensions of events.

Abolish Quasi-ecological Aims

Much attitude change research suffers from a plurality of self-defeating aims. Many studies begin as an attempt to describe the distribution of opinions among sections of the population. This purpose, however, often becomes blurred when the investigator adds to the study one or more manipulations to address some theoretical issue in attitude change theory. The net result is often a study in which there is a cryptic and inaccurate view of the distribution of opinions, and the manipulations are sufficiently gross and complex that they are difficult to interpret. Neither theory nor description are advanced when aims get mixed in this fashion.

In a sense, the argument here is the complement of the argument associated with tempered naturalness. The rationale for tempered naturalness is that laboratory and field methodologies share significant properties and that portions of both methodologies might be combined in the final design. However, combining methodological properties is *not* the same as combining questions or aims. Tempered naturalness pertains to the *refinement* of procedures, but *as* a procedure it may tempt investigators to ask questions that are less well defined. The seduction occurs because tempered naturalness typically involves a

natural setting where a person might well learn about real-world properties of an issue while he also reduces competing explanations by means
of appropriate controls. The point is that tempered naturalness does
not insure that both aims will be accomplished. The investigator still
has to assign priorities in a study. He still has to be clear just what
questions he is asking. If the intent of the study is to test theory, then
information concerning the distribution of positions in the population
will probably be less valid. Similarly, if the intent is to determine the
prevailing sentiment on an issue, intrusion into the behavioral stream
will have to be held to a subtle minimum. With lesser intrusion, theoretical propositions may be tested less precisely.

Obvious as these points may be, it seems that the running debate
within attitude change research concerning the merits of field and
laboratory studies has tempted investigators to ask, within the same
study, questions that are incompatible. Asking incompatible questions
is quite different from employing a set of procedures that involve the
best portions of various methodologies. We are simply arguing that
research will improve in this area if investigators take care to preserve
important differences in their questions while they also search for simi-
larities in strategy.

As questions become clarified, it should be possible for investigators
to engage more vigorously in "pure" ecological research, a type of
research that is essentially absent from current attitude literature. Even
though attitude change research has both field and laboratory data
relevant to its questions, there is a significant gap concerning the
ecology of natural attitude change. Attitude change theory still lacks a
thorough description such as that provided by Barker and Wright
(1955), Barker (1963), or Barker and Gump (1964), which describes
how persons in everyday life become exposed to communiques, the
settings in which exposure occurs, the associates that are around at the
time of exposure, the extent to which the issue is discussed when it
arises, and so forth. As mentioned earlier, it seems clear that attitude
change can occur through several means other than exposure to mass
media. Yet our knowledge of these additional sources of exposure is
scant, because descriptions of natural attitude change are focused on
exposures to mass media.

Persons interested in psychological ecology have recently begun to
outfit subjects with radio transmitters so that they can monitor what
occurs as these persons go about their everyday activities (e.g., Soskin
and John, 1963). It seems likely that recordings obtained under these

conditions could be scored for instances of potential and actual attitude change. With these data, investigators might discover neglected variables in the process of attitude change and learn more about factors that impede attitude change (Hovland, 1959, p. 183).

Several additional solutions could be mentioned, but perhaps these are sufficient to suggest that it may be premature to draw conclusions about limitations of the laboratory. As experimenters direct their attention to procedural details that may affect the outcomes of attempts at attitude change, they may be able to discover workable solutions. The first requirement seems to be an accurate identification of the problems. Probably one of the first beliefs that must be abandoned before we advance is the belief that "nothing beyond that which we are now doing is science" (Severin, 1965, p. 282). It would certainly be ironic, as well as a sad commentary on science, if those who devoted their lives to studying attitude change turned out themselves to be the persons who were most reluctant to change their tools for studying change.

But perhaps the best way to summarize this chapter is to return to the letter "D" that I found so useful in relieving my discomfiture at the outset. It is true that experimenters have been derelict, their energies have been diffused in needless controversy, and they have denied or disregarded many relevant criticisms out of defensiveness or despair. However, the issues explored in this chapter suggest that dismay seems unfounded and debunking seems premature. Perhaps these are merely delusions. But, if delusions can generate deliberation, discipline, and daring, perhaps we can look forward to the discovery and not the demise of the laboratory.

Part Three
INTERNAL
VALIDITY

5
Difficulties
In Implementing
Experimental Designs
With Human Subjects

As the reader will recall from the introductory chapter, the unique power of the experimental method in testing causal relationships is primarily based upon two features of experiments. First, the experimenter attempts to control at constant levels those extraneous variables he believes might affect the dependent variable. Second, by randomly assigning subjects to experimental conditions, the experimenter can assume that within the limits of chance variation, differences between experimental groups in the value of the dependent variables are not due to the operation of uncontrolled extraneous variables.

For the experimenter working with human subjects to apply the logic of experimentation in his work, certain assumptions must be met. First, all subjects within any experimental condition must be exposed to the same set of stimuli; no differences in the stimuli presented to subjects should be present except for those differences needed to manipulate the independent variable. Second, in most experimentation the manipulation of the independent variable is intended to affect some state of behavior of the subject (e.g., his or her "cognitions," his or her "perceptions"); no differences in the subjects' states should be present except for those intentionally manipulated by the independent variable treatment. Third, the researcher must be able to assume independence of observations, that is, he or she must be able to assume that the making of any given observation has not influenced the outcome of any other observation. Unless the experimenter can make such an assumption he or she will be unable legitimately to determine whether or not observed relationships were due to chance factors.

These three assumptions may be used to organize discussion of much of the work that has become known as the Social Psychology of Experiments. In this section we will consider the viability of these assumptions given the social nature of the experiment with human subjects.[1]

THE STANDARDIZATION
OF STIMULUS PRESENTATIONS

Experimenters and their assistants, like all actors trained to play a role, may display considerable variation from performance to performance. It is to this "performance varia-

---

[1] It should be noted that not all social scientists would agree that each of these assumptions must be met for experimental research to be successful. For example, some symbolic interactionists and others may not agree that all subjects within any experimental condition must be exposed to the same set of stimuli; they might hold that it is only necessary that subjects in each experimental condition be in similar states. A variety of stimuli may, of course, produce similar states in different subjects. We believe, however, that we must reject this position on methodological grounds primarily since it rests on the false premise that we can reliably and validly determine (measure) the variety of subject states studied in experimental research. Other social scientists, for example some radical behaviorists, might maintain that we need not worry—or *should* not worry—about subjects' states at all, but only about the objective stimuli to which they are exposed. Again, however, we must reject this advice on general methodological grounds since most experimentation with human beings either explicitly or implicitly presumes that *some* state of the subject is being affected by experimental stimuli. To take an absurd but clear example, when an experimenter tells a subject to "sit in that chair" he must assume that the subject "understands" the English

tion" in the behavior of researchers—within and across experimental conditions—that we now turn our attention. After discussing some potential *sources* of performance variation and possible remedies, we shall consider the *effect* of performance variation on the behavior of research subjects. While, in the social sciences, complete standardization is an ideal state which can only be approximated whenever human research personnel are employed in the experimental setting, nevertheless, to the extent to which performance variatior occurs, different stimuli are being presented to different subjects and internal validity is therefore threatened.

Performance Variation

A promising point of departure for an explanation of the source of *researcher's* performance variation is the subjects' behavior. Although experimenters *attempt* to appear and behave in a constant way, subjects are relatively free to display their entire behavioral repertoire. Since experimenters are human beings, they may be expected to react to their subjects in socially structured ways. The behavior and attributes of subjects may thus trigger variation in experimenter behavior. This is borne out by analyses of sound motion pictures of subject-experimenter interaction performed by Robert Rosenthal and his associates (see Rosenthal in this book; Friedman, 1967). Female subjects, for example, elicited more smiling behavior, eye glances, and personal references (sub-

---

language (or *some* language) sufficiently to perform the act necessary (sitting "there") for the experiment to proceed. (The serious theoretical and epistemological questions involved in the foregoing positions cannot, of course, be explored in the present context. However it can be said that if experimentation is to be viewed as a methodological strategy which, in the best philosophical and scientific tradition, should be conservatively practiced in an attempt to make only clearly warranted claims to knowledge, the assumptions we invoke should be taken seriously, given our current state of knowledge.) Finally, in regard to the assumption of independence of observations, most social scientists would note that there are standard statistical techniques for dealing with non-independent data. However, practically all would agree that none of these techniques are preferable to independence of observations, and are in fact seriously deficient when placed against that standard.

ject's name or personal pronoun) from male experimenters than did male subjects (Friedman, 1967, pp. 71–109). Further, the effect of the subject's sex seems to be complicated by the experimenter's sex, since the sex-linked behavior of either participant may provide feedback that markedly alters the ongoing experimenter-subject interaction. Conceivably many other (unstudied) subject characteristics may also evoke differential performance variation, such as the subject's emotional warmth, ego strength, mental acuteness, general appearance, and so forth. An experimenter, for example, may consciously or unintentionally allow a dull-appearing subject more time to finish a complex task than would be granted a seemingly bright subject.

Two general approaches have been suggested to deal with performance variation arising from subject factors: (1) better professional training for experimenters, or (2) substitution of taped or written instructions for "live" experimenters. The experimenters filmed by Rosenthal's researchers were mainly graduate students enrolled in an advanced educational psychology course (Rosenthal, 1966, p. 260). Had they filmed more experienced or better trained experimenters, the exorbitant amount of performance variation described by Friedman (1967, pp. 71–109) might not have been evident. Yet, the type of training typically given to experimenters and their assistants—dress rehearsals of specific experiments—is not likely to insure negligible subject-to-subject performance variation. One potential solution would be a program that trains researchers to play the role of the experimenter who enters into an objective, scientific relationship with his subject— relating not as a male to a female, not as a scholar to a pupil, not as a conservative to a radical, but as an experimenter to a subject. The same remedy—training researchers to assume a professional role by putting aside personal feelings and attitudes—has been proposed in survey research to cope with analogous problems of interviewer variability (Kahn and Cannell, 1957).

The major difficulty with implementing experimenter

training programs is that we lack a theory of social experimentation to determine which aspects of the experimenter's behavior should be standardized. As Friedman (1967) has pointed out, there are no rules or guidelines as to how subjects should be greeted, how subjects should be talked to or looked at, how much spatial and social distance should be maintained between researchers and their subjects, how subjects should be debriefed, and so forth. In particular, very little is known about the effect that nonverbal behavior (body motion) and paralinguistic behavior (voice quality) may have on experimenter-subject interaction. Of course, this is not unique to experimental situations. We do not know much in general about nonverbal behavior. A clear understanding of these features of experimenter behavior would be very useful, since any attempt to standardize additional aspects of the experimenter's behavior (for example, by providing a script for greeting subjects) may unintentionally increase the variability of unprogrammed aspects of the experimenter's behavior (for example, body motion).

A second procedure for minimizing performance variation is to substitute "canned" performances (audio or video tape, written instructions) for "live" researchers whenever possible. When completely implemented, such mechanical delivery systems assure a higher level of stimulus control than that attainable with live research personnel. Mechanical delivery systems may be applied to many experimental problems, but many practicing experimentalists believe that it is impossible or impractical to completely eliminate live personnel from the research scene. Besides assisting in the stimulus presentations, experimenters and their assistants perform several other vital functions that do not easily lend themselves to automated pre-programming—such as securing the cooperation and interest of the subject, guiding the subject through difficult instructions and making sure that he understands them (a "canned" experimenter would fail to detect subject bewilderment or misunderstanding), enhancing the credibility of dubious cover stories, and generally monitoring other aspects of the subject's behavior (signs of boredom, disbelief, obstinacy, mischievousness, and the like) that might bear upon the validity of the subject's performance (Aronson and Carlsmith, 1968, pp. 52–53).

If *subjects'* attributes and behavior were the only source of an experimenter's performance variation, the effects (if any) of performance variation could be controlled (but not eliminated) by subject randomization; that is, random assignment of the subjects to the experimental conditions would insure (within limits of chance error) equivalent patterns of performance variation within each experimental condition. But unfortunately there is considerable evidence that performance variation may also be brought about by any number of other non-randomizable factors. One such factor is the experimenter's involvement in the research.

It is reasonable to assume that the motives of research personnel will depend partly upon their position in the research program. Should they be senior researchers or graduate students pursuing research of their own invention, one would expect a high degree of project involvement. Conversely, should they be hired assistants or graduate students involved in a project not of their own choosing, they may lack the dedication necessary for successful task performance. Roth (1966) and Argyris (1968, reprinted in this book) have likened the position of the latter to that of lower-level organizational employees who perform repetitive tasks. The highly authoritarian conditions that senior researchers impose on their subordinates in the name of rigorous experimental control—such as highly structuring the role activities and restricting the decision-making participation of their subordinates—are the very things which may alienate their assistants from the research project. And, like other lower-level production employees, their assistants may adapt to these restrictive conditions by deviating from work instructions (cutting corners, cheating, and the like) and otherwise doing just enough to get by. The build-up of such disaffection from work over time, in conjunction with learning and fatigue processes, may sometimes result in "instrument decay" (Campbell and Stanley, 1963, p. 9).

A satisfactory remedy for performance variation arising from highly structured superior-subordinate research conditions has yet to be proposed. Roth (1966, p. 195) has suggested various ways to give subordinates a greater stake in the research project, including permitting them to participate in the overall planning and in the publication of the findings. Whether such incentives will motivate research assistants other than those with strong social science research interests is problematic. Hopefully, however, even those hired assistants who are uncommitted to scientific ideals would benefit, motivationally, from the opportunity to plan the details of their research tasks.

But increasing the project involvement of research assistants is not without risks: highly involved assistants may consciously or unconsciously bias the results of an experiment.

Performance Variation Effects

Performance variation on the part of research personnel is in and of itself troublesome, since it violates the assumption of standardized stimulus presentation. Moreover, since subjects may be influenced by the experimenter's behavior and since subjects' behaviors are the basic scientific product of experiments, the effects of performance variation may produce a false picture of the relationship between the independent and dependent variables.

What *are* the effects of performance variation on subject behavior? To answer this question, it is helpful to partition performance variation effects into random and systematic components. While moderate dosages of the former are generally tolerable, the latter poses a serious threat to internal validity. The presence of purely random performance variation will normally result in conservative statistical inferences.[2] Thus, if "significant" findings are produced in the

---

[2] The observed variance-based measures of association and tests of significance will be weaker than their "true" values because random performance variation will inflate estimates of variances and negligibly affect estimates of means (as random disturbances tend to cancel each other or average out to zero).

presence of random performance variation, the researcher has reason to believe that the true relationship is even more pronounced. This is not the case if systematic performance variation is also present; that is, bias which tends to accumulate rather than cancel out within the experimental conditions. Since systematic performance variation may co-vary with the experimental manipulation, its presence may lead to spurious inferences of "significant findings" in instances in which the true experimental variable has a negligible effect. Conversely, systematic performance variation may operate in the opposite direction from the experimental variable and mask a true effect.

Only recently have experimenters sought to evaluate the effects of systematic performance variation (McGuigan, 1963; Rosenthal, 1963c, Rosenthal and Fode, 1963a). One systematic influence on subject behavior—the experimenter's hypothesis or expectancy—has been identified in Robert Rosenthal's comprehensive program of research.[3] Since an extensive review by Rosenthal of his work is reprinted in this book, only a brief sketch of his experiments on experiments follows.

To demonstrate that experimenters may inadvertently communicate their expectancies and desires to their subjects, Rosenthal experimentally manipulated the hypotheses of his student experimenters. In the person-perception or empathy task (Rosenthal and Fode, 1963b), for example, half of the experimenters were told that the subjects would perceive a series of persons depicted by photographs as generally experiencing success (high ratings) while the remainder were led to expect low ratings (failure-perceiving) from their subjects. "Success-perceiving" experimenters obtained significantly higher ratings from their randomly assigned subjects than did the "failure-perceiving" experimenters.

---

[3] Surprisingly, only the expectancy effect on subject behavior, and not those aspects of performance variation that mediate the effect, has been clearly established by Rosenthal and his associates.

Although Rosenthal has largely confined his study to the person-perception task, he has also applied his basic paradigm of contradictory expectancies of success and failure to learning situations involving laboratory rats (Rosenthal and Fode, 1963a) and classroom children (Rosenthal and Jacobson, 1968). In the former experiment, students enrolled in a laboratory course in experimental psychology were deceived about the intelligence or maze-running ability of their animal subjects. In the latter field experiment, elementary school teachers were led to expect unusual potential for intellectual development in some of their students. In both studies, subjects were randomly assigned to the high- and average-ability conditions. And in both studies, it appeared that the experimenters or teachers somehow elicited from their subjects or students the behavior they had been led to expect from them.[4]

While the expectancy effect hypothesis has generally received support in somewhat over a hundred studies covering a wide range of experimental situations (animal conditioning, person perception, learning and ability, psychophysical judgments, reaction time, inkblot tests, and laboratory interviews; for details, see Rosenthal, 1969a), it has also received some vigorous criticism (Barber and Silver, 1968a, 1968b; Barber, 1969).

One criticism is that Rosenthal has failed to demonstrate his central thesis that experimenters *unintentionally* bias their results by *subtly* transmitting visual or verbal cues to their subjects. Early unsuccessful attempts to identify these mediating cues led Rosenthal to conclude that the mediation process must be extremely subtle (Rosenthal, this book). Barber and Silver (1968a), on the other hand, suggest a number of *intentional* and *overt* actions in their inventory of eleven possible modes of mediation: intentional or unintentional paralinguistic cues (voice quality), intentional or unintentional kinesic cues (body movement), intentional or

---

[4] But see Snow (1969) for a critique of the classroom study.

unintentional operant conditioning (verbally reinforcing subjects for desired responses), intentional or unintentional mis-
judgment or misrecording of the subjects' responses; and intentional experimenter cheating. Since Rosenthal has
assumed that experimenter effects are due to unintentional
paralinguistic and kinesic cues, Barber and Silver (1968a,
1968b) charge that these other possible mediators of expectancy effect may have gone undetected. In rebuttal,
Rosenthal (1969a) cites selected studies which he claims
demonstrate that expectancy effects do occur in the absence
of experimenter cheating, in the absence of recording errors,
and in the absence of operant conditioning. Furthermore, the
recent search for mediating cues has been more productive
than earlier exploratory studies. For instance, if subjects are
shielded from visual contact with their experimenter, the remaining mediation channel (presumably auditory cues) is
sufficient to bring about one half of the normal expectancy
effect in the person-perception task (Rosenthal and Fode,
1963b; Zoble, 1968). Visual cues may also be important, but
the evidence is inconclusive (Rosenthal, 1969a, pp. 253-54;
Zoble and Lehman, 1969). Also, paralinguistic analysis has
identified voice quality aspects that are moderately correlated with the expectancy effect (Duncan and Rosenthal,
1968; Duncan et al., 1969).

A second bone of contention between Rosenthal and his
critics concerns questions of statistical analysis. Barber and
Silver (1968a, 1968b) have accused Rosenthal of taking
statistical liberties by bending his analysis to favor or preserve
the expectancy hypothesis. The alleged biases in the studies
of experimenter bias include post-mortem analyses of subsets
of data that overall were not statistically significant; failure
to take into consideration changing levels of significance
when several statistical tests are performed on the same set of
data; acceptance of low levels of significance (for example,
levels greater than .10) to obtain "significant findings"; ex-
clusion of data contrary to the expectancy hypothesis from
the analysis; and improper use of various statistical tests. In

reply, Rosenthal (1968) points out errors and omissions in the Barber and Silver critique, and goes on to demonstrate that if the experiments in this research domain are jointly considered as a series, the probability that these results could have occurred by chance is infinitesimally low (p < .000000000001). Barber and Silver (1968b) are unpersuaded, however, for they maintain that Rosenthal pooled spurious values to obtain this extremely high level of significance.

The statistical controversy surrounding the expectancy effect hypothesis serves to highlight a third issue of disagreement—the generality and robustness of the phenomenon. Two questions are pertinent. Does experimental bias generally occur in the research paradigms used by Rosenthal and his associates? Does experimenter bias generally have a large enough effect to seriously bias the findings in experiments using other types of experimental tasks? As adequate empirical evidence is lacking, we can only speculate on the answers to these questions. First, the studies which have supported the expectancy effect hypothesis are too numerous to quickly dismiss as a chance occurrence. Yet the frequent inability of many investigators, including Rosenthal, to replicate this phenomenon suggests that the conditions under which it occurs are not fully understood. Failure to replicate may hinge on factors such as subject recruitment, subject-experimenter sex differences, subject-experimenter status differences, and the like (Rosenthal, 1969b).

In answer to the second question, it has been frequently observed that the Rosenthal paradigm differs substantially from the usual experiment in which the same experimenter runs subjects in all conditions and the stimulus material is less ambiguous. Aronson and Carlsmith (1968, p. 67) propose that it may be harder for an experimenter unintentionally to bias subject behavior if he is running more than one condition, as he is likely to notice systematic performance variation should it occur. Further, Rosenthal has intentionally chosen stimulus materials which are totally ambiguous; that is, on the basis of pretests, Rosenthal has selected pictures of individuals who appear neither particularly successful nor particularly unsuccessful. Lyons (1964, p. 99) has likened the person-perception task to the ambiguous stimulus in typical projective tests. Lacking a context in which to judge the pictures, the subject is susceptible to subtle cuing from the experimenter. Stimuli used in many experiments, however, are quite different from the person-perception stimuli in that they have associated with them many cues which may affect the subject's behavior. For example, subjects know that motor or mental tasks like problem-solving ought to be responded to rapidly and accurately rather than slowly and inaccurately. In general when subjects may draw upon their past experiences and knowledge to determine their responses to stimuli, experimenter bias may not be as prevalent as Rosenthal's work seems to suggest. Yet, even in those tasks involving some skill or ability, experimenters may be effective biasers if the activity is especially difficult. Zoble and Lehman (1969), for example, have demonstrated experimenter expectancy effects in a tone length discrimination task. Be that as it may, we suspect that the expectancy effect will prove to be largely insignificant outside of experiments involving ambiguous stimulus tasks.

Methodological Implications

Several special techniques have been proposed to minimize the effect of the experimenter's expectancies when it is likely to pose a problem (Rosenthal, 1966, pp. 331–400; Aronson and Carlsmith, 1968, pp. 68–70). The "double-blind" procedure entails keeping both experimenters and subjects "blind" as to the specific condition that each subject is in. When it is impossible or impractical to use the "double-blind," as when experimenters must vary their activities according to the treatment condition, it is often possible to keep experimenters "blind" during the phases of the experiment that are common across conditions. Another approach to minimize experimenter effect is to rely, as much as possible, upon taped or written instructions. Other possibilities include the use of two or more experimenters in each trial (some or all of whom are completely or partially blind to the subjects' conditions), simultaneously running the subjects in all experimental conditions, and applying sampling and randomization procedures to populations of experimenters as well as subjects.

Rosenthal (1966) has suggested another approach—the use of expectancy control groups. For each manipulation of the experimental (independent) variable, there may be control groups involving manipulation of the experimenter's expectancy:

TREATMENT (Experimental variable)		
	Experimental	Control
EXPECTANCY		
Change	A	B
No Change	C	D

In the above diagram, cells A and D represent the usual experimental design consisting of a control group (D) and an experimental group (A) in which the experimenter expects a change to occur. To permit the evaluation of the true experimental effect apart from the effect induced by the experimenter's expectancy, two additional control groups, C and B, are included. To take a pharmacological study as an illustration, group C would receive the experimental drug although the attending physicians (experimenters) would believe that a placebo (no real drug) had been administered. Any significant differences between groups C and A would be attributed to the physicians' expectancy for treatment change. Similarly, cell B physicians are misled to believe that their subjects received the real drug in order to determine if the physicians' expectancy for no change will affect the subjects' responses. Statistical methods, such as two-way analysis of variance, may then be used to differentiate real effects from expectancy effects, and to explore interactions between the two sources of effect. Rosenthal (1966, pp. 389-92) suggests var-ous ways to manipulate experimenter expectancies, such as mislabeling experimental conditions (as in the above drug example), ascribing differential characteristics to randomly assigned subjects (as in the study of "maze-bright" and "dull" rats), and misleading the experimenters to expect just the opposite outcome from that predicted by the theory under study.

Rosenthal's suggestions for adding expectancy control groups to experimental designs is representative of an emergent conception of social scientific research in which methodologically "suspect" variables in addition to the experimental (independent) variables are manipulated. A recent study of cultural influence on visual perception (Campbell, 1969, pp. 363-64) provides an excellent example of the "new" approach. To rule out performance variation in the administration of visual tasks as an alternative explanation of observed cultural differences, half of the researchers in one sample were purposely instructed to administer the tests in a manner deviating sharply from the standard instructions given to the remaining data collectors. By employing this additional control group, the investigators were able to demonstrate that differences-in-administration effects were very small compared to the observed cultural differences.

The notion of experimenter expectancy and performance variation control groups does not represent a major departure from the experimental methods developed in the natural sciences, but rather should be viewed as a step in the continuing process of adapting those methods to social research situations. For example, it was necessary for psychologists in 1907 to invent control groups to assess the effects of pretests upon subject performance (Campbell, 1969, p. 357). The addition of experimenter expectancy and performance variation control troups is representative of a general strategy of adding to the experimental design control groups for each specific set of suspected confounding factors.

The idea that it may be necessary in social scientific research to manipulate additional features apart from the independent variable in any given experiment is easily extended from conditions within experiments to replications of entire experiments. This is consistent with Rosenthal's suggestion that the value of a replication should be judged in terms of its separation from prior experiments "along such dimensions as time, physical distance, personal attributes of the experimenters, experimenters' expectancy, and experimenters' degree of personal contact with each other" (Rosenthal, 1966, p. 326).

THE RECEPTION AND INTERPRETATION OF STIMULUS PRESENTATION

The second assumption which must be met if the logic of the experimental method is to be successfully applied in the social sciences is that within experimental conditions the stimuli to which subjects are exposed should arouse in each of them similar states and that between experimental conditions subjects' states should differ only in ways intended by the experimental manipulation. While the procedures discussed in the preceding section may minimize the problems of standardized stimulus presentation, it remains true that even if objectively identical stimuli are presented to a group of subjects there will be variation in the way different subjects respond to them.

Any number of characteristics subjects bring with them to experiments may influence how they respond to experimental stimuli. For instance, it is well known that men and women in our culture respond differently to many stimuli. While few would deny that subjects may vary in their responses to objective stimuli, it is generally felt that with adequate pretesting this variability can be made inconsequential in most experiments. Even if *considerable* variability is present, it should mainly contribute to random error (because of subject randomization) and therefore "wash out" ın comparisons across experimental groups.[5] We now turn our attention to a more serious problem: unintended and systematic variation in subjects' states introduced as a function of the social character of experiments with human subjects.

Multiple Meaning

That even seemingly simple stimuli can affect subjects in a number of different ways has been called the problem of "multiple meaning" by Aronson and Carlsmith (1968, p. 13). As an example of the problem of "multiple meaning," let us consider in some detail the controversy surrounding Festinger and Carlsmith's (1959) study of how a person's private opinions change when he is forced (or, more accurately, induced) to publicly say something contrary to those opinions. They proposed, on the basis of cognitive dissonance theory, that the *larger* the reward used to elicit the public statement (beyond the minimum needed to elicit it), the *smaller* the subsequent change in the individual's private opinions. To test their hypothesis, Festinger and Carlsmith designed an experiment in which subjects were exposed to an extremely boring laboratory experience and then induced to tell the next subject (in actuality, a paid confederate) that their experience had been both interesting and enjoyable. One group of subjects was paid one dollar for lying, one group was paid twenty dollars for lying, and a control group was not asked to lie. Various measures of subjects' private opinions about their experiences were administered after they had lied. Subjects in the one dollar (small reward) condition expressed more favorable opinions about their laboratory experiences than did subjects in the twenty dollar (large reward) and control conditions.

Festinger and Carlsmith concluded that their results had strongly corroborated the hypothesis they had derived from

---

[5] Of course, if random error becomes too large, for this or any other reason, it may make obscure the relationships among variables.

cognitive dissonance theory. Critics of this study, however, have proposed several plausible rival explanations of the findings, each based on the contention that Festinger and Carlsmith's manipulations aroused in subjects states different from those intended. Several social psychologists (Chapanis and Chapanis, 1964; Janis and Gilmore, 1965) have argued that subjects in Festinger and Carlsmith's $20 condition may have become suspicious of the whole experiment because of the inordinately large amount of money they were being paid for only a few minutes of lying. If subjects in the $20 condition were more suspicious than subjects in the $1 condition, the failure of subjects in the $20 condition to change their opinions may have been due to their negative feelings about the experiment or the experimenter. Offering a different explanation, Rosenberg (1965, reprinted in this book) has suggested that subjects bring with them to experiments a general concern that the "psychologist" running them is in some way interested in evaluating their personalities. It is his contention that subjects in the $20 condition may have failed to change their opinion because of concern that such a change would make a bad impression on the experimenter; that is, he might believe that their integrity was for sale. Subjects in the $1 condition would presumably be less likely to reach such a conclusion. Both sets of criticism, then, maintain that data from subjects in Festinger and Carlsmith's high reward (low dissonance) condition may have been systematically biased in that offering subjects the large sum of $20 to lie may have aroused them in unintended and undetected ways.

Although a great deal of effort has gone into critical evaluation of Festinger and Carlsmith's study, the issue of multiple meanings contained in the $20 condition has not been resolved (for example, see Bem, 1967). Many factors contribute to the difficulty of resolving such questions. First, subjects may be unaware of or unwilling to describe accurately the states produced in them by the stimulus. Thus simply asking subjects about their interpretations of stimuli is of questionable utility. Second, the experiment when viewed as a social situation contains multiple features which in any combination may affect subjects' states. Third, the motives which subjects bring with them to the experiment may affect the way in which they interpret stimuli.

Just as the addition of appropriate control groups was suggested as a means of handling problems of standard stimulus *presentation,* the addition of control groups may be used to study problems of standard stimulus *reception* (see Wuebben, 1968, for a discussion of some appropriate designs). That is, those features of the experimental situation and those subject motivations which, despite successful standardized stimulus presentation, are thought to contribute to unintended variation in subjects' states may themselves be treated as variables through the use of appropriate control groups. For example, features of the experiment that are extraneous to the intended independent variable may be varied to ascertain if subject behavior is affected. That is, if the subject is not responding in the intended way to the independent variable, but rather is responding to extraneous features of the experiment, then modifying these features will alter his behavior.

Using such a control group approach, Orne and his co-workers (Orne, 1962, reprinted in this book; Orne and Evans, 1965; Orne and Scheibe, 1964; Gustafson and Orne, 1965) have shown that experimental subjects are acutely attentive to the subtle, unprogrammed features of experimental situations. Such cues have been called "demand characteristics." For example, in sensory deprivation experiments the typical procedure followed introduces into the experimental situation many features extraneous to the experimental manipulation (sensory deprivation). Such features may include pre-experimental screening for medical or physical disorders, emergency medical apparatus, forbidding release forms, cautious instructions and the presence of a "panic [release] button." Orne and Scheibe (1964) have shown that when such features are excluded from an experimental situation, no sensory deprivation behavior on the part of subjects occurs in the absence of actual sensory deprivation. However, the presence of such cues alone was sufficient to elicit "deprivation behavior" even though actual sensory deprivation did not take place. Thus, in the typical deprivation study, the extent to which "deprivation behavior" is a function of reduced sensory stimulation (the presumed independent variable) as opposed to demand characteristics is problematic. This study, and others in the Orne series of experiments, are described in greater detail in the Orne article reprinted in this book.

Apparently, demand characteristics may even affect physiological responses, such as the GSR (galvanic skin response), that are often assumed to be entirely beyond voluntary control. By varying the "cover story" in a psychophysiological study involving the lie detector (GSR indicator), Gustafson and Orne (1965) placed differential demands upon subjects to be detected (*or* not detected) in deception by informing them that only "psychopathic personalities or habitual liars" (*or* "highly intelligent, emotionally stable, and mature individuals") are able to fool the lie detector. It was assumed that subjects would, therefore, want to be detected (*or* not detected) to demonstrate their good character. After a first trial involving lying about numbers drawn from a deck of cards, half of the subjects in each "demand expectancy" group were told that they had fooled the lie detector. The results of the second detection trial were very striking. Subjects whose hopes had *not* been confirmed in the first trial (i.e., those who wanted to be detected but were told that they were undetected in the first trial *and* those who were detected in the first trial but needed to deceive) were easy to detect by the large GSRs they gave to the critical numbers. The remaining subjects, whose hopes had been confirmed in the first trial, were physiologically similar, both groups (detected "need-to-be-detected" and undetected "need-to-deceive" subjects) being hard to detect by their GSR.

As we said before, the states aroused in subjects by experimental stimuli are shaped not only by events that occur in the experiment but also by the motives and preconceptions that subjects bring to experiments. We turn now to a discussion of subject motivation.

The Motives of Experimental Subjects

Theoretical discussions of subject motivation may be grouped conveniently into three somewhat contradictory themes: (1) subjects in our culture are largely motivated to play the role of a "good subject" (Orne, 1962); (2) the alienating character of the typical experimental scene engenders "bad subjects" (Argyris, 1968); and (3) subjects in an experimental situation suffer from "evaluation apprehension" and wish to "put their best foot forward" (Riecken, 1962; Rosenberg, 1965). A brief discussion of each theme follows.

The model of the "good subject" is intended to explain the apparent sensitivity of experimental subjects to subtle cues ("demand characteristics"). According to Orne, the "good subject" satisfies his need to *perform well* and *advance science* by consciously or unconsciously behaving in a manner designed to validate the experimenter's hypothesis as it becomes apparent to him through demand characteristics and other extraneous cues.

The wide recognition accorded Orne's work is easily understood when it is realized that his conception of experimental subjects as active, dedicated, hypothesis-prone, information processors appeared at a time when many social scientists still viewed subjects as passive responders to experimental stimuli. Moreover, the Orne model has proven extremely useful in explaining certain empirical phenomena. Now widely evoked in post factum interpretations, the model of the "good subject" has been proposed to explain a diversity of findings ranging from the reluctance of Levy's (1967, reprinted in this book) non-naive subjects to admit pre-experimental knowledge of a verbal conditioning schedule during a post-conditioning interview (the "good subject" does not want to invalidate his performance) to the process by which Rosenthal's (1967, reprinted in this book) experimenters unwittingly communicated their expectancies to subjects (the "good subject" is responsive to subtle cues from the experimenter).

On the other hand, the major assumptions underlying the "good subject" model have not been subjected to empirical testing. For example, Orne *assumes* that subjects come to experiments with built-in motivations to help the experimenter confirm his hypothesis. Or again, Orne assumes that *because* subjects have great respect for the social sciences, they will gladly comply with almost any request an experimenter might make of them. Plausible as such assumptions seem, they are clearly speculative. Is it not equally plausible that some subjects might resent experiments and thus attempt to impede the progress of an experiment in which they find themselves? Or again, might not subjects feign naiveté to outwit the experimenter rather than to validate their performance? What is the distribution of "good subject" types among subject populations? In spite of the inherent plausibility of the "good subject" model, an assessment of its explanatory and predictive capacity must await further empirical inquiry into questions such as these.

Indeed, theorists of subject motivation frequently differ not only in their explanations of the same phenomena but often disagree over the facts involved in an issue. A striking example of this observational selectivity is evident in the divergent empirical phenomena considered by theorists of the "good subject" or "bad subject" persuasion. For every anecdotal account of the model "good subject" in the literature, there must exist an equally persuasive account of the activities of his bad brother, as the following illustrate:

> In operant conditioning, it is commonly observed that some Ss will show a nice learning curve, only to show a reversal at some point. If asked, Ss will say that they became tired of hearing "uh huh" and wanted to see what would happen if they varied the response, or they might state that they did not want the experimenter to think he could control their behavior (Masling, 1966, pp. 95–96).

> In one major university, a formal evaluation was made of the basic psychology course by nearly 600 undergraduates ... the stu-

dents were very critical, mistrustful, and hostile to the requirement [that they had to participate in experiments]. In many cases they identified how they expressed their pent-up feelings by "beating the researcher" in such a way that he never found out (Argyris, 1968, p. 188).

Observations of this sort have promoted limited specula-tion and theorizing (Argyris, 1968; Aronson and Carlsmith, 1968, p. 62; Masling, 1966, pp. 95-96; Rosenberg, 1969, pp. 340–41) about the motives and prevalence of "bad subjects," a theme to which Argyris has contributed the most system-atic treatment. Borrowing from organizational theory, Argyris (1968, p. 193) argues that rigorous experimentation tends "to place subjects in situations that are similar to those [which] organizations create for their lower level em-ployees." Unaccustomed to being subordinates in a highly authoritarian system, research subjects may react by adapting employee ploys such as covert or overt withdrawal or opposi-tion. One of these adaptive strategies, outright dependency upon the experimenter, is usually associated with the "good subject" model:

> The studies that show subjects as all too willing to cooperate are, from this point of view, examples of subject withdrawal from in-volvement and not, as some researchers suggest, signs of subjects' high involvement. To give a researcher what he wants in such a way that the researcher does not realize that the subject is doing this (a skill long ago learned by employees and students) is a sign of non-responsibility and of a lack of commitment to the effectiveness of the research (Argyris, 1968, p. 188).

In addition to their divergent interpretations of observed subject behavior, the "good subject" and "bad subject" theorists provide diametrically opposed suggestions for im-proving social experimentation. Argyris (1968) would have us adopt employee incentive techniques for the purpose of *in-creasing* subject involvement in the research project, perhaps by inviting subjects to participate in the research design and execution or by making the research more relevant to the needs of the subjects. While acknowledging that such motivational techniques might contaminate the findings, Argyris theorizes that truly involved subjects will strive to provide objective rather than biased data. Theorists of the "good subject" persuasion, in contrast, are fearful that highly involved subjects will contaminate the results by acting to confirm their perception of the experimenter's hypothesis. Believing thusly, "good subject" theorists are concerned with *decreasing* or minimizing the unintended effects of high subject commitment to the research. One common approach is to deceive the "good subject" by providing him with a false, but plausible, hypothesis about the experiment, the hypothesis being of such a nature that efforts to confirm it will not systematically affect the results of the true hypothesis under investigation (Aronson and Carlsmith, 1968, pp. 62-63). Another approach, intended to sort out the effects of "good subject behavior" from the true effects of the independent variable, involves manipulation of the social cues (demand characteristics) denoting the true hypothesis (Orne, 1962; Orne and Scheibe, 1964). These procedures for approximating the effect of demand characteristics, reminiscent of expectancy control groups, are described by Orne in the article included in this book.

The "good subject" and "bad subject" theorists are in agreement, however, on one point. This is the implausibility of the former (largely implicit) model of human subjects as passive responders to experimental stimuli. Instead, the new theorists stress the importance of subject motivation, although they disagree as to whether subjects are primarily motivated to help the experimenter (the "good subject") or themselves (the "bad subject").

Another potent motive that subjects may import to experimental situations is that of wishing to present to the experimenter a favorable self-image. Riecken (1962) and Rosenberg (1969) have proposed that experimenters, particularly psychologists, may be viewed by subjects as powerful figures who have the ability to penetrate "common human disguises" for the purpose of evaluating the subject's emotional adequacy, mental health, and other personality attributes. Whenever experimenters do anything to confirm this suspicion, the subject is likely to experience "evaluation apprehension" or concern with presenting himself in such a manner that he receives positive evaluation (and avoids negative evaluation) from the experimenter. Earlier, we described how Festinger and Carlsmith's (1959) $20 condition might arouse evaluation apprehension in subjects. Another well-replicated finding, that lends itself to a favorable self-presentation interpretation (as well as "good subject" and "bad subject" interpretations, unfortunately), is the general reluctance of non-naive subjects to admit pre-experimental knowledge of the experimental hypothesis during the post-experimental interview (Levy, 1967; Golding and Lichtenstein, 1970). It may be contended that these subjects believe that the disclosure of their failure to admit their prior knowledge to the experimenter would cast aspersions on their character or moral integrity.[6]

Rosenberg (1965, this book) holds that the influence of evaluation apprehension upon subject behavior may be circumvented by separating evaluation-arousing phases of the experiment (usually the instruction and treatment periods)

---

[6] It should be noted that Orne has recently modified and enlarged his definition of the "good subject" to include a concern with favorable self-presentation:

> To be a "good" subject may mean many things: to give the right responses, i.e., to give the kind of response characteristic of intelligent subjects; to give the normal response, i.e., characteristic of healthy subjects; to give a response in keeping with the individual's self-perception, etc., etc. If the experimental task is such that the subject sees himself as being evaluated he will tend to behave in such a way as to make himself look good ... However, when the subject's wish to look good is not directly challenged, another set of motives, one of the common bases for volunteering, will become relevant. That is, beyond idiosyncratic reasons for participating, subjects volunteer, in part at least, to further human knowledge, to help provide a better understanding of mental processes that ultimately might be useful for treatment, to contribute to science, etc. (Orne, 1969, p. 145).

The new definition represents a modification of his earlier position that subjects are more concerned with the "utility of their performance" than in "reinforcing their self-image" (Orne, 1962, this book).

from the measurement of the dependent variable by the act of disguising the two segments to appear as two unrelated studies conducted by two unrelated investigators. When this is impossible, Rosenberg (1969) suggests the techniques of altered replication or manipulated arousal and cuing, both of which involve additional experimental or control groups. In the method of altered replication, one modifies the stimulus presentations thought to arouse evaluation apprehension and repeats the experiment. In the second or "evaluation apprehension control group" method, arousal is directly manipulated by differential cuing, such as by varying the cover story to create "high" and "low" arousal conditions or to convey contradictory information about the type of behavior likely to be positively evaluated.

This discussion by no means exhausts the current models of experimental subjects. Numerous additional models have been proposed, including the "faithful subject" who remains faithful to the experimenter's instructions and refuses to seek out the true purpose of the study (Fillenbaum, 1966) and the "negativistic subject" who acts in the opposite way to the one he thinks is expected of him (Masling, 1966). More models, no doubt, are on their way. At the same time, however, research in this area is starting to move in a more productive direction. Instead of prolonged discussions over the relative merits of various subject motivational models, attention is now being given to the experimental conditions and to the subject population characteristics which may trigger one or more of the various components of subject motivation (e.g., see Silverman and Shulman, 1970).

The General Expectations of Experimental Subjects

Another potent influence on the states aroused in subjects by experimental stimuli is the set of general expectations that subjects bring to experiments. Most people probably have at least vague preconceptions about what occurs in social scientific experiments and about how research subjects should behave (Riecken, 1962, reprinted in this book). The content of subjects' imported expectations about experiments is thought to be shaped by (1) formal contact with social scientific thought and practices as well as by (2) everyday social experiences. We will consider these two potential sources of subjects' expectations in turn.

Implicit in the operating procedures of most experimenters is the notion that experimental stimuli will arouse intended states only in "naive subjects." For instance, experienced subjects who have previously been fooled in a "deception" experiment may attach different meanings to the events in a subsequent experiment than will unexperienced (undeceived) subjects. Similarly, exposure to communication channels relevant to experiments (social scientific literature, course lectures, campus gossip, etc.) is thought to jeopardize subject naiveté. Thus it is a common practice to recruit from populations thought to contain "naive subjects," such as college freshmen and sophomores who are taking their first course in sociology or psychology.

The available empirical evidence bearing upon the "naive subject" formulation is equivocal. Some studies have shown that "deceptions" and "debriefings" in earlier experiments do not appreciably affect the performance of subjects in later experiments (Fillenbaum, 1966; Cook et al., 1970). But other studies have found that performance *does* vary with previous experience (Holmes, 1967) and prior deception (Silverman et al., 1970). Prior knowledge of social scientific procedures and testing instruments has also been found to affect subject performance in a psychological testing (TAT) situation (Ismir, 1962), but not in a "deception" experiment (Cook et al., 1970).

It is difficult to reach any conclusion from such mixed findings, for the relevant studies differed in many ways that might have affected the results, including the nature of the experimental tasks employed in the prior and test experiments, the time interval between successive experiments, and the "cover" story given. There are some other findings, however, that provide some clues upon which to speculate. First, the impact of prior experimental deception may be significant only in subsequent experiments that closely resemble the earlier "deception" experiment (Brock and Becker, 1966). Second, previous experimental experience may affect subject motivation (Holmes and Appelbaum, 1970), which in turn may influence the states aroused in subjects by subsequent experimental stimuli. For example, prior deception may both arouse subjects' suspicions and decrease their interest in performing as "good" subjects. In other words, effects on subjects' states may be complex.

The "naive subject" formulation, in its emphasis on actual exposure to social scientific thought and practices, overlooks the importance of our general culture as a basis for subjects' preconceptions about experiments. Obviously, the ease with which experiments are performed is largely a function of their similarity to everyday social situations. In addition, it is the general culture that prepares subjects to expect "patterned and orderly stimulus experiences." (Alexander et al., 1970), to expect professional experimenters who will not do anything to actually harm them (Orne and Evans, 1965), to expect that the experimenter is interested in evaluating their personality (Rosenberg, 1965, this book), and so forth.[7]

The relative importance of actual exposure to social scien-

---

[7] Since this section of the book was completed, Straits and Wuebben have reported two studies which have explored subjects' expectations about and attitudes toward experiments. In the first (Straits, Wuebben, & Majka, 1972), an economical method was developed to study various influences (e.g., deception, prior experience) on subjects' perceptions of experimental research situations. After obtaining subjects' impressions of a series of "simulated" experiments, factor analysis of subjects' ratings revealed two stable orthogonal dimensions in terms of which subjects apparently evaluated the experimental situations to which they were exposed—(a) the scientific value of the experiment and (b) the value of the experiment to the subject "personally." The predominant factor was the value to science (or value to the experimenter) dimension. In the second study (Straits and Wuebben, 1973), a survey of a random sample of students/subjects showed, again, that subjects responded to their experiences in terms of both their scientific and "personal" value. Straits and Wuebben (1973, pp. 382-383) offered the following summary of the typical subject: "The subject is participating to fulfill a course requirement and has had considerable previous exposure to social scientific thought and practices through such channels as social science courses, experienced subjects, and prior experimental experiences. He may also have received some

tific thought and practices, as opposed to everyday social experiences, in affecting subjects' expectations about experiments cannot be determined with the meager empirical evidence available. If we were to speculate, however, we would predict that the "naive subject" formulation will, in the future, be less influential as a methodological guideline for conducting experiments. It appears that procedures intended to isolate "naive subjects" (for example, the post-experimental interview) have low validity and reliability (see next section) because of the overriding influence of subject motivational factors. Moreover, we suspect that motives and expectancies formed in the larger socio-cultural environment (including concern with favorable self-presentation) are more "powerful" than those formed as a result of actual exposure to social scientific thought and practices.

INDEPENDENCE OF OBSERVATIONS

If the data from any experiment are to be scientifically useful, they must have been collected in such a way that independence of observations can be assumed. That is, we must be able to assume that the making of any given observation (measurement) during the course of the experiment did not influence the outcome of any other observation. Independence of observations is important for several reasons, two of which may be conveniently discussed here. First, social scientists, like all scientists, are interested in establishing *general* laws, laws that apply to many different instances of the same phenomenon. If the same causal relationship can

---

information about the experiment from an earlier-run subject. On the basis of his previous exposure to social scientific thought and practices and his everyday social experiences, he has formed a definite set of expectancies about the social science experiment. Included in his model are beliefs that experimentation is scientifically worthwhile and will benefit mankind, that serving as an experimental subject is not always an interesting and pleasant experience, that experimenters are persons to be respected and trusted, and that sometimes experimenters should be feared for their 'psychological powers' of personality insight. If the events of an actual experiment tend to depart from the subject's preconceived model of the experiment as an 'orderly' affair, various components of subject motivation may be intensified, and the subject may exhibit unintended (from the experimenter's standpoint) behaviors."

be observed a number of times, i.e., in many subjects, we have increased confidence that we are dealing with a general phenomenon, not one peculiar to some particular set of individuals. But that confidence rests on each observation being independent of other observations.

Independence of observations is also important for a second reason—the nature of statistical tests. After data are collected, the investigator must decide if any observed differences among the experimental conditions are consistent with his hypothesis or if they are likely to have arisen through chance extraneous variation. The way he typically does this is to apply a statistical test to his data, a test that will tell him the probability that the differences were due to chance. To legitimately apply such a test, however, the observations that together comprise the data must (normally) be independent of each other.

To what extent are social scientists justified in assuming that independence of observations is usually achieved in social scientific experimentation? We may consider the question in the context of the two assumptions we have already introduced, the assumption of standard presentation of stimuli and the assumption of intended stimulus effects on subjects' states.

Early Data Returns

Rosenthal (1966) has identified experimenters' reactions to early data returns as a threat to the independence of observations. In those experiments which involve extensive subject-experimenter interaction, the experimenter's expectancies may change as a result of his inspection of data from the first few subjects, and that in turn may systematically affect his performance in later runs. Thus, later-run subjects will be responding to different stimuli from the experimenter than did earlier-run subjects. In an experiment on the effects of early data returns, Rosenthal, Persinger, Vikan-Kline, and Fode (1963a) found that if an experimenter's expectancies were confirmed by the first two "subjects" (the experimenter's confederates), data from later-run subjects were more confirmatory of the hypothesis than were data collected by experimenters whose early returns were disconfirmatory. A second study by Rosenthal and his co-workers (Rosenthal, Kohn, Greenfield, and Carota, 1965) provided indirect evidence that the factor mediating the effects of early data returns was in fact changes in the experimenter's expectancies. (The way in which those expectancies were communicated was not determined in this case, as in most other experimenter-bias experiments.)

Although it may be true that knowledge of early data returns can bias later findings, *in principle* the solution to the problem is relatively simple. Experimenters or their surrogates need only make certain that they look at none of the data until it has all been collected, or alternatively, that no one who interacts with subjects learns of early data returns. In practice, however, experimenters will frequently find it difficult to avoid contact with the data during the course of an experiment. Experimenters are of course vitally interested in the results of their studies and the temptation to inspect the data is always present. Further, for some kinds of studies it may be difficult to devise an experimental design which will prevent the experimenter from becoming aware of how subjects are responding. For example, in some studies the manipulation of the independent variable may best be done by the experimenter and he or she may also have to make observations relevant to the dependent variable. In such cases, he or she will as a matter of course form impressions of "how the study is going." Nevertheless, it may be maintained that with careful planning the potential biasing effects of early data returns may be minimized in most studies.

Inter-Subject Communication

In the "ideal" experiment, the investigator has complete control of the nature of experimental stimuli, the manner in which the stimuli are presented, and the sequence of the presentation. With such control, the probability that intended states will be produced in the subjects is maximized. For present purposes let us assume that (a) researchers *can* closely approximate complete control of everything that occurs during any given experimental run and that (b) considering the experimental situation alone, the stimuli present in it are such that they *are* capable of producing the intended states in subjects. Now let us consider still one more complicating feature of experiments in the social sciences.

Experiments with human subjects are events which take place *within* some larger socio-cultural setting, most usually a university. Participants in experiments are only "borrowed" from the larger community. That is, unlike mineral or animal subjects, "used" human subjects may not be destroyed after an experiment has been completed; rather they must be returned, unimpaired, to their natural habitat. Human beings who have served as subjects in a given experiment are therefore *of necessity* given an opportunity to *communicate to others* in the community their impressions of the events of the experiment. If a significant number of subjects do so, experimental stimuli may acquire socially structured "extra-scientific" meanings among the population which discusses them—usually the very population from which subjects are drawn for later runs of the experiment. It must be considered unlikely that experimental stimuli will produce the *intended* states in subjects with prior knowledge of (and opinions about) those stimuli.

Of course, methodologically, the most damaging form of inter-subject communication would be that in which an ex-subject informs a yet-to-be processed subject of the experimental hypothesis. But *any* information about the events of an experiment acquired by a subject prior to his participation in it threatens the independence of the observations made on that subject. For example, suppose an ex-subject tells his friend that although he wasn't able to "figure out" the hypothesis of the experiment and the experimenter didn't tell him, it must have had something to do with fear since the experimenter said he was going to be given an electric shock when in fact one was never delivered. In such a case, when the friend participates in the experiment, not only will the experimental manipulation have little impact on him (he knows he won't be shocked), but also his behavior will be a function of the definition of the study he *shares* with his friend—that it has to do with fear. In fact, the study may have nothing to do with fear, but nevertheless observations relevant to the dependent variable will not be independent of each other for these two subjects.

One must consider certain features which are typical of most experiments in the social sciences to fully appreciate the methodological implications of "illicit" post-experimental communications. In the usual experiment, successful manipulation of independent variables and/or valid measurement of dependent variables can be accomplished only if subjects are ignorant of certain aspects of the experiment. Experimenters regularly rely upon three related sets of practices in an effort to assure such ignorance. First, subjects are procured from populations which are believed to be both unknowledgeable about experiments in general and deceivable, e.g., college freshmen and sophomores who are taking their first course in sociology or psychology. Second, when subjects arrive for an experiment they are given a cover story which is designed to conceal certain true facts about the experiment while at the same time facilitating its execution (Aronson and Carlsmith, 1968). Third, since most studies process subjects *sequentially,* a "used" subject is allowed to return to the subject population only after he has promised not to tell anyone about the experiment. It is presumed that he will keep his promise and that, therefore, subjects who come to later runs of the experiment will be as naive and gullible as he supposedly was.

The tenability of the presumption that subjects keep their promises not to talk to others about experiments have been put into question by a number of recent studies (Lichtenstein, 1968b; Rokeach, Zemach, and Norrell, 1966; Straits

and Wuebben, 1972; Wuebben, 1967, 1969). These studies
indicate that (a) the proportion of subjects who break their
pledges to secrecy is very high, probably greater than 50
percent, and that (b) subjects who do talk, talk to an average
of more than two other persons. Further, Wuebben (in an
article published in this book) has shown that (a) subjects are
likely to tell others a good deal about the experiments in
which they have participated—in many cases *detailed* information is communicated—and that (b) ex-subjects talk to a
great variety of people, many of whom are potential subjects
for later runs of the experiment.

In a study of some of the factors related to whether or not
subjects talk to others about their experiences in an experiment, Wuebben (1969) found that the experimenter's request
for post-experimental silence does effectively deter some subjects from talking. Of those subjects who had received no
request for silence, 92 percent said that they had talked to
others about the experiment they had been in (one week
intervened between the experiment and the questionnaire).
However, 50 percent of the subjects who *had* received a plea
for post-experimental silence said that they had talked to no
one. Of course that leaves 50 percent of the subjects who
received the request for post-experimental silence and committed themselves to fulfill it, but who nevertheless said they
did talk. What factors were responsible for these subjects'
talking? Testing a hypothesis suggested by Festinger's (1954)
theory of social comparison processes, Wuebben exposed
roughly one half of those subjects who had committed themselves to silence to an experimental condition designed to
produce relatively great uncertainty about the correctness of
an opinion they had formed during the course of the experiment. The other subjects were in a condition designed to
produce less uncertainty. Following social comparison
theory, it was hypothesized that relative to subjects in the
low uncertainty condition, subjects in the high uncertainty
condition would be more likely to break their pledges to
secrecy in an attempt to evaluate their opinion through social

comparison processes. Findings strongly supported the prediction. Only 35 percent of the subjects in the low uncertainty condition said that they had talked to others about
the experiment. However, 65 percent of the subjects in the
high uncertainty condition admitted that they had violated
their promise not to talk.

On the basis of findings from Wuebben's study, one would
expect that anything that reduces subjects' uncertainty about
opinions formed during the experiment would also reduce
their propensity to talk to others about the experiment. And
indeed, in the only study reporting data inconsistent with the
hypothesis of widespread post-experimental talking, Aronson
(1966) found that of nine *extensively* debriefed subjects,
none revealed any information in response to a request from
the experimenter's confederate. (It should be noted however
that Aronson's small sample and the unusual degree to which
his subjects were debriefed makes questionable the represen-
tativeness of his results.)

Taken together, then, the relevant studies suggest that
most subjects do *not* honor their promises of silence. Thus it
must be considered likely that at least some later-run subjects
in the typical experiment will have received illicit information about the study prior to their participation in it. But if
this conclusion is correct, what can account for the fact that
most investigators report finding only an occasional subject
who had "heard about the experiment before"? In most
cases, it may be contended, the number of subjects who
possess prior information about an experiment is greatly
underestimated. Experimenters typically check the naiveté of
their subjects by simply asking them (before, during, or, typically, after the experiment) whether they have heard of, or
are familiar with, the research procedures. If a subject should
answer "yes," he is of course dropped from the study. However, if he answers "no," it is assumed that he is, in truth,
naive. Evidence which has recently become available suggests
that this assumption is unwarranted.

Several studies (Denner, 1967; Levy, reprinted in this

book; Lichtenstein, 1968a; Golding and Lichtenstein, 1970) have directly addressed the question of the extent to which subjects will admit their prior knowledge of an experiment. These studies have all employed the same basic experimental design. Posing as a subject who has just completed the experiment, a confederate of the experimenter informs waiting subjects of the nature of the experimental task (e.g., "What they want you to do is to make up sentences with the words 'I' and 'we' in them"). After completing the experiment, the subjects are asked if they knew anything about the study before they participated in it. Only about 5 percent admit their knowledge of the experimentally crucial prior information. An extensive, probing interview produces only a slight increase, to a range of 10 to 15 percent, in the proportion of subjects who will admit all that they have been told. Only about 50 percent of subjects will admit to having known *anything at all* about the experiment.

It must be noted, further, that informed subjects have been found to produce the "same" kind of data as do presumably naive subjects. That is, the same *pattern* (although not necessarily the same numerical values relevant to the dependent variable) of statistically significant differences between experimental groups is found for both "naive" subjects and informed subjects (Levy, reprinted in this book; Lichtenstein, 1968a; Golding and Lichtenstein, 1970)! If further research were to show that in most studies presumably naive subjects and informed subjects respond to experimental stimuli in the same way, the theoretical import of any set of findings would be rendered ambiguous. For any given experiment, one would be unable to dismiss the possibility that the effective variable operating in the "naive" subject population was their knowledge of the experimenter's hypothesis rather than the independent variable the experimenter manipulated.

The methodological problem inherent in the circumstance that experimentation occurs within a larger social context may now be succinctly stated. If an experiment is to produce valid results, the subjects who participate in it must be naive and manipulable, and observations on each of them must be independent of observations on the rest. In most experiments, subjects must be processed sequentially. In all experiments, "used" subjects must be allowed to return to the subject population. Once released from the laboratory, many subjects violate their pledges not to talk to others about the experiment in which they have taken part. It is therefore likely that some unknown (and perhaps considerable) proportion of later run subjects will have heard about the experiment before participating in it. It is *not* likely that even an extensive interview will enable an experimenter to reliably distinguish those of his subjects who were truly naive from those who had prior knowledge of the experiment. Between-runs-independence of observations cannot be safely assumed and present techniques of post-experimental interviewing are such that the reliable empirical determination, of which subjects in fact are naive, is impossible (see Wuebben, on pp. 173-176, for further discussion of these points).

Before discussing ways of dealing with lack of independence in experimental observations, a word of caution is in order. Although the rather discouraging conclusions stated in the preceding paragraph are warranted by presently available evidence, the problem may be less severe than it appears. First, although previous studies have fairly consistently found that a majority of subjects talk to others, we have no notion of what proportion of subjects *come to* experiments with prior information. Since subjects refuse to admit prior information when we know they have it, finding ways to determine the "typical" proportion of informed subjects may be very difficult. In any case the proportion of "contaminated" subjects may be expected to vary widely with any number of factors. For example, if an experimenter's subject pool consists of 150 students in an introductory psychology course, he might expect that by the time he has processed his fiftieth subject a high percentage of the remaining students will have heard about the study. On the other hand, if subjects are recruited at random from a student body of 25,000, the proportion of later run subjects who have prior information may be exceedingly small.

It should also be noted that various features associated with different kinds of experiments may influence the extent to which subjects will talk about a study in which they have participated. For example, studies which are particularly "interesting," which are obviously "relevant" to larger social concerns, and which are particularly involving may be expected to provoke a good deal of "illicit" information exchange. Other kinds of studies may be talked about to a lesser extent. Finally, it must be noted that even if some later run subjects do have prior information, the methodological consequences for some kinds of studies may be inconsequential.

At the present time, the most prudent position on intersubject communication would seem to be one in which researchers are counseled not to *assume* that they have achieved independence of observations. Rather, experimenters should seriously question that assumption and take all possible steps (a) to assure independence and (b) to devise means of empirically addressing the question, e.g., by routinely comparing data collected early in an experiment with data collected later.

Of course a general solution to the dual problem of subjects' talking about experiments and subjects' refusing to admit what they know of experiments awaits further research into the general phenomenon of the handling of "secret" information and into the peculiarities of the experimental situation as a social interaction between subject and researcher. However, in the meantime several "partial" solutions may be suggested. First, since asking subjects not to talk does apparently deter some of them from talking, experimenters should continue to secure the pledge to secrecy. Second, those studies which can be run without processing subjects sequentially have no problems with communication between first and later run subjects since all subjects are processed simultaneously. More studies should be run in such a way. Third, at the conclusion of the experiment, subjects should be given an extensive "debriefing" so that they have an opportunity to reduce any and all uncertainties they might have developed about the experiment and about anything that occurred during the experiment. When ethical considerations demand it, the true hypothesis under investigation must, of course, be exposed, e.g., when the experimental manipulations caused subjects psychological discomfort through deception, the deception must be revealed. However, when ethical concerns are not paramount and when the experimental cover story has not been "blown" during the course of the experiment, the true hypothesis being studied should not be disclosed. Rather, subjects' questions about the experiment should be answered within the context of the deception originally employed. Thus, if subjects do talk about the experiment, they will, hopefully, communicate to prospective subjects information consistent with the study's cover story. Fourth, new means of conducting post-experimental interviews should be employed in an effort to achieve accurate measurement of prior knowledge. For example, subjects might be led to believe that a "lie detector" to which they are attached will expose any attempt on their part to conceal what they knew of the experiment. Other innovations should also be pursued. Finally, more attention should be paid to the composition of subject pools—for example, friends and acquaintances might be excluded from participation in the same study.

INTRODUCTION TO REPRINTED ARTICLES

In the pages immediately following, the reader will find reprinted articles that deal with some of the problems of successfully executing experiments with human subjects. The first article, by Riecken, may be regarded as the manuscript in which the social psychology of the experiment was first given definition as a legitimate and important area of concern. Rosenthal, in the next article, reviews much of the literature on experimenter expectancy effects and explores the implications of that work for the social psychology of interpersonal relations. In the following article, Orne discusses demand characteristics and stresses subjects' motivations to be "good subjects" and to "figure out" the hypothesis. Next, in Argyris' article, factors related to subjects developing "bad subject" motivations are discussed and the future development of the relationship between subjects and experimenters is explored. Wuebben, in an article specially prepared for this volume, then reports findings which indicate that the nature of deceived and debriefed subjects' postexperimental communications with others may present a major methodological problem in many experiments.

Verbal conditioning, conformity, and cognitive dissonance are central substantive concerns in contemporary social psychology. Each of the articles reprinted in the latter part of this section represents an empirical demonstration that typical experimental paradigms in these areas may be subject to "social psychology of the experiment" problems.

In the first article, Levy analyzes the impact of prior information about the hypothesis in a standard verbal conditioning design. He shows not only that subjects who are known to have been informed will not admit their prior knowledge of the hypothesis, but also that very similar learning curves are produced by uninformed and informed subjects.

Schulman's work with the classic Asch conformity paradigm demonstrates that the subject's behavior is in part a function of the experimenter's position as an observer. In the Asch design, giving the same objectively incorrect answer as the group of confederates has been taken as a measure of the subject's conformity to the group. Schulman suggests that such responses may also reflect conformity to the experimenter.

Rosenberg's study raises serious questions about the appro-

priateness of "forced compliance" studies as tests of dissonance theory. In "forced compliance" studies, subjects are
typically given differential amounts of inducement to behave
publicly in ways contrary to their private opinions. While
differential inducements are intended to create differences in
cognitive dissonance, Rosenberg suggests that they may instead create differences in the subjects' perception of the
experimenter's purpose. Such differences in subjects' definition of the situation may in part account for the results of
"forced compliance" studies.

6
A Program
For Research
On Experiments
In Social Psychology

Henry W. Riecken

The present paper is a first attempt to outline a problem in empirical social psychology and to suggest some ways of attacking it.[1] Stated abstractly, the problem is the identification and analysis of some sources of unintended variance in the data collected during an experiment. In more concrete terms, we may think of the problem as understanding those features of persons, situations and events that are unintentionally (from the point of view of the experimenter) present or introduced into the process of data collection and that are responsible for unexpected (and, usually, undesired) variation in the behavior of subjects.

Such variation is ordinarily regarded as "error," reflecting some mistake in procedure on the part of the investigator. From this standpoint, the problem under scrutiny can be seen as an investigation of ways of improving experimentation. On the other hand, a broader perspective on the problem reveals it as a series of more fundamental questions about human interaction, interpersonal relations, or social behavior.

[1] The present paper is a shortened version of a background paper prepared at the Behavioral Sciences Conference at the University of New Mexico in the summer of 1958. The conference was supported by the Air Force Office of Scientific Research, Behavioral Sciences Division, under contract AF 49(638)-33. The assistance provided by AFOSR and the University of New Mexico is hereby gratefully acknowledged.

Reprinted with permission of author and publisher from *Decisions, Values, and Groups,* Norman F. Washburne, ed. (Elmsford, N.Y.: Pergamon Press, 1962), pp. 25-41.

The process of collecting data about human behavior is itself a social process and shares features in common with other situations and events of human interaction. Accordingly, the process of data collection can be studied as a particular type of interaction in a particular social situation. A major task of this paper will be to examine the particular features of the social situation in which data are collected and the processes of negotiation[2] between investigator and subject through which they come to understand how to behave in the situation.

In fact, the range of interest in this paper will be narrower than the process of data collection in general. I want to confine attention to matters that typically arise in experimental social psychology in American universities, omitting for the moment the interesting problems that occur in participant observation, public opinion poll interviewing and field studies of communities, organizations and social processes. This restriction comes from both my interest in and familiarity with laboratory experiments and from the need to cut the task down to manageable size. At a later time I hope to deal with the specific problems of these other types of research.

Furthermore, I want to concentrate on certain aspects of the laboratory experiment that have been largely overlooked or underemphasized, namely those assumptions and inferences that experimenter and subject make about the social character of each other and about the nature of the experiment as a social situation. In other words, I want to examine how subject and experimenter "make sense of" the situation of the experiment and of each other as social types. Some of the possible sources of unintended variance have been occasionally glimpsed, by design or by accident, in social psychological research; and the citation of some examples may clarify the nature of my interest. For example, the relationship between subject and experimenter may make a difference in subject's behavior. Birney's (1958) replication of Lowell's research on need achievement and task performance demonstrates that a faculty experimenter induces different performance levels in subjects than does a graduate student experimenter. Elinor Sachs' (1952) study of measured intelligence in nursery school children indicates that a warm, friendly relation between subject and test administrator can "elevate" a child's IQ, while a cold, distant relationship may have an oppo-

[2] I am indebted to Harold Garfinkel for calling my attention to this notion which he encountered in some unpublished material of Erving Goffman's. In addition, I should like to thank Dr. Garfinkel for suggestions and helpful criticism at many other points in the paper.

site effect. Concrete evidence of this sort does not occur frequently in the literature; but similar sorts of effects are known or suspected by many practicing experimenters, whose anecdotes, hunches, suspicions and speculations can further the inquiry at hand. The first job, however, is to provide a framework for organizing these casual observations and impressions.

The framework I should like to adopt is suggested by Goffman (1959) in his analysis of everyday interaction, namely the appearance (or "image" or "impression") that people in social contact with each other try to create and maintain. Goffman puts it this way: "I shall consider the way in which the individual in ordinary ... situations presents himself and his activity to others, the ways in which he guides and controls the impressions they form of him, and the kinds of things he may and may not do while sustaining his performance before them" (preface). (It should be noted that this way of putting things does not imply either an interest in the correspondence between "appearance" and "reality"; nor a necessary implication that people in ordinary social interaction are deliberately and self-consciously "playing a part.")

Goffman's view of interaction is echoed in a statement by Kahn and Cannell (1957) in the course of describing communication in the interview:

> ... we have developed ways and habits of reacting to each other that are not intended to simplify or facilitate the process [of communication]. They are designed in large part to help us protect ourselves against making some undesirable revelation or against putting ourselves in an unfavorable light. They are man's methods of defending himself against the possibility of being made to look ridiculous or inadequate. And in most cases we are not content merely to avoid looking inadequate, we also want to appear intelligent, thoughtful, or in possession of whatever other virtues are relevant to the situation from our point of view. We want to put our best foot forward.

Precisely. Everyone wants to put his best foot forward and certainly subjects in an experiment want to display "whatever other virtues are relevant." The crucial question is: how does the subject in an experiment decide what virtues are relevant and what faults must be concealed? To find our answer to this question we shall look first at the features of the experiment as a social situation and second at the process of negotiation between subject and experimenter whereby the former decides what qualities he will see as "relevant."

THE EXPERIMENT AS A SOCIAL SITUATION

The most outstanding feature of the experiment as a social situation is that it is an invitation for one person to behave under the scrutiny of another. It is usually an invitation rather than a command and the fact that the invitation is accepted implies that the subject anticipates or seeks some rewards for his participation. Sometimes these rewards are obvious: pay, academic credit, opportunity to win a prize or simply the gratitude of the experimenter. There is reason to believe that these "obvious" rewards do not exhaust the possible returns a subject can get, however, for there is some evidence that subjects also see the experiment as an opportunity to learn more about how psychology is practiced; to learn some things about himself—his traits, abilities and defects as a person, as these are revealed by psychological techniques; and even to receive some help in solving personal problems. In one sense, then, the subject may have his own set of private reasons or purposes for participating in the experiment. To be sure, these purposes and the corresponding expectations on the part of the subject as to what opportunities the experiment will offer for his purposes to be fulfilled are ordinarily "specifically vague."

The major reason they are "specifically vague" comes from a second feature of the experiment, namely that the terms of the invitation to behave are usually not well specified. In his initial invitation, the experimenter usually specifies only a few items, such as the time, place and duration of the experimental session and, at most, outlines vaguely the "purpose" of the experiment. He leaves much to be revealed progressively as the experimental session itself unfolds. On the other hand, the subject is not completely unprepared for what is going to happen in the session for he usually has some notions about both what psychologists are interested in and how they go about gratifying these interests; he also has some ideas about the limits of appropriate behavior. (Just what the contents of these notions are is not presently clear, but presumably they could be investigated.)

The third feature of the experiment I want to examine is the nature of the personages (or roles) involved. In most cases the experimenter is a professor and the subject a student. They have a relationship that has a history and a socially defined character.

The experimenter is a teacher who offers no course but may nonetheless teach the subject something—about himself. While he has no grade to give, the experimenter may still "grade" the subject in terms of quality of performance, co-operativeness, effort and the like. Like the earlier figures who have stood *in loco parentis* for the subject, this experimenter-professor has responsibilities toward his students and is bound to protect as well as guide them. He is, in the common sense meaning of the term, trustworthy. Furthermore, he is rational, serious and purposive. He may be eccentric; but he is not a lunatic, a prankster or an idler. His behavior is explicable in terms of the scheme of motives, purposes, and norms that govern the academic community.

But this particular professor has another aspect, for he is also a psychologist, whose job it is to poke and pry into recesses of the person that are not ordinarily open to view. The things a psychologist may uncover about one may be gratifying or shame-provoking, but they are likely to be true since the psychologist reputedly has special tools and techniques that enable him to penetrate at least the common human disguises. He can see more than one wants him to see. There is some suspicion that his techniques are incompletely effective and that he makes mistakes, but also an uneasy feeling that he may make fewer mistakes than his victims joke about.

The experimenter then is a powerful figure. He has two kinds of power: as a professor, he is a member of the superordinate group that has the power of effective evaluation over students; as a psychologist he has the power of insight into the subject. Furthermore, one can afford to feel ambivalent toward him. On the one hand, he is trustworthy in that he will not knowingly risk the subject's life, steal or physically attack him. On the other hand, he is up to the same trick that all teachers are up to: divining the true character of the pupil, assessing his worth and passing judgment on him. In so doing he may expose the subject's pretenses, inflict humiliation and mental pain. Furthermore, he is especially able to do all these things becaues he has fortified himself with the skills and paraphernalia of "modern psychology."

Such a picture is, of course, one-sided. Teachers and psychologists can be gulled; and they can, with some risk, be defied. If defied in an experiment psychologist-teachers have rather limited means of retaliation: withholding gratitude, academic credit or pay. These penalties may not be enough to dissuade defiance when the task demanded or the insult delivered is great. On the other hand, the appearance of docility and co-operativeness (within limits) may be a superior strategy for the subject who is playing safe by trying to get a good evaluation of himself from the professor.

A fourth important feature of the experiment as a social situation is that it is temporally and spatially set apart from everyday life—at least from the point of view of the experimenter. The experimenter usually wants to use the subject as an instance of behavior, use him just one time, and then forget everything about him except the data he has produced. He views the subject as a more or less typical human being and his behavior as a more or less typical instance of what human beings would do under the conditions of the experiment. He is ordinarily not interested in the subject's past or his future prospects but sees him only as a producer of raw data.

It may be that the subject sees the situation differently, however, and may either hope for or fear greater continuity. In the first place, the subject may be unable to accept the indignity of being viewed as just another instance of general human behavior and may wish to be appreciated for the unique individual that he considers himself to be. Thus, he may see the experiment as an opportunity to make a good impression on a member of the faculty at his university or as an opportunity to be inducted into the mysteries of behavioral science and thus begin a career (however peripheral) as an "insider." In the second place, the subject may fear that the experimenter cannot or will not take such a detached view of him but will, instead, take an evaluative view of his performance and will make some use of this information to affect some future enterprise in which the subject may be engaged. It is probably difficult for subjects to accept fully the assurances of the experimenter about anonymity and protection of personal data from the scrutiny of those who could use it to evaluate the subject. Further, in all his previous experience with teachers the subject has undoubtedly learned that they are capable of invoking past performances both "in" and "out" of school as the basis for present judgments and recommendations for the future. The nature of the subject's anxieties may be vague and far ranging: he may believe that his performance in the experiment will literally become a part of his academic record; or he may simply entertain the vague notion that in future occasional or accidental encounters the experimenter will treat him in terms of how he performed in the experiment. In any event, the subject's question is: "What will he think of me?"

Finally, I want to call attention to a fifth feature of the experiment as a social situation, namely the one-sided distribution of information. Even after the experimental session has begun and the task has been explained to the subject, the experimenter typically withholds information and the subject knows that he is doing so. The experimenter may conceal or misrepresent the purpose of his experiment; but even when he does not, he still conceals "the right answer." He plays, almost like an examiner, a serious game with the subject, inviting the latter to behave under specified conditions but revealing neither what the experimenteer regards as the "right answer" nor even the criteria by which a particular answer will be judged. The experimenter may provide some hints by indicating what a *relevant* answer is—e.g., when he provides a questionnaire or rating scale—and these hints may help the subject guide his interpretation of the situation, but "the right answer" remains the property of the master of these ceremonies until the program is over.

Sometimes the psychologist tells the subject: "There is no right or wrong answer. The best answer is your own opinion." In one sense, the psychologist literally means this instruction; yet in another he does not, for he ordinarily knows what interpretation will be given to each possible answer. Now the subject is not such a fool as the experimenter wants to make him out. He suspects that various answers are right and wrong to the extent that they represent him to the experimenter in the light that he (the subject) wishes to appear—that there are answers that will enhance and that will diminish his value as a person.

The fact that the experimenter controls the information available to the subject and that he never reveals completely what he is trying to discover and how he will judge what he observes—this feature gives the experiment much of its character as a game or contest. It leads to a set of inferential and interpretive activities on the part of the subject in an effort to penetrate the experimenter's inscrutability and to arrive at some conception of the meaning that the unrevealed categories of response have for the latter.

In the light of these five features of the experiment—its invitational quality, the unspecified nature of the invitation's terms, the attributes of the relationship between the two principal personages (subject and experimenter), the temporal and spatial segregation of the experience and the one-sidedness of the distribution of information—it is easy to see how the subject is impelled to "put his best foot forward." He attempts to appear in the best possible light within the constraints imposed by the situation, by concealing or exhibiting, exaggerating or belittling those qualities he believes will be positively and negatively evaluated in the particular experiment.

Granted this much, the problem now becomes: how does the subject decide in a particular instance what he will see as relevant to the situation and what sign (positive or negative) he will see any relevant act as having? The general answer will be that the subject decides the answers to these questions progressively as the interaction between himself and the experimenter proceeds. I believe that the subject enters the experimental situation with rather broad and vague expectations that become progressively more explicit (although perhaps never fully explicit) and definite as the experiment proceeds. That is, the subject has formed, at any particular point in the sequence of events of the experiment, a working definition of the situation, which is open to change and elaboration as the experiment proceeds (and even after it is over). The working definition is assembled from the material at hand, namely what the subject knows, believes or suspects about psychological experimentation before he starts the experimental session; what the experimenter says, does (and perhaps leaves unsaid); and what the scene—the physical and social environment—furnishes in the way of information. I want to conceive the process of forming a working definition of the situation as a process of negotiation between subject and experimenter, and I should like to begin examining this negotiation by looking at what the experimenter says and does in the conjectural light of how his words and deeds are interpreted and used by the subject to govern the "line" that the latter will take.

Negotiating an Understanding Between Experimenter and Subject

In order to understand the process of negotiating a definition of the experimental situation, we must examine what happens during the experimental session, especially in its early phases, from the viewpoint of both the subject and the experimenter; and we must understand one important aspect of the process, namely its overt one-sidedness and the predetermined course.

Just as the distribution of information is one-sided, so is the negotiation. Characteristically, the experimenter gives the instructions, decides when the action starts and stops and hands out the measuring instruments. The experimenter does the talking while the subject listens. The latter is a status subordinate who presumably listens in order to find his place in the situation—a situation that is oriented around the experimenter's purposes. Typically, the subject asks, "What do you want from me?" Furthermore, the experimenter assumes that the subject will take this attitude and will manifest "co-operativeness" by listening, understanding and accepting the instructions. By "accept" here is meant that the subject will make the sense of the instructions that the experimenter intends and will then act as if he believed this sense was correct and binding upon him.

The experimenter will not listen to any attempt on the subject's part to change the conditions of the experiment, nor does he grant the subject's wishes and needs a legitimate status as an element of the bargain. Ordinarily the subject is permitted only to ask questions of clarification, and these are ordinarily answered by repeating a portion of the instructions. In other words, the experimenter limits what the subject may do and what he may know and, furthermore, makes the assumption that the instructions are clear and sufficient.

In assuming the sufficiency of the instructions, the experimenter usually has a good technical reason: standardization of procedure. He assumes he is presenting a standard set of conditions to a standard person and that what he tells the subject, together with what is readily available from the scene, will be the same for all subjects, i.e., will be interpreted in the same way by all subjects. (In practice, the experimenter believes that there will be individual differences that he hopes will be randomly distributed over subjects and can be treated as "error.")

The assumption of sufficiency really incorporates more than notions of standardized procedure, however, for it asserts that what the experimenter tells the subject is all the subject needs to know. Further, the assumption implicitly demands that the subject will suspend his doubts or questions about aspects of the procedure and the scene and will treat as irrelevant his own (the subject's) purposes, needs and reservations. Simply stated, the experimenter's assumption is that for the subjects "things are what they seem," and that what he has been told in the instructions and what he can see for himself are true and that there is nothing more to the situation than this.

Finally, let us note about the experimenter that he is inflexible in his behavior. Ideally, at least, the experimenter's every move in an experiment has been predetermined and can be said to be "programmed." He has decided in advance on the task to set for all subjects, on the range of behavior he will attend to—i.e., on what he will treat as "data" and what behavior he will ignore—and on every one of his actions. He has a script that provides lines and business. The script cannot be revised or adapted to meet the exigencies of particular subjects or events and every experimental session must be either a "success" in that the events occurring during it come acceptably close to the ideal program or a "failure" that must be discarded. The period of reflection has passed for the experimenter once the series of trials gets under way; and his activities are, indeed, a mechanical program of activities.

The world appears somewhat different to the subject. In the first place, it seems doubtful that the subject always assumes the docile, cooperative and credulous stance that the experimenter wishes him to take. Some subjects probably do not find the experimental instructions sufficient, but are left with doubts, reservations and questions. Further, they may not suspend their own purposes. Rather, I think the subject enters the experiment with three major aims: first, he wants to accomplish his private purposes or get his rewards—e.g., pay, course credit, satisfaction of curiosity, self-insight, help with a problem and so on; second, he wants to penetrate the experimenter's inscrutability and discover the rationale of the experiment—its purposes and the types of judgment that will issue from it; and, finally, he wants to accomplish this second aim in order to achieve a third, namely in order to represent himself in a favorable light or to "put his best foot forward."

The subject must accomplish these three aims within the restriction that he is present primarily in order to accomplish the experimenter's purposes, which purposes may be initially quite vague to him. The accomplishment of the experimenter's purposes is one of the conditions that makes possible the achievement of one of the subject's aims, namely the discernment of these purposes. That is, the true nature of the situation will be revealed progressively as it goes along or at the end. Thus, like a stranger at a ceremonial or a man who cannot speak the native tongue, the subject comes to know what is going on only insofar as he participates in the action and does as he is told. His own actions have some effect upon the outcomes of the situation, but he can have only partial knowledge of the effect of his action until the whole situation has been played out.

The subject, therefore, must adopt a peculiar posture. He must be (or appear to be) co-operative in order to find out the meaning of his own actions as these are given meaning by the experimenter's interpretations. Yet he must have some basis for deciding how to act before he knows what his acts mean. He must make some approximation of the meaning of the situation in order to take a step that will yield some information that permits him to revise (or confirm) his first approximation. He must, necessarily, adopt a cut-and-try or iterative procedure for solving his problem.

In truth, the subject has more than one problem. One is the "task" that the experimenter sets. Another is what we may, for convenience, call his "deutero-problem," meaning his personal problem as defined by the three aims mentioned above: attainment of reward, divination of experimenter's true purposes and favorable self-presentation. The extent to which the deutero-problem occupies the subject is not uniform across subjects. When it becomes the salient feature of the situation, we describe the subject as "neutrotically defensive," "hyper-suspicious" or even "over-sophisticated." When it is minimal, we rejoice in having a truly "naive" subject. But I claim that the deutero-problem plays some role in all experimental situations and for all subjects and may, on some occasions, be more important than the "task" or the "treatment" in explaining results.

Finally, let me make it clear that the subject does not approach the deutero-problem without preconceptions to help him define the situation nor without hints furnished by the experimenter's actions, the instructions, and the scene. I propose that the subject's preconceptions are properly a matter of empirical investigation and below I suggest some techniques for such investigation. On the other hand, the matter of what hints and clues does the subject get from the ongoing procedure seems to have some conceptual properties worth exploring before we go to collecting data.

I suggest that there are two general types of experimental (i.e., "task") problems that provide subjects with different kinds of hints as to how to put their best foot forward or, in effect, urge subjects to adopt one or another "set" toward the experiment. Let me distinguish these problems and sets by calling one type "task-ability" and the other "self-quality," and by characterizing them further as follows:

A "task-ability" set is characterized adopted when the experimenter presents the work to be done as involving some ability, skill or capacity to perform. The task may be motor or mental, simple or complex, familiar or strange, e.g., estimating the number of dots on a card, judging "auto-kinetic" movement distances, judging the personality of another or solving "human relations problems." The outstanding feature of such assignments is that there is no upper limit on the amount of skill or capacity the subject "ought" to display. The nature of the task tells the subject: "You can't do too much in proving your worth." Furthermore, the positively valued end of the ability continuum is easily discerned by the subject in most cases. If he does not or if two rivalrous dimensions of ability confront him, the experimenter will ordinarily instruct the subject on which dimension he is to maximize performance, e.g., whether speed or accuracy will be considered more important. Finally, it is impossible for the subject to do more than his best; the only possibility for misrepresentation lies in under-achievement or concealment of a skill. Ordinarily under-achievement arises from some failure to motivate the subject adequately or from the subject's failure to see the relevance of the ability being tested either to the experimental purpose or to the assessment of his own worth. In short, try as he may, the subject can distort or misrepresent his performance in only one direction. He has only partial voluntary control over his performance.

Quite different in nature are the "self-quality" problems, which can be characterized in general as being concerned with opinions and beliefs; with responses to frustration, insult, and failure; with conformity-independence, choice-rejection of others; or with qualities such as dogmatism, authoritarianism, punitiveness and the like. The differences between "self-quality" performances and those in the "task-ability" area are several. First, the dimensions of behavior do not have simply one "good" and one "bad" end point; rather, they tend to have two "bad" extremes and a "good" point located somewhere between the two extremes, though not necessarily in the "middle." For example, it is possible to be over- or under-conforming, too acceptant of others or too rejecting. Thus, the second aspect of "self-quality" situations is that the subject cannot be sure how extreme a behavior will be considered maximally worthy. Unlike task-ability situations, the subject does not have a guarantee that he "cannot do too much." In order to know how to maximize the worth of his behavior, a subject must either draw from his pool of common sense knowledge about what "anyone knows" is a worthy way to behave; or, to be perfectly sure, he would have to know the scheme of relevances that the experimenter is employing: the hypothesis being tested, the categories into which behavior will be placed, the criteria for such placement, and the value assigned to the category. The fact that the experimenter conceals these items, while the subject is pushed by his own aims to try to discover them, tends to maximize the negotiation between subject and experimenter. It is the third feature of self-quality experiments that makes negotiation possible, namely that the behavior under scrutiny can be under the voluntary control of the subject at least within broad limits. The subject can both inhibit a behavior and can stimulate it, depending on how he believes a particular kind of behavior will be judged by the experimenter.[3]

[3] Experimenters are aware of these features of "self-quality" problems and often disguise such problems as "task-ability" situations (e.g., the TAT is pre-

RESEARCH PROPOSALS

Given the foregoing characterization of the experimental situation and some of the features of the process of negotiation between subject and experimenter, it seems probable that the behavior of the subject in dealing with his "deutero-problem" can be investigated further; and can be most profitably investigated in the area of "self-quality" problems. The strategy of investigation proposed arises from viewing the negotiation process as one in which the subject progressively elaborates a definition of the experimental situation. Further, it assumed that the definition grows out of (1) what the subject knows or believes about experimental psychological procedure before he takes part in an experiment; (2) what the experimenter says and does and also what he believes, expects or wishes; and (3) the remaining features of the scene, including the physical properties of the experimental setting, its temporal characteristics, the apparatus, the other people present and the events that occur during the experiment. At any particular point, the subject has some definition or understanding of the situation, although it may be so vague that he can say little about it. As the experiment proceeds, his definition becomes more elaborated until, at the end of the session, the subject can usually give some coherent account of what he thinks happened. The fundamental strategy is to investigate subjects' interpretations at various points throughout the sequence of events in the experiment.

Preconceptions

Since the subject's expectations of what will occur during an experi-

---

sented as "a *test* of imagination"); or misdirect the subject's attention by initiating and overtly carrying out a "task-ability" procedure that at some point is apparently inadvertently intruded upon by some event to which the subject must respond. Hopefully, the subject responds spontaneously; and the experimenter attends to this response while ignoring the "task-ability" performance.

In this connection it is worth noting that occasionally the experimenter encounters what can be called "inter-set interference," meaning that the adoption of one set by the subject precludes his noticing or responding adequately to a phenomenon that would appear relevant to him under a different set for example, Milton Rosenbaum (personal communication) reports that subjects engaged in the "task" of judging stimulus persons may be so task-directed that they appear to ignore insulting remarks directed by the stimulus person toward the subjects. Rosenbaum also mentions an experiment in a military setting in which a strong instruction to adopt a task set apparently "took" so well that the subjects were inattentive to social-emotional events later introduced into the situation as part of the experimental procedure.

ment are likely to be vague, they should be studied by a "recognition" rather than a "recall" technique. Specifically, then, the questioning procedure should involve presenting subjects with lists of items and asking them to respond to each, rather than an "open-end" interview.

Knowledge

First, it is important to find out what subjects know about experimental procedure and findings in social psychology. How knowledgeable are they about common features of experiments? Can subjects correctly identify or describe certain facts, terms, descriptions of procedure, and the like? The list of items might include such things as: control group, autokinetic phenomenon, cohesiveness, use of tape recordings, one-way screens, authoritarianism, sociometric tests, some brief statements of experimental findings (some true, some invented) for the subject to judge true or false together with an estimate of his confidence, and the like.

Expectations of Legitimate Activity

The second kind of expectations needing study are what the subject considers ordinary or unusual or impossible events in an experiment. Using brief descriptions of activities, the subject could be asked to indicate for each whether he thought it could be a normal occurrence in an experiment. The list might include such items as: receiving an electric shock, telling his home address, getting experimenter a pack of cigarettes with the subject's money, drinking a liquid of unknown composition, jumping into the university pool with all his clothes on.

Expectations of Purpose

A somewhat more general kind of expectation is what the subject conceives the experimenter's purpose to be. This conception, if it can be educed, might provide the general framework within which knowledge and expectations of legitimate activity are organized. The details of procedure have not been worked out here and "open-end" interviewing may be the best way to start.

What the Experimenter Says and Does

One way of investigating what subjects make of experimental situations is to study their interpretations of various events as they occur sequentially during an experimental procedure: the initial instructions, subsequent ones and various tests, questionnaires and the like. At least two lines of procedure suggest themselves:

Paper and Pencil Tasks

The subject might be presented with a series of written descriptions of experimental situations, instructions and of events occurring during an experiment and asked to indicate: what he thinks the experimenter's purposes are, what the significant response categories are and how the experimenter would evaluate each of them.

The same sort of procedure could be used to study the insight that subjects have into many of the standard or classical measuring devices of social psychology. What does the subject make of the F-scale, the Study of Values, self-esteem scales, and the like? What does the subject think the instrument is measuring? How accurately can he state what would be a "high" or a "low" score? What responses does he think describe an esteemed person?

Partial Procedures and Replicated Variations

Instead of submitting a written version of the experimental procedure to the subject, it might be useful to run subjects through varying length portions of actual experimental sequences, interrupting the procedure at some point to interview the subject and get his impressions of what is going on, in the terms outlined above. Another obvious move suggested by this line of reasoning is a program of interviewing subjects following the completion of some experiment that another investigator is conducting for his own purposes. On the basis of hunches obtained from such interviewing, one might attempt deliberate variation of some portion of the instructions or procedure to determine the effects on subjects' understanding.

Personal and Social Attributes of Experimenters

We know that the academic position of the experimenter seems to make a difference in subjects' motivation in a task-ability problem. Are there parallel differences in the area of self quality problems? Will subjects demonstrate more or less conformity, credulity, co-operativeness for a faculty experimenter than for a graduate student? Will they be more or less hostile to an instigating agent depending on his status?

A warm, friendly test administrator seems to induce higher performance among nursery school children. Will a friendly administrator induce more acceptance in sociometric tests than a cold person? Do subjects read an experimenter's style and manner of behavior for cues as to what is "appropriate" behavior? Will an experimenter whose overt mannerisms, clothing and speech exude social orthodoxy produce greater conformity than one whose appearance is "radical" or "bohemian"? Does a white laboratory coat make a "scientist" out of a psychologist?

All of the foregoing questions can be answered by replicating standard experiments with variations in experimenters' appearance, status, or actions. But one wonders if subjects can perhaps read even more subtle cues than the foregoing.

Experimenter's Attitudes Toward the Experiment

Robert Zajonc reports (personal communication) experiments in which the instructions clearly implied the attitude that experimenter took toward the hypothesis being tested. When the instructions implied that the experimenter was convinced of the truth of the hypothesis, the results supported the hypothesis; but when he implied that he believed it was wrong, the results did not support the hypothesis. In Zajonc's experiment the experimenter's attitude was made almost explicit; but one wonders if perhaps more subtle communication can still affect results, as when the experimenter holds an opinion but tries to disguise it. An experiment is called for here.[4]

Two other attitudinal areas ought to be investigated also. One is boredom with the procedure, increasing as a long series of trials progresses. Aside from simple sloppiness in procedure during later trials, is it possible that there are other effects? Does experimenter's lack of interest, restlessness, and lack of excitement affect the subject's performance, perhaps in the direction of reducing motivation? The other attitudinal area is one manifested during the early part of a series of trials, when the experimenter may experience anxiety about the efficacy of his procedure or feel guilt about the deception he is practicing on subjects. Just precisely what consequences these feelings might have for subjects' performances is uncertain, but one can speculate that such feelings on experimenter's part would generate discomfort and confusion in subjects and might increase the variety of their interpretations of the experiment and hence increase variance in their behavior.

As with experimenters themselves, so perhaps with their confederates too. Insufficient attention has been given to the effects of certain non-role characteristics of stooges, although analysis has sometimes shown significant inter-stooge differences. In addition, the very process of taking the stooge role seems to have some consequences,

---

[4] When this article was written, the author was unaware that a relevant experiment was being conducted by Peggy Cook (1958). In addition the independent work of Rosenthal (1958b) and Orne (1959b) are relevant here.

though their effects on the outcomes of the experiment are obscure. Theodore Mills reports (personal communication) that his confederates experienced guilt over their rejecting and unsupportive role-behavior toward a naive subject. Mills had to provide tension-release sessions to keep his team functioning. Richard DeCharms reports (personal communication) the case of a confederate who had to act stupid and fail before people whom he considered his intellectual inferiors. The man "took it out" on his wife in displays of ill-temper, reckless driving, sulkiness, etc. Seymour Feshbach (personal communication) has also commented on tension and irritability in role-players. The possibility that such tensions can be altogether excluded from actual role performance in the experiment seems remote, yet the actual effects on subjects are unstudied.

The Scene

Finally, a brief comment should be made about how the physical environment, properties and apparatus in view may affect the subject's understanding of the experiment. Unfortunately, little is known about this aspect of things, although experimenters have fairly strong opinions about how elaborate the staging of the experiment ought to be. On the face of it, it might seem reasonable to believe that the more intricate, elaborate and "realistic" the setting was, the greater the impact of the treatment would be on the subjects. Yet, many experimenters work with the baldest kind of verbal directives, make no attempt to dramatize the scene, and still get results. And there have been cases of elaborately rigged experiments that simply failed to produce the desired effects. It seems at least possible that an elaborately staged experiment may simply provide the subject with more cues than he has time or attention span to interpret. Perhaps as complexity of the desired effect increases, the consequence of shifting the burden of communication from verbal instructions to portions of the scene is merely to confuse the subject and to produce irrelevant or wrong interpretations. It seems worthwhile at least to study the relative impact of instructional and scenic communication, perhaps by performing the "same" experiment in two versions: one using simple verbal instructions to create the desired effect, the other depending maximally upon the scene—props and cast—to carry the informational burden.

7
Covert
Communication
In The Psychological
Experiment [1]

Robert Rosenthal

Psychological laboratories and the psychological experiments conducted there are not the only scenes or means whereby we learn of human behavior. There is no doubt, however, that in our discipline as in others, the laboratory experiment is a preferred mode for the observation of nature. It is so preferred because of the greater control it gives us over the inputs to the experimental subject. Unlike the usual situation in the field or in the "real world," when we observe the behavior of the subject of a psychological experiment we are in a position to attribute his behavior to the antecedent conditions we have ourselves arranged.

In the paradigm psychological experiment, there is a subject whose behavior is to be observed and an experimenter whose functions include

[1] The research described in this paper has been supported by research grants (G-17685, G-24826, GS-177, GS-714) from the Division of Social Sciences of the National Science Foundation. An earlier version of this paper was presented at the symposium "Ethical and Methodological Problems in Social Psychological Experiments," American Psychological Association, Chicago, September 1965.

Reprinted with permission of author and publisher from *Psychological Bulletin*, 67, no. 5 (1967):356-67.

the control of inputs to the subject. (The experimenter also often functions as a recorder of the subject's output, but this function of the
experimenter is not important to the present discussion. It may be
assumed for present purposes that the subject's response is recorded
directly by an error-free automated system.) As part of the experimenter's function of controlling the subject's inputs, he engages in a
variety of intended, programmed, overt communications with the subject. Such communications include the "instructions to subjects." Although the instructions are highly programmed, they, along with
aspects of the physical scene (Riecken, 1962) and the overall design of
the experiment as perceived by the subject, may unintentionally communicate to the subject something of what the experimenter is after.
Such unintended information transmission has been discussed most
fully by Orne (1962), who referred to such sources of cues as the
demand characteristics of the experimental procedures. To the extent
that these unintended cues tend to be systematic for a given experiment, and do not depend for their operation on *differential* communication to subjects by experimenters, they are not discussed here.
Instead, the focus will be on variations in the covert and unintended
communications that occur in the psychological experiment. Such
variations are not random and are predictable to some extent from a
knowledge of various characteristics of the experimenter and the subject.

One purpose of this paper is to illustrate the fact that unintended
covert communications are the norm in psychological experiments. To
the extent that the experimenter communicates unintentionally and
differentially with his subjects he has lost some measure of control over
the inputs. Since such control is a major reason for our reliance on the
experimental method, there are serious implications. Serious as these
implications may be for our interpretation of the results of experiments, it should not surprise us that different experimenters engage in
different covert communication with different subjects. We should, in
fact, be more surprised if such covert communication did not occur.
Covert communications occur routinely in all other dyadic interactions;
why then, should they not occur in the dyad composed of the experimenter and his subject?

The evidence for the experimenter's covert communication with his
tacitly understanding subject comes from a program of experiments on
experiments (Rosenthal, 1964b). One purpose of this research program
is primarily methodological. By taking account of the covert commu-

nication processes in the psychological experiment, techniques may be developed which will permit the drawing of more valid substantive conclusions about those experimental inputs about whose effects on the subject's behavior we want to learn. Another purpose of this research program is less methodological and more substantive. What we learn about the covert communication between experimenter and subject may teach us something about covert communication processes in other dyadic interactions as well. Laboratories need not simply be those places where we test, in simplified form, the hypotheses derived from the "real world." Laboratories, as Mills (1962) has pointed out, are just as "real" as the rest of the world.

THE EXPERIMENTER AS COVERT COMMUNICATOR

Covert communication between experimenter and subject could be demonstrated simply by showing that different experimenters behave differently toward their subjects in their conduct of a specific experiment and that these individual differences in behavior affect the subject's response. But it seems late in the history of psychology simply to demonstrate individual differences in behavior even when the people happen to be experimenters. It seems more useful, therefore, to concentrate on those cases of covert communication in which we can predict, more or less, just how he will communicate covertly with his subjects, before the experimenter even enters the laboratory.

Experimenter's Sex

There is a good deal of evidence that the sex of the experimenter can affect the responses of the experimental subject (Rosenthal, 1966; Sarason, 1965; Stevenson, 1965). What we have not known, however, is whether the effect of the sex of the experimenter was passive or active. By "passive effect" is meant that subjects respond differently to and for male and female experimenters simply because they are male or female. By "active effect" is meant that subjects respond differently to and for male and female experimenters because male and female experimenters treat the subjects differently. The best way to determine the extent to which any effects of the experimenter are active or passive is to make observations of the experimenter as he or she conducts an experiment.

In our research program we have employed two types of observers. One type of observer has been the subject himself. In several experiments, subjects have been asked to describe the behavior of their experimenter during the experimental transaction. An advantage of such observations by the subject himself is that there is no one closer to the experimenter during the experiment than the subject, and he is in a good position to see what the experimenter does. A disadvantage of such observations by the subjects themselves is that they may be contaminated by the responses subjects made during the experiment itself. Thus, if a subject has made conforming responses during an experiment in verbal conditioning, he may describe his experimenter as a more forceful, dominant person, not because the experimenter really was, but because that would justify to the subject and to others the subject's having conformed.

Another type of observer has been employed who was not a participant in the experiment itself. Instead, graduate and undergraduate students have observed sound motion pictures made of experimenters interacting with their subjects. Neither experimenters nor subjects knew that their interaction was being observed. The films were of five different samples of experimenters and subjects involving altogether twenty-nine experimenters (five of whom were females) and eighty-six subjects (of whom twenty-one were males). The details of the experiments which were filmed are given elsewhere (Rosenthal, Persinger, Mulry, Vikan-Kline, & Grothe, 1964a, 1964b). It is enough to know that in all the experiments filmed the task was the same. The experimenters presented to each of their subjects a series of ten standardized photos of faces. Each face was to be judged as to how successful or unsuccessful the person appeared to be. All experimenters were to read the same instructions to their subjects and this reading lasted about a minute, on the average. Before reading the instructions, experimenters asked subjects for their name, age, major field, and marital status. This brief pre-instructional period lasted on the average about half a minute.

Analysis of the films showed that even during this brief preinstructional period, male and female experimenters treated their subjects in a significantly different manner. Male experimenters interacting with either male or female subjects were a good deal more friendly in their interaction than were female experimenters ($r_{pb} = .47; p < .05$). Support for this finding comes from a different study employing the same experimental task. This time the observers of the experimenters' behavior were the subjects themselves. Suzanne Haley made the data available for this analysis. Her eighty-six female subjects judged their twelve male experimenters to be more friendly during the course of the experiment than their two female experimenters (r_{pb} = .32, $p < .005$). Regardless of whether we ask external observers or the subjects themselves, male experimenters are observed to behave differently from female experimenters. Such systematic differences in the treatment of subjects suggest that though experimenters may read the same instructions to their subjects, subjects contacted by male experimenters and subjects contacted by female experimenters are simply not in the same experiment. It should not surprise us, therefore, when male and female experimenters obtain different responses from their subjects. Whenever the warmth or friendliness of the experimenter can affect the subject's response, and that happens often (Gordon & Durea, 1948; Luft, 1953; Reece & Whitman, 1962), we may look also for the effect of the experimenter's sex.

The effect of the experimenter's sex is complicated by the effect of the subject's sex. Male and female subjects evoke different behavior from their experimenters. Neil Friedman (1964) made observations of the smiling behavior of the experimenters who had been filmed which were made available for this analysis. During the brief half-minute preceding the reading of the instructions, female subjects evoked more smiling behavior from their experimenters than did male subjects ($p < .05$). Only 12 percent of the experimenters smiled even a little at any male subject, but 70 percent of the experimenters smiled at least a little at their female subjects. From this evidence and from some more detailed analyses which suggest that female subjects may be more protectively treated by their experimenters (Rosenthal, 1966), it might be suggested that in the psychological experiment, chivalry is not dead. This news may be heartening socially, and it is interesting social psychologically, but it is very disconcerting methodologically. Sex differences are well established for many kinds of behavior. But a question must now be raised as to whether sex differences which emerge from psychological experiments are due to the subject's genes, morphology, enculturation, or simply to the fact that the experimenter treated his male and female subjects differently so that, in a sense, they were not really in the same experiment at all.

Male and female experimenters remember and respond to their subject's sex. They also remember their own sex. Female experimenters show a pattern of behavior which might be called "interested modesty" when interacting with their male subjects, while male experimenters show a pattern which might more simply be called "interested" when interacting with their female subjects. An indirect assessment of this interest comes from an analysis of the time spent in performing the preparations to show the subject the next stimulus photo. The timing of these portions was done by Richard Katz (1964), who made the data available for the present analysis. When male experimenters were contacting female subjects, it took them 16 percent longer to prepare to present the next stimulus than when they were contacting male subjects ($p < .01$). When female experimenters were contacting male subjects, it took them 13 percent longer to prepare the next stimulus for presentation than when they were contacting female subjects, though this difference was not significant statistically. Though the absolute amounts of time involved were measured in a few seconds, it appeared that among male experimenters especially, there was a tendency to stretch out the interaction with the opposite-sexed subject. This same finding of a prolongation of opposite sex experimental interactions has also been reported recently by Shapiro (1966) in an experiment on verbal conditioning.

Among our own female experimenters, evidence for their "modesty" in the motor channel of communication comes from observations of the degree to which experimenters leaned toward their subjects during the experimental transaction. (These observations were made by R. Katz, who made them available for this analysis.) Male and female experimenters leaned toward their female subjects to about the same degree. However, when the subjects were males, female experimenters did not lean as close as did their male colleagues ($p < .05$).

Further evidence for this relative modesty of female experimenters when contacting male subjects comes from a different, still preliminary sort of analysis. Observations of experimenters' friendliness were now made by two different groups of observers. One group watched the films but did not hear the sound track. Another group listened to the sound track but did not see the films. From this, a measure of motor or visual friendliness and an independent measure of verbal or auditory friendliness were available. (The correlation between ratings of friendliness obtained from these independent channels was only .29.) The results of this analysis are shown in Table 1. Among male experimenters, there was a tendency, not statistically significant, for their movements to show greater friendliness than their tone of voice, and to be somewhat unfriendly toward their male subjects in the auditory channel of communication. It was among the female experimenters that the more striking effects occurred. They were quite friendly toward their female subjects in the visual channel but not in the auditory channel. With male subjects, the situation was reversed significantly ($p < .05$). Though not friendly in the visual mode, female experimenters showed remarkable friendliness in the auditory channel when contacting male subjects.

The quantitative analysis of sound motion pictures is not yet far enough developed that we can say whether such channel discrepancy in the communication of friendliness is generally characteristic of women in our culture, or only of advanced women students in psychology, or only of female experimenters conducting experiments in person perception. Perhaps it would not be farfetched to attribute the obtained channel discrepancy to an ambivalence over how friendly they ought to be. Quite apart from considerations of processes of covert communication in the psychological experiment, such findings may have some relevance for a better understanding of communication processes in general.

Other Attributes

We have seen that the sex of the experimenter, a variable shown often to affect subjects' responses, is associated with different patterns of communication in the psychological experiment, patterns which may account in part for the effects on the subjects' responses. Further, we have seen that the sex of the subject affects the experimenters' behavior, so that it is hard to tell whether different responses obtained from male and female subjects are due to the subjects' difference in sex or to the differences in the behavior of the experimenters. There are many other characteristics of experimenters and of subjects which should be

TABLE 1

Experimenter Friendliness in Two Communication
Channels as a Function of
Experimenter and Subject Sex

Experi-menter sex	Subject sex	Communication channel		
		Visual	Auditory	Difference
Male	Male	3.00	-0.50	3.50
	Female	2.81	1.32	1.49
	Mean	2.90	0.41	
Female	Male	0.44	2.96	-2.52
	Female	1.75	0.25	1.50
	Mean	1.10	1.60	

analogously investigated. Some beginnings have been made and some results have been reported (Rosenthal, 1966). Here we present brief examples of differences in the experimenter's behavior toward the subject of the experiment, differences which are predictable from a knowledge of various attributes of the experimenter. The examples are chosen from only those experimenter variables which have been shown by various investigators to affect the subjects' responses.

There is considerable evidence that the anxiety of the experimenter, as measured before he enters the laboratory, can be a significant determinant of his subjects' responses (e.g., Rosenthal, 1966; Sarason, 1965). But what does the more anxious experimenter do in the experiment that leads his subjects to respond differently? We might expect more anxious experimenters to be more fidgety, and that is just what they are. Experimenters scoring higher on the Taylor (1953) Manifest Anxiety scale are observed from their films to show a greater degree of general body activity ($r = .41$, $p = .09$) and in addition, to have a less dominant tone of voice ($r = -.43$, $p = .07$). What effects just such behavior on the part of the experimenter will have on the subjects' responses depends no doubt on the particular experiment being conducted and, very likely, on various characteristics of the subject as well. In any case, we must assume that a more anxious experimenter cannot conduct just the same experiment as a less anxious experimenter. It appears that in experiments which have been conducted by just one experimenter, the probability of successful replication by another investigator is likely to depend on the similarity of his personality to that of the original investigator.

Anxiety of the experimenter is just one of the experimenter variables affecting the subjects' responses in an unintended manner. Crowne and Marlowe (1964) have shown that subjects who score high on their scale of need for approval tend to behave in such a way as to gain the approval of the experimenter. Now there is evidence that suggests that experimenters who score high on this measure also behave in such a way as to gain approval from their subjects. Analysis of the filmed interactions showed that experimenters scoring higher on the Marlowe-Crowne scale spoke to their subjects in a more enthusiastic tone of voice ($r = .39$, $p < .10$) and in a more friendly tone of voice ($r = .47$, $p < .05$). In addition, they smiled more often at their subjects ($r = .44$, $p = .07$) and slanted their bodies more toward their subjects than did experimenters lower in the need for approval ($r = .39$, $p < .10$).

THE EXPERIMENTER AS REACTIVE COMMUNICATOR

Experimenter's Experience

The kind of person the experimenter is *before* he enters his laboratory can in part determine the responses he obtains from his subjects. From the observation of experimenters' behavior during their interaction with their subjects there are some clues as to how this may come about. There is also evidence that the kind of person the experimenter becomes *after* he enters his laboratory may alter his behavior toward his subjects and lead him, therefore, to obtain different responses from his subjects.

In the folklore of psychologists who do experiments, there is the notion that sometimes, perhaps more often than we might expect, subjects contacted early in an experiment behave differently from subjects contacted later in an experiment. There may be something to this bit of lore even if we make sure that subjects seen earlier and later in an experiment come from the same population. The difference may be due to changes over the course of the experiment in the behavior of the experimenter. From what we know of performance curves we might, in fact, predict both a practice effect and a fatigue effect on the part of the experimenter. There is evidence for both. In the experiments which were filmed, experimenters became more accurate ($r = .25, p = .07$) and also faster ($r = .31, p = .03$) in the reading of their instructions to their later-contacted subjects. That seems simply to be a practice effect. In addition, experimenters became more bored or less interested over the course of the experiment as observed from their behavior in the experimental interaction ($r = .31, p = .02$). As we might also predict, experimenters became less tense with more experience ($r = -.26, p = .06$). The changes which occur in the experimenters' behavior during the course of their experiment affect their subjects' responses. In the experiments which were filmed, for example, subjects contacted by experimenters whose behavior changed as described rated the stimulus persons as less successful ($r = .31, p = .02$).

Subjects' Behavior

The experimenter-subject communication system is a complex of intertwining feedback loops. The experimenter's behavior, we have seen, can affect the subject's next response. But the subject's behavior can also affect the experimenter's behavior, which in turn affects the subject's behavior. In this way, the subject plays a part in the indirect determination of his own next response. The experimental details are given elsewhere (Rosenthal, 1966; Rosenthal, Kohn, Greenfield, & Carota, 1965). Briefly, in one experiment, half the experimenters had their experimental hypotheses confirmed by their first few subjects, who were actually accomplices. The remaining experimenters had their experimental hypotheses disconfirmed. This confirmation or disconfirmation of their hypotheses affected the experimenters' behavior sufficiently so that from their next subjects, who were bona fide and not accomplices, they obtained significantly different responses not only to the experimental task, but on standard tests of personality as well. These responses were predictable from a knowledge of the responses the experimenters had obtained from their earlier-contacted subjects.

There is an interesting footnote on the psychology of the accomplice which comes from the experiment alluded to. The accomplices had been trained to confirm or to disconfirm the experimenter's hypothesis by the nature of the responses they gave the experimenter. These accomplices did not, of course, know when they were confirming an experimenter's hypothesis or, indeed, that there were expectancies to be confirmed at all. In spite of the accomplices' training, they were significantly affected in the adequacy of their performance as accomplices by the expectancy the experimenter had of their performance, and by whether the experimenter's hypothesis was being confirmed or disconfirmed by the accomplices' responses. We can think of the accomplices as experimenters and the experimenters as their targets or "victims." It is interesting to know that experimental targets are not simply affected by experimental accomplices. The targets of our accomplices, like the subjects of our experimenters, are not simply passive responders. They "act back."

Experimental Scenes

One of the things that happens to the experimenter which may affect his behavior toward his subject, and thus the subject's response, is that he falls heir to a specific scene in which to conduct his experiment. Riecken (1962) has pointed out how much there is we do not know about the effects of the physical scene in which an experimental transaction takes place. We know little enough about how the scene affects the subject's behavior, we know even less about how the scene affects the experimenter's behavior.

The scene in which the experiment takes place may affect the subject's response in two ways. The effect of the scene may be direct, as when a subject judges others to be less happy when his judgments are made in an "ugly" laboratory (Mintz, 1957). The effect of the scene may also be indirect, as when the scene influences the experimenter to behave differently and this change in the experimenter's behavior leads to a change in the subject's response. The evidence that the physical scene may affect the experimenter's behavior comes from some data collected with Suzanne Haley. We had available eight laboratory rooms which were varied as to the "professionalness," the "orderliness," and the "comfortableness" of their appearance. The 14 experimenters of this study were randomly assigned to the eight laboratories. Experimenters took the experiment significantly more seriously if they had been assigned to a laboratory which was both more disordered and less comfortable ($R = .73$, $p = .02$). These experimenters were graduate students in the natural sciences or in law school. Perhaps they felt that scientifically serious business is carried on best in the cluttered and severely furnished laboratory which fits the stereotype of the scientist's ascetic pursuit of truth.

In this same experiment, subjects described the behavior of their experimenter during the course of the experiment. Experimenters who had been assigned to more professional appearing laboratories were described by their subjects as significantly more expressive-voiced ($r = .22$, $p = .05$), more expressive-faced ($r = .32$, $p = .005$), and as more given to the use of hand gestures ($r = .32$, $p = .005$). There were no films made of these experimenters interacting with their subjects, so we cannot be sure that their subjects' descriptions were accurate. There is a chance that the experimenters did not really behave as described but that subjects in different appearing laboratories perceive their experimenters differently because of the operation of context effects. The direct observation of experimenters' behavior in different physical contexts should clear up the matter to some extent.

Principal Investigators

More and more research is carried out in teams and groups so that the chances are increasing that any one experimenter will be collecting data not for himself alone. More and more there is a chance that the data are being collected for a principal investigator to whom the experimenter is responsible. The basic data are presented elsewhere (Rosenthal, 1966), but here it can be said that the response a subject gives his experimenter may be determined in part by the kind of person the principal investigator is and by the nature of his interaction with the experimenter.

More specifically, personality differences among principal investigators, and whether the principal investigator has praised or reproved the experimenter for his performance of his data-collecting duties, affect the subjects' subsequent perception of the success of other people and also affect subjects' scores on standardized tests of personality (e.g., Taylor Manifest Anxiety scale).

In one experiment, there were 13 principal investigators and 26 experimenters. When the principal investigators collected their own data it was found that their anxiety level correlated positively with the ratings of the success of others (pictured in photographs) they obtained from their subjects ($r = .66$, $p = .03$). Each principal investigator was then to employ two research assistants. On the assumption that principal investigators select research assistants who are significantly like or significantly unlike themselves, the two research assistants were assigned to principal investigators at random. That was done so that research assistants' scores on the anxiety scale would not be correlated with their principal investigator's anxiety scores. The randomization was successful in that the principal investigators' anxiety correlated only .02 with the anxiety of their research assistants.

The research assistants then replicated the principal investigators' experiments. Remarkably, the principal investigators' level of anxiety also predicted the responses obtained by their research assistants from their new samples of subjects ($r = .40$, $p = .07$). The research assistants' own level of anxiety, while also positively correlated with their subjects' responses ($r = .24$, ns), was not as good a predictor of their own subjects' responses as was the anxiety level of their principal investigator. Something in the covert communication between the principal investigator and his research assistant altered the assistant's behavior when he subsequently contacted his subjects. We know the effect of the principal investigator was mediated in this indirect way to his assistant's subjects because the principal investigator had no contact of his own with those subjects.

Other experiments show that the data obtained by the experimenter depend in part on whether the principal investigator is male or female, whether the principal investigator makes the experimenter self-conscious about the experimental procedure, and whether the principal investigator leads the experimenter to believe he has himself performed well or poorly at the same task the experimenter is to administer to his own subjects. The evidence comes from studies in person perception, verbal conditioning, and motor skills (Rosenthal, 1966).

As we would expect, these effects of the principal investigator on his assistant's subjects are mediated by the effects on the assistant's behavior toward his subjects. Thus, experimenters who have been made more self-conscious by their principal investigator behave less courteously toward their subjects, as observed from films of their interactions with their subjects ($r = -.43$, $p = .07$). In a different experiment, involving this time a verbal conditioning task, experimenters who had been given more favorable evaluations by their principal investigator were described by their subsequently contacted subjects to be more casual ($r = .33$, $p < .01$), and more courteous ($r = .27$, $p < .05$). These same experimenters, probably by virtue of their altered behavior toward their subjects, obtained significantly more conditioning responses from their subjects. All 10 of the experimenters who had been more favorably evaluated by their principal investigator showed conditioning effects among their subjects ($p = .001$) but only 5 of the 9 experimenters who felt unfavorably evaluated obtained any conditioning ($p = 1.00$).

THE EXPERIMENTER AS HYPOTHESIS COMMUNICATOR

Ever since Pfungst's (1911) brilliant series of experiments with Clever Hans, we have known that the experimenter's hypothesis can be communicated quite unintentionally to his subject. Hans, it will be remembered, was that clever horse who could solve problems of mathematics and musical harmony with equal skill and grace, simply by tapping out the answers with his hoof. A committee of eminent experts testified that Hans, whose owner made no profit from his horse's talents, was receiving no cues from his questioners. Of course, Pfungst later showed that this was not so, that tiny head and eye movements were Hans's signals to begin and to end his tapping. When Hans was asked a question, the questioner looked at Hans's hoof, quite naturally so, for that was the way for him to determine whether Hans's answer was correct. Then, it was discovered that when Hans approached the correct number of taps, the questioner would inadvertently move his head or eyes upward—just enough that Hans could discriminate the cue, but not enough that even trained animal observers or psychologists could see it.

The "Clever Hans" phenomenon has also been demonstrated to occur in more ordinary and more recent experiments. The details are found elsewhere (Rosenthal, 1966). Briefly, the expectancy or hypothesis of the experimenter has been shown to be a significant determinant of the results of his research in studies of person perception, verbal conditioning, personality assessment, and animal learning. The basic paradigm for such studies has been to divide a sample of experimenters into two equivalent groups and to create in each an expectancy for the data they would obtain which was opposite in direction to the expectancy induced in the other group of experimenters. Thus in the animal learning studies, half the experimenters were told that their rats were from the special "Berkeley Stock" and were specially bred for maze brightness or "Skinner-box brightness." The remaining experimenters were told that their animals had been specially bred for maze or "Skinner-box dullness." The rats run by experimenters expecting good performance performed significantly better than did the rats run by experimenters expecting poor performance. This was equally true in maze learning and in operant learning experiments.

In the person perception studies, half the experimenters were told that their subjects (humans now) had been selected because they tended to see photos of people as reflecting a great deal of past success, while the remaining experimenters were told that their subjects had been selected for the perception of failure in other people's faces. Subjects were then randomly assigned to their experimenters who subtly communicated their expectancies to their subjects in such a way that subjects expected to be success perceivers became success perceivers while subjects expected to be failure perceivers became failure perceivers. We can safely say that the communication processes whereby subjects learned of experimenter expectations were subtle ones because for the last five years we have been analyzing films of such experiments and we have yet to find the specific cues that mediate the Clever Hans phenomenon to human subjects. This is not for want of careful observation. The films have been observed by dozens of psychologists, graduate students, and undergraduate students; and two doctoral dissertations were based on the analysis of these films (Friedman, 1964; Katz, 1964). We all wish Pfungst were here to help us now, though there is some experimental evidence that human subjects are not using the same sort of cues that Clever Hans employed.

What we do know of the communication to subjects of the experimenter's expectancy has been learned as much from experiments as from the analysis of films. The details of the research are available elsewhere (Rosenthal, 1966). To summarize briefly, we know that both visual and auditory cues are helpful to the subjects in their tacit understanding of the experimenter's covertly communicated messages. We know that the communication of expectancies can occur before the subject makes even his first response so that verbal or nonverbal reinforcements of desired responses will not do as an explanation. There are not yet sufficient data to be sure of this point, but there are indications that experimenters learn during the course of an experiment how better to communicate their expectancies to their subjects. Subjects contacted later in the experiment, therefore, tend to give responses more biased in the direction of their experimenter's hypothesis.[2]

Such a finding makes good sense. It may be asked, if the experimenter is learning to communicate unintentionally, who is the teacher? Most likely, the subject is the teacher. It seems to be rewarding to have one's expectations confirmed (Aronson, Carlsmith, & Darley, 1963; Carlsmith & Aronson, 1963; Harvey & Clapp, 1965; Sampson & Sibley, 1965). Therefore, whenever the subject responds in accordance with the experimenter's expectancy, the likelihood is increased that the experimenter will repeat any covert communicative behavior which may have preceded the subject's confirming response. Subjects, then, may quite unintentionally shape the experimenter's unintended communicative behavior. Not only does the experimenter influence his subjects to respond in the expected manner, but his subjects may well evoke just that unintended behavior which will lead subjects to respond as expected. As the work of Hefferline (1962) suggests, such communication may not fall under what we commonly call "conscious control."

When it was mentioned earlier that the observation of the films of experimenters interacting with their subjects had not solved the modern riddle of Clever Hans, it was not meant that the films had not been worthwhile. There has already been frequent reference to things learned about experiments and experimenters from these movies. There is a good deal more. One of the most exciting findings was that it was possible to predict whether an experimenter would subsequently in-

---

[2] For three experiments with a total of 54 experimenters, the combined p was less than .001, but it must be pointed out that in these studies we could not always be sure that there were no systematic subject differences which could have accounted for a greater effect of the experimenter's expectancy among later-contacted subjects.

fluence his subjects to respond in accordance with his hypothesis from the experimenter's behavior during the first half-minute of his interaction with the subject. Experimenters who were more likeable, dominant, personal, relaxed, and important-acting during these initial seconds of the interaction and less given to leg movements, later obtained data significantly biased in the direction of their hypothesis (all the correlations exceeded .30 but were less than .43 and all p's were less than .05).

Observations were made of the sound films by one group of observers, of the silent films by another group, and of the sound track alone by a third group. Interestingly, during this phase of the experiment, it did not help the observers at all to have access to the sound track. None of the observations made by the group with access only to the sound track was predictive of subsequent effects of the experimenter's expectancy. The group of observers with access only to the silent films did just as well in predicting subsequent biasing as did the observers who had access to the sound films. During this brief preinstructional phase, then, tone of voice variables seemed to be of little consequence.

Observations of the experimenter's behavior during the instruction-reading period showed much the same pattern of variables to be predictive of subsequent biasing of the subject's responses. Only now there was a great many more predictor variables which reached significance, and the correlations became larger. (The largest of the newly significant predictors of subsequent biasing was the variable of professionalism of manner, $r = .45$, $p < .005$.) The details are presented elsewhere (Rosenthal, 1966), but one interesting phenomenon must be mentioned. During the instruction-reading period of the experiment, a number of tone of voice variables became significant predictors of the experimenter's subsequent unintended biasing effects. Very often, the direction of the predictive correlation with a variable judged from the sound track alone was in the opposite direction from the correlation with the same variable judged from the films without sound track. One example must do. Experimenters who later biased their subjects' responses more were *seen* as more honest ($r = .40$, $p < .01$) in the films but were *heard* as less honest ($r = -.30$, $p < .05$). Current work in the search for the cues mediating the Clever Hans phenomenon has turned to a closer examination of the implications for unintended communication processes of such channel discrepancy. Such an examination may have consequences for areas other than the social psychology of the psychological experiment. It is, for example, part of clinical lore, though the evidence is scanty (Ringuette & Kennedy, 1966), that such channel discrepancies may have important consequences for the development of psychopathology (Bateson, Jackson, Haley, & Weakland, 1956).

The clinical and social importance of a better understanding of discrepancies among communication channels has been recently implied in a study of the treatment of alcoholism. Tape recordings were made of nine physicians' voices as they talked about their experiences with alcoholic patients. There was no relationship between the amount of hostility judges perceived in the doctors' speech and the doctors' effectiveness in getting alcoholics to accept treatment. However, when the content was filtered out of the tape recordings, the degree of hostility found in the doctors' tone of voice alone was found to correlate significantly and negatively with his success in influencing alcoholics to accept treatment ($r = -.65, p = .06$; Milmoe, Rosenthal, Blane, Chafetz, & Wolf, 1967).

BEYOND THE EXPERIMENTER-SUBJECT DYAD

The particular patterns of covert communication which have been described as relevant to the experimenter's communication of his expectancy to his subject are no doubt specific to the type of experiment being performed. We are in no position to speak for the generality of any of these findings across different experiments, much less for their generality in the other "real world," that one outside the laboratory. But there are some conclusions to be drawn from the data presented here and from the program of research which has investigated the effects of the experimenter's expectancy.

Perhaps the most compelling and most general conclusion is that human beings can engage in highly effective and influential unprogrammed and unintended communication with one another. If such communication is responsible in the psychological experiment for the fulfillment of the experimenter's expectancy, it might also be responsible for the fulfillment of other expectancies held by humans outside the laboratory. If rats learn better when their experimenter thinks they will, then children may learn better if their teachers think they will.

The experiment, a longitudinal one, is not yet completed, but the results for the first year can be given (Rosenthal & Jacobson, 1966).

The procedure was exactly as in the experiments on the effects of the experimenter's expectancy. All the children in an elementary school were given an intelligence test which was disguised as a test which would predict academic "blooming." There were eighteen classes, three at each of six grade levels. By the use of a table of random numbers, about 20 percent of the children in each class were chosen for the experimental condition. The experimental treatment consisted of telling their teachers that they had scored on the predictive achievement test such that they would show unusual intellectual development within the next academic year. At the end of the academic year the children were retested with the same test of intelligence. For the eighteen classes combined, children whose teachers expected them to gain in performance showed a significantly greater gain in IQ than did the control children, ($p < .02$), though the mean relative gain in IQ was small (3.8 points). Teachers' expectancies, it turned out, made little difference in the upper grades. But at the lower levels the effects were dramatic. First graders purported to be bloomers gained 15.4 IQ points more than did the control children ($p = .002$), and the mean relative gain in one classroom was 25 points. In the second grade, the relative gain was 9.5 IQ points ($p < .02$), with one of the classes showing a mean gain of 18 points. These effects were especially surprising in view of the large gains in IQ made by the control group, which had to be surpassed by the experimental groups. Thus first graders in the control group gained 12 IQ points and second graders gained 7 IQ points, somewhat larger than might simply be ascribed to practice effects. More likely, the entire school was affected to some degree by being involved in an experiment with consequent good effects on the children's performance.[3]

Experimenters, teachers, probably psychotherapists, and probably "ordinary" people can affect the behavior of those with whom they interact by virtue of their expectations of what that behavior will be. Of course we must now try to learn how such communication takes place—how teachers communicate their expectations to their pupils. Considering the difficulties we have had in trying to answer that same

[3] These findings raise the question of what proportion of the effects of contemporary educational programs are due to the content of the programs rather than to the administrators' and teachers' expectancies. The social importance of these programs, to say nothing of the financial costs, make it appear important that program evaluations employ some form of "expectancy control group" (Rosenthal, 1966).

question for the case of experimenters, whose inputs into the experimenter-subject interaction could be much more easily controlled and observed, we should not expect a quick or an easy solution. But there may be consolation drawn from the conviction that, at least, the problem is worth the effort.

8

On The Social Psychology
Of The Psychological Experiment:
With Particular Reference
To Demand Characteristics
And Their Implications

Martin T. Orne

It is to the highest degree probable that the subject['s] ... general attitude of mind is that of ready complacency and cheerful willingness to assist the investigator in every possible way by reporting to him those very things which he is most eager to find, and that the very questions of the experimenter ... suggest the shade of reply expected.... Indeed ... it seems too often as if the subject were now regarded as a stupid automaton. ...

A. H. Pierce (1908)

Since the time of Galileo, scientists have employed the laboratory experiment as a method of understanding natural phenomena. Generically, the experimental method consists of abstracting relevant variables

* This paper was presented at the symposium "On the Social Psychology of the Psychological Experiment," American Psychological Association Convention, New York 1961. The work reported here was supported in part by a Public Health Service Research Grant, M-3369, National Institute of Mental Health.

I wish to thank my associates Ronald E. Shor, Donald N. O'Connell, Ulric Neisser, Karl E. Scheibe, and Emily F. Carota for their comments and criticisms in the preparation of this paper.

Reprinted with permission of author and publisher from *American Psychologist*, 17 (1962), pp. 776–83.

from complex situations in nature and reproducing in the laboratory segments of these situations, varying the parameters involved so as to determine the effect of the experimental variables. This procedure allows generalization from the information obtained in the laboratory situation back to the original situation as it occurs in nature. The physical sciences have made striking advances through the use of this method, but in the behavioral sciences it has often been difficult to meet two necessary requirements for meaningful experimentation: reproducibility and ecological validity.[1] It has long been recognized that certain differences will exist between the types of experiments conducted in the physical sciences and those in the behavioral sciences because the former investigates a universe of inanimate objects and forces, whereas the latter deals with animate organisms, often thinking, conscious subjects. However, recognition of this distinction has not always led to appropriate changes in the traditional experimental model of physics as employed in the behavioral sciences. Rather the experimental model has been so successful as employed in physics that there has been a tendency in the behavioral sciences to follow precisely a paradigm originated for the study of inanimate objects, i.e., one which proceeds by exposing the subject to various conditions and observing the differences in reaction of the subject under different conditions. However, the use of such a model with animal or human subjects leads to the problem that the subject of the experiment is assumed, at least implicitly, to be a *passive responder* to stimuli—an assumption difficult to justify. Further, in this type of model the experimental stimuli themselves are usually rigorously defined in terms of what *is done* to the subject. In contrast, the purpose of this paper will be to focus on what the human subject *does* in the laboratory: what motivation the subject is likely to have in the experimental situation, how he usually perceives behavioral research, what the nature of the cues is that the subject is likely to pick up, etc. Stated in other terms, what factors are apt to affect the subject's reaction to the well-defined stimuli in the situation? These factors comprise what will be referred to here as the "experimental setting."

Since any experimental manipulation of human subjects takes place within this larger framework or setting, we should propose that the above-mentioned factors must be further elaborated and the parameters

---

[1] Ecological validity, in the sense that Brunswik (1947) has used the term: appropriate generalization from the laboratory to nonexperimental situations.

of the experimental setting more carefully defined so that adequate controls can be designed to isolate the effects of the experimental setting from the effects of the experimental variables. Later in this paper we shall propose certain possible techniques of control which have been devised in the process of our research on the nature of hypnosis.

Our initial focus here will be on some of the qualities peculiar to psychological experiments. The experimental situation is one which takes place within the context of an explicit agreement of the subject to participate in a special form of social interaction known as "taking part in an experiment." Within the context of our culture the roles of subject and experimenter are well understood and carry with them well-defined mutual role expectations. A particularly striking aspect of the typical experimenter-subject relationship is the extent to which the subject will play his role and place himself under the control of the experimenter. Once a subject has agreed to participate in a psychological experiment, he implicitly agrees to perform a very wide range of actions on request without inquiring as to their purpose, and frequently without inquiring as to their duration.

Furthermore, the subject agrees to tolerate a considerable degree of discomfort, boredom, or actual pain, if required to do so by the experimenter. Just about any request which could conceivably be asked of the subject by a reputable investigator is legitimized by the quasi-magical phrase, "This is an experiment," and the shared assumption that a legitimate purpose will be served by the subject's behavior. A somewhat trivial example of this legitimization of requests is as follows:

A number of casual acquaintances were asked whether they would do the experimenter a favor; on their acquiescence, they were asked to perform five push-ups. Their response tended to be amazement, incredulity and the question "Why?" Another similar group of individuals were asked whether they would take part in an experiment of brief duration. When they agreed to do so, they too were asked to perform five push-ups. Their typical response was "Where?"

The striking degree of control inherent in the experimental situation can also be illustrated by a set of pilot experiments which were performed in the course of designing an experiment to test whether the degree of control inherent in the *hypnotic* relationship is greater than that in a waking relationship.[2] In order to test this question, we tried to

---

[2] These pilot studies were performed by Thomas Menaker.

develop a set of tasks which waking subjects would refuse to do, or would do only for a short period of time. The tasks were intended to be psychologically noxious, meaningless, or boring, rather than painful or fatiguing.

For example, one task was to perform serial additions of each adjacent two numbers on sheets filled with rows of random digits. In order to complete just one sheet, the subject would be required to perform 224 additions! A stack of some 2,000 sheets was presented to each subject—clearly an impossible task to complete. After the instructions were given, the subject was deprived of his watch and told, "Continue to work; I will return eventually." Five and one-half hours later, the *experimenter* gave up! In general, subjects tended to continue this type of task for several hours, usually with little decrement in performance. Since we were trying to find a task which would be discontinued spontaneously within a brief period, we tried to create a more frustrating situation as follows:

Subjects were asked to perform the same task described above but were also told that when finished the additions on each sheet, they should pick up a card from a large pile, which would instruct them on what to do next. However, every card in the pile read,

> You are to tear up the sheet of paper which you have just completed into a minimum of thirty-two pieces and go on to the next sheet of paper and continue working as you did before; when you have completed this piece of paper, pick up the next card which will instruct you further. Work as accurately and as rapidly as you can.

Our expectation was that subjects would discontinue the task as soon as they realized that the cards were worded identically, that each finished piece of work had to be destroyed, and that, in short, the task was completely meaningless.

Somewhat to our amazement, subjects tended to persist in the task for several hours with relatively little sign of overt hostility. Removal of the one-way screen did not tend to make much difference. The postexperimental inquiry helped to explain the subjects' behavior. When asked about the tasks, subjects would invariably attribute considerable meaning to their performance, viewing it as an endurance test or the like.

Thus far, we have been singularly unsuccessful in finding an experimental task which would be discontinued, or, indeed, refused by subjects in an experimental setting.[3,4] Not only do subjects continue to perform boring, unrewarding tasks, but they do so with few errors and little decrement in speed. It became apparent that it was extremely difficult to design an experiment to test the degree of social control in hypnosis, in view of the already *very high degree of control in the experimental situation itself.*

The quasi-experimental work reported here is highly informal and based on samples of three or four subjects in each group. It does, however, illustrate the remarkable compliance of the experimental subject. The only other situations where such a wide range of requests are carried out with little or no question are those of complete authority, such as some parent-child relationships or some doctor-patient relationships. This aspect of the experiment as a social situation will not become apparent unless one tests for it; it is, however, present in varying degrees in all experimental contexts. Not only are tasks carried out, but they are performed with care over a considerable period of time.

Our observation that subjects tend to carry out a remarkably wide range of instructions with a surprising degree of diligence reflects only one aspect of the motivation manifested by most subjects in an experimental situation. It is relevant to consider another aspect of motivation that is common to the subjects of most psychological experiments: high regard for the aims of science and experimentation.

A volunteer who participates in a psychological experiment may do so for a wide variety of reasons ranging from the need to fulfill a course requirement, to the need for money, to the unvoiced hope of altering his personal adjustment for the better, etc. Over and above these motives, however, college students tend to share (with the experimenter) the hope and expectation that the study in which they are participating will in some material way contribute to science and perhaps ultimately to human welfare in general. We should expect that many of the characteristics of the experimental situation derive from the peculiar role relationship which exists between subject and experi-

---

[3] Tasks which would involve the use of actual severe physical pain or exhaustion were not considered.

[4] This observation is consistent with Frank's (1944) failure to obtain resistance to disagreeable or nonsensical tasks. He accounts for this "primarily by Ss unwillingness to break the tacit agreement he had made when he volunteered to take part in the experiment, namely, to do whatever the experiment required of him" (p. 24).

menter. Both subject and experimenter share the belief that whatever
the experimental task is, it is important, and that as such no matter
how much effort must be exerted or how much discomfort must be
endured, it is justified by the ultimate purpose.

If we assume that much of the motivation of the subject to comply
with any and all experimental instructions derives from an identification with the goals of science in general and the success of the experiment in particular,[5] it follows that the subject has a stake in the outcome of the study in which he is participating. For the volunteer
subject to feel that he has made a useful contribution, it is necessary for
him to assume that the experimenter is competent and that he himself
is a "good subject."

The significance to the subject of successfully being a "good subject" is attested to by the frequent questions at the conclusion of an
experiment, to the effect of, "Did I ruin the experiment?" What is most
commonly meant by this is, "Did I perform well in my role as experimental subject?" or "Did my behavior demonstrate that which the
experiment is designed to show?" Admittedly, subjects are concerned
about their performance in terms of reinforcing their self-image; nonetheless, they seem even more concerned with the utility of their performances. We might well expect then that as far as the subject is able,
he will behave in an experimental context in a manner designed to play
the role of a "good subject" or, in other words, *to validate the experimental hypothesis.* Viewed in this way, the student volunteer is *not*
merely a passive responder in an experimental situation but rather he
has a very real stake in the successful outcome of the experiment. This
problem is implicitly recognized in the large number of psychological
studies which attempt to conceal the true purpose of the experiment
from the subject in the hope of thereby obtaining more reliable data.
This maneuver on the part of psychologists is so widely known in the
college population that even if a psychologist is honest with the subject,
more often than not he will be distrusted. As one subject pithily put it,
"Psychologists always lie!" This bit of paranoia has some support in
reality.

The subject's performance in an experiment might almost be concep-
tualized as problem-solving behavior; that is, at some level he sees it as

---

[5] This hypothesis is subject to empirical test. We should predict that there
would be measurable differences in motivation between subjects who perceive a
particular experiment as "significant" and those who perceive the experiment as
"unimportant."

his task to ascertain the true purpose of the experiment and respond in a manner which will support the hypotheses being tested. Viewed in this light, the totality of cues which convey an experimental hypothesis to the subject become significant determinants of subjects' behavior. We have labeled the sum total of such cues as the *"demand characteristics of the experimental situation"* (Orne, 1959a). These cues include the rumors or campus scuttlebutt about the research, the information conveyed during the original solicitation, the person of the experimenter, and the setting of the laboratory, as well as all explicit and implicit communications during the experiment proper. A frequently overlooked but nonetheless very significant source of cues for the subject lies in the experimental procedure itself, viewed in the light of the subject's previous knowledge and experience. For example, if a test is given twice with some intervening treatment, even the dullest college student is aware that some change is expected, particularly if the test is in some obvious way related to the treatment.

The demand characteristics perceived in any particular experiment will vary with the sophistication, intelligence, and previous experience of each experimental subject. To the extent that the demand characteristics of the experiment are clear-cut, they will be perceived uniformly by most experimental subjects. It is entirely possible to have an experimental situation with clear-cut demand characteristics for psychology undergraduates which, however, does not have the same clear-cut demand characteristics for enlisted army personnel. It is, of course, those demand characteristics which are perceived by the subject that will influence his behavior.

We should like to propose the heuristic assumption that a subject's behavior in any experimental situation will be determined by two sets of variables: (a) those which are traditionally defined as experimental variables and (b) the perceived demand characteristics of the experimental situation. The extent to which the subject's behavior is related to the demand characteristics, rather than to the experimental variable, will in large measure determine both the extent to which the experiment can be replicated with minor modification (i.e., modified demand characteristics) and the extent to which generalizations can be drawn about the effect of the experimental variables in nonexperimental contexts (the problem of ecological validity [Brunswik, 1947]).

It becomes an empirical issue to study under what circumstances, in what kind of experimental contexts, and with what kind of subject populations, demand characteristics become significant in determining the behavior of subjects in experimental situations. It should be clear that demand characteristics cannot be eliminated from experiments; all experiments will have demand characteristics, and these will always have some effect. It does become possible, however, to study the effect of demand characteristics as opposed to the effect of experimental variables. However, techniques designed to study the effect of demand characteristics need to take into account that these effects result from the subject's *active* attempt to respond appropriately to the *totality* of the experimental situation.

It is perhaps best to think of the perceived demand characteristics as a contextual variable in the experimental situation. We should like to emphasize that, at this stage, little is known about this variable. In our first study which utilized the demand characteristics concept (Orne, 1959b), we found that a particular experimental effect was present only in records of those subjects who were able to verbalize the experimenter's hypothesis. Those subjects who were unable to do so did not show the predicted phenomenon. Indeed we found that whether or not a given subject perceived the experimenter's hypothesis was a more accurate predictor of the subject's actual performance than his statement about what he thought he had done on the experimental task. It became clear from extensive interviews with subjects that response to the demand characteristics is not merely conscious compliance. When we speak of "playing the role of a good experimental subject," we use the concept analogously to the way in which Sarbin (1950) describes role playing in hypnosis: namely, largely on a nonconscious level. The demand characteristics of the situation help define the role of "good experimental subject," and the responses of the subject are a function of the role that is created.

We have a suspicion that the demand characteristics most potent in determining subjects' behavior are those which convey the purpose of the experiment effectively but not obviously. If the purpose of the experiment is not clear, or is highly ambiguous, many different hypotheses may be formed by different subjects, and the demand characteristics will not lead to clear-cut results. If, on the other hand, the demand characteristics are so obvious that the subject becomes fully conscious of the expectations of the experimenter, there is a tendency to lean over backwards to be honest. We are encountering here the effect of another facet of the college student's attitude toward science. While the student wants studies to "work," he feels he must be honest in his report; otherwise, erroneous conclusions will be drawn. Therefore, if the subject becomes acutely aware of the experimenter's expectations, there may be a tendency for biasing in the opposite direction. (This is analogous to the often observed tendency to favor individuals whom we dislike in an effort to be fair.)[6]

Delineation of the situations where demand characteristics may produce an effect ascribed to experimental variables, or where they may obscure such an effect and actually lead to systematic data in the opposite direction, as well as those experimental contexts where they do not play a major role, is an issue for further work. Recognizing the contribution to experimental results which may be made by the demand characteristics of the situation, what are some experimental techniques for the study of demand characteristics?

As we have pointed out, it is futile to imagine an experiment that could be created without demand characteristics. One of the basic characteristics of the human being is that he will ascribe purpose and meaning even in the absence of purpose and meaning. In an experiment where he knows some purpose exists, it is inconceivable for him not to form some hypothesis as to the purpose, based on some cues, no matter how meager; this will then determine the demand characteristics which will be perceived by and operate for a particular subject. Rather than eliminating this variable then, it becomes necessary to take demand characteristics into account, study their effect, and manipulate them if necessary.

One procedure to determine the demand characteristics is the systematic study of each individual subject's perception of the experimental hypothesis. If one can determine what demand characteristics are perceived by each subject, it becomes possible to determine to what extent these, rather than the experimental variables, correlate with the observed behavior. If the subject's behavior correlates better with the demand characteristics than with the experimental variables, it is probable that the demand characteristics are the major determinants of the behavior.

The most obvious technique for determining what demand characteristics are perceived is the use of postexperimental inquiry. In this

---

[6] Rosenthal (1961), in his recent work on experimenter bias, has reported a similar type of phenomenon. Biasing was maximized by ego involvement of the experimenters, but when an attempt was made to increase biasing by paying for "good results," there was a marked reduction of effect. This reversal may be ascribed to the experimenters' becoming too aware of their own wishes in the situation.

regard, it is well to point out that considerable self-discipline is necessary for the experimenter to obtain a valid inquiry. A great many experimenters at least implicitly make the demand that the subject not perceive what is really going on. The temptation for the experimenter, in, say, a replication of an Asch-group pressure experiment, is to ask the subject afterwards, "You didn't realize that the other fellows were confederates, did you?" Having obtained the required, "No," the experimenter breathes a sigh of relief and neither subject nor experimenter pursues the issue further.[7] However, even if the experimenter makes an effort to elicit the subject's perception of the hypothesis of the experiment, he may have difficulty in obtaining a valid report because the subject as well as he himself has considerable interest in appearing naive.

Most subjects are cognizant that they are not supposed to know any more about an experiment than they have been told and that excessive knowledge will disqualify them from participating, or, in the case of a postexperimental inquiry, such knowledge will invalidate their performance. As we pointed out earlier, subjects have a real stake in viewing their performance as meaningful. For this reason, it is commonplace to find a pact of ignorance resulting from the intertwining motives of both experimenter and subject, neither wishing to create a situation where the particular subject's performance needs to be excluded from the study.

For these reasons, inquiry procedures are required to push the subject for information without, however, providing in themselves cues as to what is expected. The general question which needs to be explored is the subject's perception of the experimental purpose and the specific hypotheses of the experimenter. This can best be done by an open-ended procedure starting with the very general question of, "What do you think that the experiment is about?" and only much later asking specific questions. Responses of "I don't know" should be dealt with by encouraging the subject to guess, use his imagination, and in general, by refusing to accept this response. Under these circumstances, the overwhelming majority of students will turn out to have evolved very definite hypotheses. These hypotheses can then be judged, and a correlation between them and experimental performance can be drawn.

Two objections may be made against this type of inquiry: (a) that the subject's perception of the experimenter's hypotheses is based on his own experimental behavior, and therefore a correlation between

[7] Asch (1952) himself took great pains to avoid this pitfall.

these two variables may have little to do with the determinants of behavior, and (b) that the inquiry procedure itself is subject to demand characteristics.

A procedure which has been independently advocated by Riecken (1958) and Orne (1959a) is designed to deal with the first of these objections. This consists of an inquiry procedure which is conducted much as though the subject had actually been run in the experiment, without, however, permitting him to be given any experimental data. Instead, the precise procedure of the experiment is explained, the experimental material is shown to the subject, and he is told what he would be required to do; however, he is not permitted to make any responses. He is then given a postexperimental inquiry as though he had been a subject. Thus, one would say, "If I had asked you to do all these things, what do you think that the experiment would be about, what do you think I would be trying to prove, what would my hypothesis be?" etc. This technique, which we have termed the pre-experimental inquiry, can be extended very readily to the giving of pre-experimental tests, followed by the explanation of experimental conditions and tasks, and the administration of postexperimental tests. The subject is requested to behave on these tests as though he had been exposed to the experimental treatment that was described to him. This type of procedure is not open to the objection that the subject's own behavior has provided cues for him as to the purpose of the task. It presents him with a straight problem-solving situation and makes explicit what, for the true experimental subject, is implicit. It goes without saying that these subjects who are run on the pre-experimental inquiry conditions must be drawn from the same population as the experimental groups and may, of course, not be run subsequently in the experimental condition. This technique is one of approximation rather than of proof. However, if subjects describe behavior on the pre-inquiry conditions as similar to, or identical with, that actually given by subjects exposed to the experimental conditions, the hypothesis becomes plausible that demand characteristics may be responsible for the behavior.

It is clear that pre- and postexperimental inquiry techniques have their own demand characteristics. For these reasons, it is usually best to have the inquiry conducted by an experimenter who is not acquainted with the actual experimental behavior of the subjects. This will tend to minimize the effect of experimenter bias.

Another technique which we have utilized for approximating the effect of the demand characteristics is to attempt to hold the demand characteristics constant and eliminate the experimental variable. One way of accomplishing this purpose is through the use of simulating subjects. This is a group of subjects who are not exposed to the experimental variable to which the effect has been attributed, but who are instructed to act *as if* this were the case. In order to control for experimenter bias under these circumstances, it is advisable to utilize more than one experimenter and to have the experimenter who actually runs the subjects "blind" as to which group (simulating or real) any given individual belongs.

Our work in hypnosis (Damaser, Shor, & Orne, 1963; Orne, 1959b; Shor, 1959) is a good example of the use of simulating controls. Subjects unable to enter hypnosis are instructed to simulate entering hypnosis for another experimenter. The experimenter who runs the study sees both highly trained hypnotic subjects and simulators in random order and does not know to which group each subject belongs. Because the subjects are run "blind," the experimenter is more likely to treat the two groups of subjects identically. We have found that simulating subjects are able to perform with great effectiveness, deceiving even well-trained hypnotists. However, the simulating group is not exposed to the experimental condition (in this case, hypnosis) to which the given effect under investigation is often ascribed. Rather, it is a group faced with a problem-solving task: namely, to utilize whatever cues are made available by the experimental context and the experimenter's concrete behavior in order to behave as they think that hypnotized subjects might. Therefore, to the extent that simulating subjects are able to behave identically, it is possible that demand characteristics, rather than the altered state of consciousness, could account for the behavior of the experimental group.

The same type of technique can be utilized in other types of studies. For example, in contrast to the placebo control in a drug study, it is equally possible to instruct some subjects not to take the medication at all, but to act as if they had. It must be emphasized that this type of control is different from the placebo control. It represents an approximation. It maximally confronts the simulating subject with a problem-solving task and suggests how much of the total effect could be accounted for by the demand characteristics—assuming that the experimental group had taken full advantage of them, an assumption not necessarily correct.

All of the techniques proposed thus far share the quality that they depend upon the active cooperation of the control subjects, and in some way utilize his thinking process as an intrinsic factor. The subject does *not* just respond in these control situations but, rather, he is required *actively* to solve the problem.

The use of placebo experimental conditions is a way in which this problem can be dealt with in a more classic fashion. Psychopharmacology has used such techniques extensively, but here too they present problems. In the case of placebos and drugs, it is often the case that the physician is "blind" as to whether a drug is placebo or active, but the patient is not, despite precautions to the contrary; i.e., the patient is cognizant that he does not have the side effects which some of his fellow patients on the ward experience. By the same token, in psychological placebo treatments, it is equally important to ascertain whether the subject actually perceived the treatment to be experimental or control. Certainly the subject's perception of himself as a control subject may materially alter the situation.

A recent experiment[8] in our laboratory illustrates this type of investigation. We were interested in studying the demand characteristics of sensory deprivation experiments, independent of any actual sensory deprivation. We hypothesized that the overly cautious treatment of subjects, careful screening for mental or physical disorders, awesome release forms, and, above all, the presence of a "panic (release) button" might be more significant in producing the effects reported from sensory deprivation than the actual diminution of sensory input. A pilot study (Stare, Brown, & Orne, 1959), employing preinquiry techniques, supported this view. Recently, we designed an experiment to test more rigorously this hypothesis.

This experiment, which we called Meaning Deprivation, had all the accoutrements of sensory deprivation, including release forms and a red panic button. However, we carefully refrained from creating any sensory deprivation whatsoever. The experimental task consisted of sitting in a small experimental room which was well lighted, with two comfortable chairs, as well as ice water and a sandwich, and an optional task of adding numbers. The subject did not have a watch during this time, the room was reasonably quiet, but not soundproof, and the duration of the experiment (of which the subject was ignorant) was four hours. Before the subject was placed in the experimental room, ten tests previously used in sensory deprivation research were administered. At the completion of the experiment, the same tasks were again administered. A microphone and a one-way screen were present in the room, and the subject was encouraged to verbalize freely.

---

[8] See Orne and Scheibe (1964).

The control group of ten subjects was subjected to the identical treatment, except that they were told that they were control subjects for a sensory deprivation experiment. The panic button was eliminated for this group. The formal experimental treatment of these two groups of subjects was the same in terms of the objective stress—four hours of isolation. However, the demand characteristics had been purposively varied for the two groups to study the effect of demand characteristics as opposed to objective stress. Of the 14 measures which could be quantified, 13 were in the predicted direction, and 6 were significant at the selected 10 percent alpha level or better. A Mann-Whitney U test has been performed on the summation ranks of all measures as a convenient method for summarizing the overall differences. The one-tailed probability which emerges is $p = .001$, a clear demonstration of expected effects.

This study suggests that demand characteristics may in part account for some of the findings commonly attributed to sensory deprivation. We have found similar significant effects of demand characteristics in accounting for a great deal of the findings reported in hypnosis. It is highly probable that careful attention to this variable, or group of variables, may resolve some of the current controversies regarding a number of psychological phenomena in motivation, learning, and perception.

In summary, we have suggested that the subject must be recognized as an active participant in any experiment, and that it may be fruitful to view the psychological experiment as a very special form of social interaction. We have proposed that the subject's behavior in an experiment is a function of the totality of the situation, which includes the experimental variables being investigated and at least one other set of variables which we have subsumed under the heading, demand characteristics of the experimental situation. The study and control of demand characteristics are not simply matters of good experimental technique; rather, it is an empirical issue to determine under what circumstances demand characteristics significantly affect subjects' experimental behavior. Several empirical techniques have been proposed for this purpose. It has been suggested that control of these variables in particular may lead to greater reproducibility and ecological validity of psychological experiments. With an increasing understanding of these factors intrinsic to the experimental context, the experimental method in psychology may become a more effective tool in predicting behavior in nonexperimental contexts.

9
Some Unintended Consequences Of Rigorous Research

Chris Argyris

Rigorousness is to a researcher what efficiency is to an executive: an ideal state that is always aspired to, never reached, and continually revered. Much literature exists regarding the best ways to approach both rigorousness and efficiency. In the case of efficiency, executives have traditionally assumed that when organizations are not efficient it is usually because the members have not been adhering to an efficient organizational strategy. One of the contributions of organizational behaviorists has been to study how executives and employees actually behave (not limit themselves to how they say they behave). One major result of these studies has been to show that a good deal of inefficiency may occur precisely when and because the members are following closely the most accepted strategies for efficiency.

Recently a new literature has been, and continues to be, developed by scholars studying the research situation (Friedman, 1967; Rosenthal, 1966). They too have not limited themselves to what researchers say they do in conducting research. They have studied research in terms of

Reprinted with permission of author and publisher from *Psychological Bulletin*, 70, no. 3 (1968), pp. 185-197.

The author wishes to express his appreciation to his colleagues Douglas Hall, Richard Hackman, Edward Lawler, Lyman Porter, and Betty Ann Nunes for their many helpful suggestions.

how it is actually carried out. As a result, they have reported dysfunctions and opened up important new questions.

An exploration of this literature from the viewpoint of an organizational theorist suggests that his field may be able to make a modest contribution in terms of a theoretical framework to organize the existing findings and suggest other possible conclusions that have yet to be documented systematically. This framework conceives of the researcher-subject relationship as a systemic one, be it temporary. By borrowing from the established literature on research methodology, we shall attempt to show that the properties of this temporary system are remarkably similar to the properties of formal organizations. Moreover, many of the dysfunctions reported between experimenter and subject are similar to the dysfunctions between management and employee.

THE UNDERLYING ASSUMPTIONS
ABOUT RIGOROUS RESEARCH

Let us begin by asking what are the underlying assumptions for conducting rigorous research. The first is that rigorousness is an ideal state which one can only approximate. The second assumption is that rigorousness is more closely approximated as the researcher is able to define unambiguously his problem and the relevant variables. Moreover, the more easily the variables can be observed and measured, the greater the reliability, the greater the probability for future public verifiability, the more rigorous will be the research. The third assumption is that the more control a researcher has over his variables, the more rigorous will be his research.

THE NATURE OF THE RELATIONSHIP
BETWEEN RESEARCHER AND SUBJECT

These assumptions provide the basis for elegant research designs. Like management principles, the designs are expected to work if subjects cooperate. It is precisely at the point when people are brought into the picture that the difficulties arise. Why is this so?

In order to answer this question let us examine the basic qualities of rigorous research. Most methodologists agree with Edwards (1954) that rigorous research tends to occur when:

1. The research is deliberately undertaken to satisfy the needs of the researcher and where the pace of activity is controlled by the researcher to give him maximum possible control over the subjects' behavior.

2. The setting is designed by the researcher to achieve his objectives and to minimize any of the subjects' desires from contaminating the experiment.

3. The researcher is responsible for making accurate observations, recording them, analyzing them, and eventually reporting them.

4. The researcher has the conditions so rigorously defined that he or others can replicate them.

5. The researcher can systematically vary the conditions and note the concomitant variation among the variables.

These conditions are remarkably similar to those top management defines when designing an organization. Top management (researcher) defines the worker's (subject's) role as rationally and clearly as possible (to minimize error) and as simply as possible (to minimize having to draw from a select population, thereby reducing the generalizability of the research findings); provides as little information as possible beyond the tasks (thereby minimizing the time perspective of the subject); and defines the inducements for participating (e.g., a requirement to pass a course, a plea for the creation of knowledge, or money). Indeed, if Edwards' description is valid, the rigorous research criteria would create a world for the subject in which his behavior is defined, controlled, evaluated, manipulated, and reported to a degree that is comparable to the behavior of workers in the most mechanized assembly-line conditions.

THE UNINTENDED CONSEQUENCES
OF RIGOROUS RESEARCH DESIGNS

If this similarity between conditions in organizations and those in research systems does exist, then the unintended consequences found in formal organizations should also be found, in varying degree, in the temporary systems created by research. These consequences have been discussed in detail elsewhere (Argyris, 1964). Briefly they are:

1. Physical withdrawal which results in absenteeism and turnover.

2. Psychological withdrawal while remaining physically in the research situation. Under these conditions the subject is willing to let the researcher manipulate his behavior, usually for a price. The studies that show subjects as all too willing to cooperate are, from this point of view, examples of subject withdrawal from involvement and not, as some researchers suggest, signs of subjects' high involvement. To give a researcher what he wants in such a way that the researcher does not realize that the subject is doing this (a skill long ago learned by em-

ployees and students) is a sign of nonresponsibility and of a lack of commitment to the effectiveness of the research.

3. Overt hostility toward the research. Openly fighting the research rarely occurs, probably because the subjects are "volunteers." If they are not volunteers, they may still feel pressured to participate. If so, they would probably not feel free to fight the researcher openly.

4. Covert hostility is a safer adaptive mechanism. It includes such behavior as knowingly giving incorrect answers, being a difficult subject, second-guessing the research design and trying to circumvent it in some fashion, producing the minimally accepted amount of behavior, coercing others to produce minimally, and disbelief and mistrust of the researcher.

5. Emphasis upon monetary rewards as the reason for participation.

6. Unionization of subjects.

Organizational theory would suggest that the exact degree to which any of these conditions would hold for a given subject would be, in turn, a function of:

1. The degree to which being dependent, manipulated, and controlled is "natural" in the lives of the subjects (e.g., research utilizing children or adults in highly authoritarian cultures may be more generalizable).

2. The length of time that the research takes and the degree of subject control it requires.

3. The motivations of the subjects (e.g., for the sake of science, to pass a course, to learn about self, for money).

4. The potency of the research (the involvement it requires of the subject).

5. The possible effect participation in research or its results could have on the subject's evaluation of his previous, and perception of his future, life.

6. The number of times the subject participates in other research.

7. The degree to which the research situation is similar to other situations in which the subject is immersed, about which he has strong feelings, few of which he can express. For example, in the case of students, the role in a lecture class is similar to the role of a subject in a psychological experiment. (The teacher controls, has the long-range perspective, defines the tasks, etc.) To the extent that he is unable to express his frustration in relation to the class, he may find it appropriate, if indeed he does not feel himself inwardly compelled, to express these pent-up feelings during the research.

Some may question if these feelings would come out in such research situations because participating in an experiment, being interviewed, filling out a questionnaire tend to take a short time. This view may be questioned. Has not the reader watched how quickly people become involved in parlor games and noted how easy it is for them to surface competitive needs, power aspirations, and fears of failure? Indeed, is it not the fundamental assumption of the researcher that an experiment is genuinely involving? Is it not accepted that the data would hardly be generalizable if the subjects could be shown to be involved only peripherally because of the shortness of time? As Sales (1966), a proponent of experimentation pointed out, the

> "brevity" argument is not valid ... the entire science of experimental social psychology rests upon the assumption that experimental periods are sufficiently lengthy for treatments to "take," an assumption which is supported in every significant finding obtained in the experimental laboratory [p. 28].

If experimental conditions "take" in short periods, then why should not the psychological conditions implicit in the researcher-subject relationship also "take"?

ILLUSTRATION OF THE EXISTENCE OF ADAPTIVE STRATEGIES

The next question is, to what extent are subjects beginning to adapt in ways suggested by the theoretical framework? Orne (1962), Mills (1962), and Rosenthal (1963c) have presented evidence that subjects are willing to become dependent upon and submissive to the experimenter and, as Kiesler (in press) suggested, overcooperative with the researcher. Unfortunately, little systematic research exists beyond these studies. Some anecdotal evidence was collected by the writer at his own institution. The students have increasingly emphasized the importance of being paid for participating in research. This trend can be predicted by an organizational theory. The "market orientation" (so common among lower level employees in industry) is an inevitable consequence of being in a formal organization (Argyris, 1964).

Second-guessing and beating the researcher at his own game may also be becoming commonplace, especially in dissonance experiments. Many experiments have been reported where it was crucial to deceive the students. Naturally, in many cases the students were carefully debriefed (although to the writer's knowledge few, if any, researchers have provided evidence which was collected as rigorously for this assertion as were the data directly related to the goal of the experiment). One result that has occurred is that students now come to experiments expecting to be tricked. The initial romance and challenge of being subjects has left them and they are now beginning to behave like lower level employees in companies. Their big challenge is to guess the deception (beat the management). If one likes the experimenter, then he cooperates. If he does not, he may enjoy botching the works with such great skill that the experimenter is not aware of this behavior. This practice is frequent enough for Burdick (1957) to make it the subject matter of an entire chapter in his best seller, *The Ninth Wave.* He describes the hero who outguessed the experimenters and was eventually rejected by them. He also describes another subject who pleased the experimenters but who, it turned out, hated the experimenters deeply. In one major university a formal evaluation was made of the basic psychology course by nearly 600 undergraduates. They were given three topics from which they could choose one to evaluate thoroughly. The senior professor responsible for the course reported an overwhelming majority of the students focused on the requirement, in the course, that they had to participate as subjects. The students were very critical, mistrustful, and hostile to the requirement. In many cases they identified how they expressed their pent-up feelings by "beating the researcher" in such a way that he never found out (an activity frequently observed among frustrated employees).

These examples, incidentally, also serve to illustrate that students can generate strong feelings about experimentation in a very short time. They also raise the question, do we need systematic data showing that the briefing each subject received actually generated not only the correct cognitive maps but the proper psychological set upon which the experiment depends (Friedman, 1967)?

Another example of how students are beginning to react like employees is illustrated by a request received by the writer recently from a senior social psychologist at Yale. He had concluded that to identify an experiment openly and honestly would lead to a set of attitudes among students that would be harmful to the experiments. He wanted to know if a place could be found for him to conduct his experiment in an organizational setting. He assumed that people in an organizational setting are not so contaminated as students (especially along the dimension of expecting to be tricked). As we shall see, this assumption is not necessarily valid.

A graduate student was recently able to design an experiment with no deception and one in which he could honestly advertise (as he did) that the students might learn about themselves as a result of participating in the research. His experiment was a ten-hour T-group. In the first four sessions at least three hours were spent by the members trying to deal with the students' deep beliefs that the ad was phony, that they were to be tricked, and that the researcher didn't really mean what he had said.

Recently, Kelman (1967) raised similar issues. He doubts that the subjects will remain naive. He quoted one subject as saying, "Psychologists always lie!" He also suggested, and this would be predicted by an organizational theory, that the subjects may come to resent the experimenter and throw a monkey wrench in the experiment.

Brock and Becker (1966) attempted to prove that deception may not have the harmful effects suggested by Kelman (1967). Their work is open to serious question. Nowhere do they provide evidence that the subjects were not dutifully playing the role of subject and doing everything asked of them. One could argue that they signed the petition; after being told they had just ruined the experimenter's mechanical box (which was contrived to blow up when a button was pressed), because they saw through the hoax and went along with the game. An explanation for those who refused to sign the petition could be that since they did not blow up the box they saw little reason to go along with the researchers. One would predict that the subjects might openly resist if they were given a rational opportunity to do so. This turned out to be the case. There was high resistance to the experimenter when it was possible to connect the massive debriefing with participation in the second experiment.

Two points require emphasis at this juncture. First, these adaptive strategies are predictable by organizational theory because the relationship between the researcher and the subject is similar to the one between the manager and the employee in formal organizations. Moreover, the adaptive strategies may well lead to internal psychological states, on the part of the subjects, that can significantly alter their perception of the research and their response to it. If this is the case, then the generalizability of the results may be seriously limited unless the researcher can show "rigorously" that he has been able to control the existence of subjects' adaptive strategies.

One way a researcher may respond to the problem of controlling these adaptive strategies is to obtain a large sample of subjects. He may assume that these kinds of behavior are "noise" that can be partialed out. If our theoretical view is valid, then any increase in the sample may simply tend to increase the difficulties, not decrease them. Moreover, as the "noise" increases it may eliminate any "real" effect that might be there. Another response may be to increase the controls over the subjects' behavior. According to this analysis, the problems would then be compounded.

As another illustration of dysfunctions, some enterprising students at two major universities have begun to think about starting a student organization that would be similar to Manpower or, if this were resisted by the university, similar to a union. Instead of secretaries, they would offer subjects. They believe that they can get students to cooperate because they would promise them more money, better debriefing, and more interest on the part of the researcher (e.g., more complete feedback). When this experience was reported to some psychologists their response was similar to the reactions of business men who have just been told for the first time that their employees were considering the creation of a union. There was some nervous laughter, a comment indicating surprise, then another comment to the effect that every organization has some troublemakers, and finally a prediction that such an activity would never succeed because "the students are too disjointed to unite."

To continue the comparison with business men, is there not a strong similarity of the attitudes held by the early lumber kings and those held presently by many researchers? The lumber kings consumed trees without worrying very much about the future supply. Researchers (field and experimental) seem to consume subjects without worrying very much about their future supply. For example, as was shown above, simple debriefing may not be enough. Students who serve as subjects talk about their experiences with other students; they may even magnify them as they are prone to do a fraternity initiation rite. The impact upon future subjects can be deadly and difficult to overcome.

An experience the writer had several years ago illustrates how much the formal, authoritarian, pyramidal relationships are endemic in many social science generalizations even though they are never made explicit.

A world-renowned learning theorist met with a group of executives. To his surprise, one of these, a senior corporate officer, had attempted to utilize the learning theorist's views in his workplace. For example, he wanted to see what would happen if he related to his subordinates in a more systematic way, that is, by following a carefully thought-through

reinforcement schedule of rewards. He reported the following difficulties:

First, it was difficult to infer any guidelines or criteria as to what
would be a valid schedule. Nevertheless, with the help of an advanced
graduate student, one was developed. It was not too long before the
executive found that he spent the majority of his time simply monitoring the schedules and giving the appropriate rewards according to
schedule.

Although all subordinates seemed to respond favorably, there was an
unexpected differential reaction. Many men, unlike the subjects in the
experiment, reacted positively to their boss and to his rewards. They
would say in effect, "Thank you, sir. I certainly appreciate your
thoughtfulness." This genuine response tended to complicate matters
for two reasons. First, being able to show gratitude toward a superior
may in itself be gratifying. Second, such a warm response normally calls
for an equally positive response from the recipient, such as "It's always
a pleasure, Smith, to reward excellent behavior." In either case the
subject is experiencing rewards that would not be in the reinforcement
schedule.

The executive, although pleased with the "subject's" reaction, strove
to minimize the pleasure so that the original reinforcement schedule
would not be confounded. In doing this he found that he was creating a
world where his subordinates had a relationship to him that was similar
to the one rats (or children) have to an experimenter. This relationship
was one in which the subordinate was dependent and had a short time
perspective. The schedule, if it were to work, required a fundamentally
authoritarian relationship!

To make matters worse, the "subjects" were constantly having their
lives bombarded with meaningful rewards and penalties from other employees as well as from such administrative procedures as budgets. The
executive began to realize that if these were to be systematically controlled, he would have to become a little Hitler, control the world of his
subordinates completely, to the point that they would be isolated from
the system in which they were embedded.

It is important to note that nowhere did the learning theorist state
these conditions in his generalizations. For example, he had concluded
that a specified reinforcement schedule seemed to lead to a specific
level of learning. He failed to specify that this generalization held only
if the subject was in a specified relationship to the one doing the
rewarding and penalizing, namely, one that is similar to that of an

experimenter with a rat. Thus, we see that the nature of person-to-person relationships and the nature of the research situation can serve as potent moderators of the variable relationships we often study. If this is the case, the generalizations from rigorous research studies of the types described above ought to "work" (in the sense that they account for substantial portions of the non-random variance) only in life situations which are analogous to the experimental situations in which the original data were collected. The analogous situations are those that contain authoritarian relationships and provide for social isolation of the participants. These generalizations ought not to hold up (and indeed ought not to be expected to hold up), however, in those cases where a controlling party and the object of control are engaged in a relationship which is of a qualitatively different type than that of the experimenter and subject in the experimental situation which gave rise to the data, and where the characteristics of the situation (i.e., of the task and social environment) are substantially different in the life situation than in the experimental situation.

RESEARCH IN FIELD SETTINGS

The problems discussed above also hold true for the researcher-subject relationship in field settings; indeed, in some cases the problems are compounded.

During the past several years, while conducting field research, the writer has interviewed thirty-five lower level employees and thirty upper level executives on the subject of how they heard about the research, how they felt coming to be interviewed or filling out the questionnaire, and how they felt while being interviewed or filling out a questionnaire.

The most consistent finding was the unanimity of responses. Apparently research conducted in organizations may create even deeper problems for subjects. Although the data are admittedly anecdotal, it seems appropriate to use them as suggestive of the problem. In doing so, it is important to keep in mind that in all the field studies from which these data were developed, the management at all levels had been briefed by the researcher in small groups with ample time for questions, and letters of explanation had gone to each employee from the president, as well as being displayed on all the bulletin boards.

Although the managers at the lower levels felt they understood the research program and were in favor of it, when it came to telling the employee such a seemingly simple thing as that he was scheduled to be interviewed the next day, many felt very uncomfortable in doing so. They did not feel they could honestly describe the research, nor did they feel they could answer employee anxieties, and more importantly, they reported, they did not want to try. This attitude is understandable because most managers tend to emphasize "getting the job done"; they rarely inquire about their interpersonal impact on the employees, nor about interpersonal problems (Argyris, 1962; 1965). Thus to discuss a research project that could arouse emotional responses would place the manager in an interpersonal situation that would be uncomfortable for him.

Instead of running the risk of engaging in possible difficult conversation with an employee, most managers reported (and employees confirmed) that they simply went up to the employee and notified him that he would be interviewed the next day at a particular time. Over 75 percent of the employees reported that their superiors either ordered them to go to be interviewed or said it in such way that they implied that they did not want any "noise." Thus, most employees felt they (the employees) knew very little about the research. Few reported open resentment (after all, they were always being ordered to do something). Many reported feeling anxious.

The reasons for anxiety seemed to vary enormously. "Why did they pick on me? Who picked me? Are they going to ask personal questions? Are they trying to get rid of me? Whose crazy idea was this? Will I be able to understand a professor or a researcher? Will the questions be too difficult? Will they ask me to write? How open should I be? Will it get anyone (including me) in trouble? What effect will this have on my wages earned for the day? What effect will my absence have upon others who are working and depend on me?" In some cases the anxiety was compounded by informal employee kidding and discussion about the research. "Who goes to see the headshrinkers first?" "I hear they place a hot towel on your head and send electrical currents through you to make sure you don't lie." "They have a guy who can read your mind."

Few of these anxieties were openly stated and fewer were dealt with. Many employees, who came to be interviewed or to fill out the questionnaire with varying degrees of anxiety, attempted to cope with their feelings by becoming resigned ("They do things to me unilaterally all the time"), or by mild hostility and cautious withdrawal or non-involvement.

The feelings of being controlled, or being pushed around, and of anxiety were reduced more quickly in the interview situation because the interviewer was able to answer many of their questions (without their having to raise them), helped them to feel that they did not have to participate, and encouraged them to alter the questions or the sequence in which they were asked, as well as to feel free to refuse to answer any questions. The negative feelings, reported the subjects, persisted over a longer period in the questionnaire situation. They reported that they felt more controlled, pushed around, and dealt with at a distance, while filling out the questionnaire. For example, many reported questions that arose in their minds but they hesitated to discuss them openly.

The reported feelings of being controlled, being dependent, and submissive to a researcher tended to decrease as one went up the hierarchy and with more participation people had in learning about the research and in deciding if permission was to be granted for its execution. Moreover, the fear of intellectual incompetence to participate was almost negligible. However, there were some anxieties about how open to be, how much risk to take, and how much to level with the interviewer. As in the case of the lower level employees, the (properly executed) questionnaire situation irritated a significantly higher proportion of the managers than did a (properly executed) interview. The executives reported that they resented the unilateral dependence that they experienced in filling out a questionnaire.

It seems that the research process, in a field setting, tends to place subjects in a situation vis-à-vis the researcher that is similar to the superior-subordinate relationship. This is not a neutral encounter for most people, especially for employees of organizations, and especially if the research is being conducted within the organization and during working time.

There is another impact that the research process tends to have upon people that has the effect of creating a double bind. Bennis (1966) has summarized the position of many scientists and philosophers of science that the underlying spirit of scientific research is the spirit of inquiry. It is the irresistible need to explore, the hypothetical spirit. The norm to be open, to experiment, is also crucial in the spirit of inquiry. Also there is a fundamental belief in the gratification derived from gaining knowledge for its own sake as well as the sharing of knowledge with all.

If we compare these conditions with those found in the living systems of organizations we find that the organizations tend to create the opposite conditions. For example, it has been shown that interpersonal openness, experimentation, and trust tend to be inhibited in organizations (Argyris, 1962). The same may be said for the concern for truth for its own sake. The sharing of knowledge is not a living value since that could lead to one's organizational survival being threatened. Thus, the subject is in a double bind. He is expected to be open, manifest a spirit of inquiry, and take risks when he is placed in a situation that has many of the repressive characteristics of formal organizations, which he has long ago learned to adapt to by not being open or taking risks.

The degree to which this double bind exists probably varies enormously with the living system of the organization, the personal and organizational security of the subjects, their intellectual competence, their position in the system as well as the research methods, research style, and the interpersonal skills of the researcher. However, the position being taken here is that these forces and binds should be taken into account by the researchers in designing, introducing, executing, analyzing, and feeding back the data to the subjects.

To complete the picture we should mention the relationship between the senior researcher and the junior members of a research team. After all, they too form a system in which superior-subordinate relationships exist. If our model is valid, we would expect that some of the adaptive mechanisms predicted above would be found in these relationships. Unfortunately, little systematic data exist on this subject. Recently, Roth (1966) presented some data that illustrate the writer's predictions. He presented evidence that the graduate students saw much of their work as being boring and tedious. In several cases the students adapted by withdrawing from work and by cheating. Observation time was cut, the number of observations reduced, and finally fake observations were submitted for full time periods. In other cases Roth suggests that guilt was reduced by becoming less able to hear what the people said and by reducing the richness of the observations on the (conscious) grounds that there was less going on. In still other cases, researchers who missed appointments or skipped questions, filled out their forms later by putting down what they thought the respondent should have answered. Of course, none of these informal behaviors was ever revealed to the senior researcher. As Roth correctly points out, the researchers acted pretty much like lower level employees in plants who perform repetitive tasks.

Recently, Rosenthal (1964a) suggested another possibility which, if confirmed, is even more serious. He suggested that, in some cases, the junior investigator may be in such a dependency relationship to the senior investigator that he may, unknowingly, be more sensitized to instances that confirm his superior's views than to those that do not. These data raise serious questions about the standards usually accepted for checks on reliability and validity (i.e., the use of friends, colleagues, wives).

Before this discussion is ended, it may be helpful to note an important problem identified by research in organizations that social scientists may be faced with when conducting research in ongoing systems. The problem stems from the fact that in organizations, at the higher and lower levels, openness, concern for feelings, self-awareness, interpersonal experimentation, and trust tend to be suppressed. The reason for this, at the lower levels, is the technology which ties an employee to a highly molecularized and specialized job permitting little expression of self. At the upper levels, the technology decreases as a causal factor and the values executives hold about effective interpersonal relationships become dominant causal factors. In both cases therefore, organizational theory predicts, and to date the data support the prediction, that employees (lower and upper) will tend to be programmed to behave interpersonally more incompetently than competently, and to be unaware of this fact.

For example, in 35 different groups, with 370 participants, in 265 problem-solving and decision-making meetings, tackling issues ranging from investments, production, engineering, personnel, foreign policy, case discussions, new products, sales promotion, to physical science research discussions, it was found that the participants were unable to predict their interpersonal behavior accurately. Ninety-two percent predicted that the *most frequently* observed categories would be owning up, concern, trust, individuality, experimentation, helping others, and openness to feelings. The actual scores (in a sample of 10,150 units) showed that their prediction was accurate only in the case of owning up to ideas. The prediction was moderately accurate in the case of concern for ideas. Trust, experimentation, individuality, helping others, and the expression of positive or negative feelings—all the behaviors that they predicted would be frequent—were rarely observed. Conformity, a category which they predicted would be low in frequency, was the second most frequently observed category (Argyris, 1966). These data have been replicated with groups of students, clergy, nurses, teachers, and physical scientists. If these data continue to be replicated, then the researchers who are studying interpersonal relationships may have to include observational data of the subject's actual behavior because the interview or questionnaire data could be highly (but unknowingly) distorted.

To summarize up to this point: Organizational theory is an appropriate theory to use to understand the human system created by rigorous research designs. The theory predicts that the correct use of rigorous designs, in experimental or field settings, will tend to place subjects in situations that are similar to those organizations create for the lower level employees. Also predicted is that the research assistants may be placed in situations that are similar, at worst, to the low-skill and, at best, to the high-skill employees in organizations.

These conditions lead to unintended consequences. The subjects may adapt by becoming dependent. They may also fight the research by actively rejecting a positive contributive role or by covertly withdrawing this involvement and thereby provide minimally useful data. The subjects may also band together into an organization that may better represent their interest. Finally, an organized society may unintentionally program people who may be asked to be interpersonally incompetent and unaware of the fact.

SUGGESTIONS TO OVERCOME THE PROBLEMS

If the unintended consequences of rigorous research reside in the degree of control the researcher has over the subject and the subject's resultant dependence, submissiveness, and short time perspective, then theoretically it would make sense to reduce the researcher's control over the subject. It would also follow from the theoretical framework that it would make sense to provide the subject with greater influence, with longer time perspective regarding, and greater internal involvement in, the research project.

It is understandable that researchers resist these action suggestions. They argue that all research could be ruined if subjects had greater influence.

These arguments are almost identical with the reactions of many executives when asked to consider giving greater influence to their employees in administration of the firm. However, after much research the executives have begun to learn that the situation is not as bleak as they pictured it would be. They have learned that workers do not demand nor desire complete control. They do not want to manage the entire plant. They wish greater influence, longer time perspective, and an opportunity for genuine participation at points and during time spans where it makes sense.

The same may be true of subjects. They would not tend to see the issue as one of complete versus no involvement. They would be willing to react reasonably if the researchers could show, by their behavior, that they assumed the subjects could be reasonable and are to be trusted.

Managers have developed from research an increasing number of guideposts regarding the conditions under which employee participation is helpful and harmful to the employee and to the organization. Unfortunately similar research is lacking in the area of conducting research. We have few data regarding when it is in the interests of the researcher and of the subject to invite the subject to participate in the design and execution of the research. It may be that, as a first step, much can be accomplished by having worker representative groups (in organizations) and student representative groups (in universities) to help in the design and execution of research as well as in the attraction and involvement of subjects in the research.

The most important fear expressed by researchers when considering subject influence is the fear of contamination of research. This is a legitimate fear. As we have seen, if subjects know what the research is about they may give the researcher what he wants. However, it should be noted in the studies where these results have been found they were *not* studies where the subject was to gain personally from participating (e.g., voting or marketing studies, Hyman, Cobb, Feldman, Hart, & Stember, 1954). One must be careful in generalizing from these studies to situations where the subject feels genuinely involved in the research.

There are further two points that may be worth considering about this position. Subjects *are* trying to please the researcher even when they are not told what the research is about. This means that much time and energy are being spent by the subject in second-guessing the researcher. If this is so, the researcher runs the risk of compounding the problem of unintended contamination.

The second point to be made about contamination is that it is inevitable. The issue therefore is *not* contamination versus no contamination. *The issue is under what conditions can the researcher have the greatest awareness of, and control over, the degree of contamination.*

Is it possible to create a psychological set on the part of the subject so that he is involved in giving as accurate replies as he can *and* in keeping the researcher informed as to when he (subject) is becoming defensive or could become defensive? Can the subject be helped to become as objective and verbal as he can about his subjectivity? Under what conditions can subjects be motivated to be so involved in the research that they strive to give valid data and warn the researcher when they (or others) may not be giving valid data?

Perhaps subjects will be motivated when they believe that it is in their interests to be so. Perhaps researchers may wish to consider designing research in such a way that the subject can gain from participating in the research (a gain that goes beyond simple feedback of results).

Motivating subjects by offering some possible help could make the situation more threatening rather than less threatening. For example, there are studies to show that people lie to their physicians when they describe their problems if they fear that there is something seriously wrong with them and they may be asked to undergo some stressful therapy like surgery. This is most certainly the case with employees who mistrust their management and would fear participation in research feedback and cooperating with management. In no case will valid research data be obtained where the subjects are fearful of the research or its consequences. If they are fearful, however, would it not be better to know this early in the relationship? Decisions could be made to drop the research or somehow account for the influence the fear would have upon the subjects' participation.

In field research, the biggest fear that we have discovered is that the research will not be relevant to their lives. They tend to see the researcher as a "long-hair" who wants to use them as guinea pigs and who, at most, promises a feedback session to give them the results and leaves them with the more difficult problem (for them) of what to do about their feelings. For example, the writer interviewed about fifty employees in a bank to test certain hypotheses. As an expression of gratitude he wrote a nontechnical report to the officers, who liked it so much that they provided the support to enlarge the study. In enlarging the number interviewed, twenty-five of the original sample were reinterviewed. The results showed that many of their answers were drastically different from their original answers to the same questions. When the subjects were confronted they replied as followes: During the first study they saw the writer as a researcher who wanted to use them as guinea pigs; during the second study the officers had described the research as helping them to make the bank a more effective system.

"Now," they continued, "you could really make a difference in our lives, so we had to tell you the truth!"

In our experience the more subjects are involved directly (or through representatives) in planning and designing the research, the more we learn about the best ways to ask questions, the critical questions from the employees' views, the kinds of resistances each research method would generate, and the best way to gain genuine and long-range commitment to the research (Argyris, 1958). Moreover, subjects have told interviewers why they felt the interviewers were biasing their answers, so that they wondered if giving an answer during an interview might not bias an interviewer in his observations (which they expected since they had participated in the design of the research). Or, they have hesitated to tell the researcher certain information in the interview because they thought it might bias his observations. In reading protocols of interviews where feedback and help in exploring their problems are promised to subjects, one can find a great number of comments that indicate the subject is trying to be very careful not to distort his responses. For example, subjects have told the writer when they were not certain about an answer, or when they were biased, or how we should check their views with certain individuals.

Researchers are also concerned about telling subjects about the research lest such feedback influence them to change their behavior. In our experience this fear is more valid when the subject does *not* perceive the feedback of the results as relevant to his life or when he is asked to provide data that he perceives as inconsequential and nonrelevant. Also, the degree to which a subject can vary his response is much less if one is studying his behavior through observations rather than his reports of his behavior (either through interviews or questionnaires). For example, telling the subjects the plan of a study did not alter their behavior. The subjects were unable to alter their behavior even when asked, told, cajoled, required to do so (Argyris, 1965). In one case ten executives were observed for three months without telling them the variables that were being studied or the results. Their behavior showed no change during this period. Two men were then asked to alter their behavior in the direction that would make them more effective group members. They agreed to try and both were unable to do so. One man became so frustrated with himself that he wrote a large note to keep in front of himself with appropriate reminders (e.g., to listen more, to cut people off less, etc.). In the first ten minutes of a meeting a topic was raised that centrally involved him and he returned immediately to his original style.

In another case (Argyris, manuscript in preparation) feedback was given to a group of executives about their behavior. After the feedback session, they spent three hours deciding what behavior they wanted to change. Three of them committed themselves to work together to change their behavior. The researcher acknowledged their constructive intent but told them he doubted they could change their behavior. They became annoyed and insisted they could. Subsequent research showed that their behavior patterns never changed.

These observations should not be surprising to anyone who has to help people change behavior that is internalized, highly potent, and related to their feelings of intellectual and interpersonal competence, as well as to their career survival. Put in another way, the more researchers study such behavior, the less they may need to worry about such contamination.

Even if this were not the case, the researcher still has many ways to check as to whether involving the subject and offering help contaminate the research. For example, if the analysis is valid, predictions can be made as to how subordinates will respond on a superior's behavior (or vice versa), or how people will behave under particular conditions. If these predictions are not confirmed, then one can doubt the validity of the diagnosis.

It should be emphasized that we are not suggesting that we must swing from little subject influence and control to total subject influence and control. The major suggestion is that research needs to be conducted to learn more about the conditions where subject influence and control are possible and under what conditions more rigorous research (in the sense that the researcher has greater awareness and control over contamination) can be accomplished.

We may also have to reexamine the meaning of our present concepts of rigorousness and preciseness. They may imply a degree of precision about the nature of our universe which may not be the case. Is not the universe of human behavior more accurately characterized by redundancy and overdeterminedness? Human beings may design and build their interpersonal relationships the way engineers design and build bridges. The latter usually figure out precisely the stresses and strains and then triple their figures as a safety factor. Bridges are "overbuilt"; and behavior may be overdetermined. Human beings build their interpersonal relationships with the use of many imprecise and overlapping units. As Herbert A. Simon has pointed out, people's problem-solving processes may be quite sloppy; they neither maximize nor optimize; they satisfice. However, he has also shown that these sloppier processes are subject to systematic understanding.

This view is similar to von Neumann's (1958) thesis that one of the crucial differences between the computer and the brain is the brain's capacity to be accurate with a lot of noise going on in its circuits. The brain can operate relatively accurately with a calculus that, for the computer, is relatively sloppy. Indeed, the computer would probably break down if it had to use the calculus characteristic of the brain. Perhaps what social science methodology needs to do is take on more of the characteristics of human problem solving. It would then enter a realm of overlapping, redundant concepts and thus be able to operate and predict in the world in which we live even though it is full of noise.

In closing, it may be worth noting that high validity and reliability scores with these concepts are best obtained with observers who manifest a relatively high degree of competence in the variables being studied. For example, in the development of a system of categories in organization and innovation, observers with relatively high degree of interpersonal openness and trust were able to develop interobserver reliability scores with these variables ranging from 80 percent to 94 percent within eight hours of scoring. Two of these observers were able within two hours to reproduce the score of 74 percent agreement after one year of not using the scoring system. However, two observers with relatively low capacity to be open and trusting were never able to reach a higher observer interreliability score than about 50 percent. The possession of the higher level of interpersonal competence made it possible for the first pair to see the interpersonal world more accurately and reliably. These findings are similar to Meehl's (1965) and Barron's (1965). They have suggested that the most reliable and valid raters of "creativity" were people who themselves were creative. Reliable and valid observation of interpersonal phenomena may also require a certain level of interpersonal competence.

Research is needed to help us understand more precisely how social scientists can develop valid theories and rigorous operational measures in a universe which may be composed of overlapping and redundant parts; where interrelationships are so complex that concepts of steady state are needed to conceptualize them; where objective observations may be limited to researchers who already manifest a relatively high competence in the phenomena under study.

10
Dissemination
Of Experimental Information
By Debriefed Subjects:
What is Told to Whom, When

Paul L. Wuebben

Deceiving subjects is considered necessary in the experimental study of many forms of behavior. Stricker (1967), in a survey of studies published in leading social psychological journals, found that deception is widely practiced in all experimental research and is particularly prevalent in experiments relevant to certain theoretical formulations, e.g., cognitive dissonance. Similarly, Carlson (1971), in reviewing reports of experimental research published in the *Journal of Personality and Social Psychology* and in the *Journal of Personality,* found that deception was employed in 73 percent of the studies in his sample.

Deception is typically used in an effort to keep subjects ignorant of certain features of an experiment, features which if known would prevent effective manipulation of independent variables and/or valid measurement of dependent variables. The effectiveness of deception depends not only upon maintenance of the credibility of the experimental "cover story" during the time the subject is participating, but also upon prevention of "outside" dissemination of information about the experiment by those who are privy to it.[1] The presumption that research personnel do not, in most cases, talk to "unauthorized" others about an experiment while it is in progress is probably correct, although in the author's experience such communication has occurred. (A graduate student teaching assistant told students in his introductory sociology discussion sections "all about" an experiment in which he was involved; unfortunately, subjects for the experiment were being recruited from the same course.) However, the presumption that *subjects* do not tell others about an experiment in which they have participated is almost certainly incorrect. Several studies have shown that even though subjects readily promise not to tell others about an experiment in which they have participated, most subjects do not honor their pledges to secrecy (Lichtenstein, 1970; Rokeach, Zemach, and Norrell, 1966; Straits and Wuebben, 1973; Wuebben, 1967, 1969; but see Aronson, 1966).

The extent to which experimental results may be rendered invalid by post-experimental communication undoubtedly varies widely from study to study depending upon such obvious factors as the size of the subject pool, the nature of the experimental design, the manner in which subjects are recruited, etc. However, certain features characteristic of *most* studies suggest that the problem may be both serious and general. First, as we have noted, deceiving subjects is considered necessary for the successful execution of many, if not most, researches. Even if subjects are not intentionally deceived, it is the rare study that does not depend upon subject ignorance of the experimental hypothesis. Second, although a cover story may be effective during the course of an experiment, subjects often are able to discern the true hypothesis being investigated once they have completed the often "reactive" experimental procedures (Campbell, 1965; Wuebben,

[1] Information about some studies, for example Asch's studies of conformity, may be so widely diffused that finding naive subjects may be difficult in any case.

1968). Even if they are not formally and fully debriefed as often as might be expected (Carlson, 1971; Straits and Wuebben, 1973), ex-subjects thus are usually in possession of experimentally crucial knowledge. Finally, since most studies employ college students as subjects (Carlson, 1971; Schultz, 1969), subject pools are typically composed of individuals who have ample opportunity in their day-to-day routines to speak with one another about their experimental experiences.

Before concluding, however, that post-experimental communication is *in fact* the methodological problem it *potentially* is, additional data are needed. The central question is, of course, what proportion of subjects come to later runs of an experiment with extensive prior knowledge of it. The "obvious" way to seek an answer to this question is simply to ask subjects if, prior to their participation, they had heard anything about the experiment. Unfortunately this procedure is almost totally ineffective. Several studies have shown that of those subjects who are *known* to be in possession of critical information prior to their participation, most will not reveal, even in an extensive post-experimental interview, what they had heard (Denner, 1967; Levy, 1967; Lichtenstein, 1968a; Golding and Lichtenstein, 1970; Schulman and Freed, in preparation; White and Shumsky, 1972; Wuebben, Straits, and Crowle, in preparation). At present, then, the best method of exploring the dimensions of the methodological problem caused by "illicit" dissemination of experimental information may be the determination of who is likely to be told what. The present study is concerned with that topic.

Previous studies that attempted direct measurement of post-experimental communication have either employed experimental "stooges" who questioned ex-subjects about an experiment (Aronson, 1966; Lichtenstein, 1970), or have asked ex-subjects to report whether or not they talked to others (Straits and Wuebben, 1973; Wuebben, 1967, 1969). The first of these methods probably results in relatively precise measurement of whether or not subjects will talk about an experiment when directly questioned by someone whom they believe to be another student. However, it does not permit generalization about the post-experimental communication that "naturally" occurs. The second method is, of course, subject to all of the methodological difficulties associated with self-report, i.e., problems of recall, deliberate falsification, etc. Studying self-reported talking does, however, allow estimation of both the *pattern* and *content* of "everyday" post-experimental communication. Further, the measurement error involved in the self-report method should be in the direction of underestimation of the extent of talking since most apparent sources of bias should work to deflate self-reported communication (i.e., one is asking subjects to admit that they broke a promise to the experimenter, describing those talked to requires "work" while denying talking doesn't, failure to recall talking should be more likely than falsely remembering talking, etc.). Data from the present study are subjects' self-reported communications about an experiment in which they had been deceived and fully debriefed. Information was collected not only about the extent of subjects' talking, but also about the previously unexplored topics of whom they told what, when.

METHOD

Subjects

Subjects were 75 first-born or only-child female students who volunteered to participate in an experiment for extra credit in their elementary sociology courses. Female firstborn or only-child students were employed for reasons not related to the present report. Previous studies of postexperimental communication have found no sex-linked differences in subject talking behavior; one study found that first-born or only-child subjects talked to fewer others than did later-born subjects (Wuebben, 1967). Twins and adopted children were excluded. Subjects who knew one another were not included in the same experimental session; from four to six subjects were utilized in each session. Over 90 percent of those students asked to participate in the study did so.

The experiment in which subjects participated consisted of a replication and elaboration of Schachter's (1959) studies on the relationship of anxiety and affiliation. After all subjects had arrived at the experimental room, a middle-aged man in a white laboratory coat, stethoscope dangling, entered and proceeded to unveil an "impressive" electrical machine. After turning on the machine, manipulating voltage dials, and engaging various switches, the man introduced himself as Dr. Gregor Zilstein, a psychologist and neurologist. He explained that the "university-wide" study he was conducting had to do with the effects of electric shock on both physiological and psychological functioning. He then said:

> "Now what we will ask each one of you to do is very simple. We'd like to give each of you a series of electric shocks. I feel I must be completely honest with you and tell you exactly what you are in for. These shocks will hurt; they will be painful, but they will not be harmful; they will do no permanent damage. We will . . . hook you into an apparatus such as this [indicating the machine] and take various measures, such as your pulse rate, blood pressure, respiration, etc. We are also interested in the effect of electrical shock on certain performance skills, so we will take measures of your manual dexterity and ability to judge emotions."

After answering various questions about how anxious they felt about being shocked, subjects were led to individual cubicles where Dr. Zilstein's "assistants" administered (fake) tests of manual dexterity or ability to judge emotions. After the tests were scored, subjects were told that they had scored very high or very low on the test; the assistants also told subjects either that the shocks would indeed be very painful or that they weren't really as bad as Dr. Zilstein had said. Subjects were then led back to the experimental room to fill out a questionnaire. One of the questions was whether or not subjects wished to continue in the experiment (five indicated

that they didn't) and was introduced by Dr. Zilstein's remarks:

> "I know I've talked before about your freedom of choice in this
> experiment, but obviously the only real freedom of choice is
> whether or not you wish to take part in this experiment. We would
> find it perfectly understandable if there are some of you who do not
> wish to take part in this experiment. We would find it perfectly
> understandable if there are some of you who do not wish to take
> part in an experiment in which you will be subjected to electric
> shock. If this is the case, just let us know. Turn to the fourth sheet.
> If you do wish to continue, check yes, if you do not wish to take
> part, check no, and you may leave. A few of you are in classes in
> which you get credit; if you leave I can't give you credit."

Immediately after answering the question about whether
or not they wished to continue in the experiment, subjects
were completely debriefed and pledged to secrecy. Dr. Zilstein said:

> "Now, girls, I have something to tell you that I am sure will not
> make you unhappy. The experiment is over as of now and none of
> you will be shocked. I repeat: the experiment is now finished and
> you will not be shocked. By the way, Dr. Gregor Zilstein doesn't
> exist; I'm an actor.
> "Let me explain to you what we have actually been doing here.
> What we were really interested in from the start was not how you
> would react while actually being shocked, but rather how you would
> react when you *thought* you were going to be shocked later on. As
> you can see, in order for us to do our research we had to try to make
> you believe that you really were going to be shocked. I certainly
> hope that we have caused no one any severe mental anguish or
> worry. If we did, we apologize and hope you won't think badly of us
> . . . This research is important from a number of viewpoints . . . So
> your help with this experiment may be of direct benefit to others,
> although in a different way than you thought. We appreciate your
> cooperation very much. By the way, whether you were told you did
> well or poorly on your [manual dexterity or emotion judgment] test
> was all faked. It had *no* relation to your actual performance.
> "Now as you can see, if we are going to get any useful results
> when other girls participate in this experiment, it is absolutely essen-
> tial that they don't know what it is really about. In other words, if
> any girl comes to this experiment knowing that she is really *not*
> going to be shocked at all, we can get no useful information for our
> research whatsoever. The whole experiment depends upon the fact

that the subjects believe they really *will* be shocked. If they have heard that they won't be shocked, the considerable amount of time and money that the university has invested in this experiment will all be wasted.

"All this means that your participation in this experiment is not yet over in the sense that we need the cooperation of each and every one of you in a pledge not to talk about this experiment to *anyone*, even if you know they're not in the experiment. You never know who might hear about things indirectly. Don't even talk to each other, or to someone you know has participated in the experiment— you may be overheard . . . So I'll ask each of you to promise not to mention what this experiment is about, or what happens during the experiment. Will that be okay? Thank you very much.

"Now did anyone know anyone else in this room before tonight? Has anyone here heard about the experiment before? Good. Any questions? Thank you. Please do not talk *even to each other* on the way out, as the next group of subjects will be coming in."

Each subject readily indicated that she would not speak to anyone about the experiment. All subject questions about the study were fully answered. As expected, no subject indicated that she had heard about the experiment before.

Dependent Variables

Approximately one month was required to complete all runs of the experiment. Three weeks after all sessions had been completed, a questionnaire designed to measure various dimensions of subjects' post-experimental communications was distributed. The instructions were as follows:

(The information you give on this questionnaire will be held in strict confidence.)

As you will recall, at the end of "Dr. Zilstein's" experiment in which you participated earlier in the quarter, you were asked not to mention to anyone what the experiment was about or what happened during the experiment. Quite frankly, we knew it would be natural for many people to talk about the experiment; however, the usefulness of the results was *not* diminished even though a few subjects did know about the experiment beforehand.

Some of us find it hard to be completely quiet about an experience such as you had; others of us find it easy to do so. If you did talk to others, it would help us to know certain facts about them. No one will be penalized or rewarded in any way for having talked. Please give us, to the best of your ability, the information called for below.

Name _____

Did you tell (or write) anyone at all, here or elsewhere, that you had participated in the experiment?

Yes_____ No_____

If you talked to one or more persons, please answer the following questions about each of them.

A table followed in which space was provided for subjects to indicate for each person to whom they talked: (a) his relationship to the subject—illustrative categories were parent, date, fiancé, classmate in this sociology class, roommate, casual acquaintance, etc.; (b) the amount of time that passed between participation in the experiment and the time at which the talking took place—suggested categories were immediately after the experiment, the night of the experiment, the next day, two days later, n days later; (c) what was communicated—illustrative categories were *only* that the subject was in an experiment, *generally* what the experiment was about, *in detail* what the experiment was about; (d) sex of the communication's recipient. The decision not to ask directly if the experiment's "real" hypothesis had been revealed was made on the basis of previous teaching and research experience which suggested that beginning students, as most of the subjects were, frequently are not certain of the meaning of the term "hypothesis." Various demonstration or pilot studies conducted by the author have shown, further, that even when subjects indicate on a questionnaire that they had told someone only "in general" what an experiment was about, the information conveyed invariably includes statements about the deceptions employed and "what they were really studying."

Most subjects returned their completed questionnaires within a week of receiving them; however, as many as four requests for filled-in questionnaires were necessary in a few cases. Two individuals who had withdrawn from the university were not contacted and one student could not be persuaded to cooperate. Of 75 subjects who participated in the experiment, 72 provided information about their postexperimental communications.

RESULTS AND DISCUSSION[2]

Results

Although all subjects had promised not to talk to anyone about the experiment "until it was announced in class that it was over," 54 subjects, or 75 percent, admitted that they had talked to at least one other person about the study. Those who did talk talked to a mean of 2.39 people—129 people were told—about the research (range 1 to 10). Comparing the results of the present study with those of relevant previous studies, the generally close agreement is striking. In a sample survey of the undergraduate students at one university, Straits and Wuebben (1973) found that 64 percent admitted breaking their promises to keep silent about the last experiment in which they had participated. Wuebben (1967, 1969), in two studies which measured the extent of talking that occurred during seven days immediately following an experiment, found that 64 percent and 50 percent of the exsubjects confessed that they had broken their pledges to secrecy. In the present study, 62 percent of the subjects indicated that they had talked within the first seven days following the experiment.

From a methodological standpoint not all forms of postexperimental communication are potentially damaging. Unfortunately, data from the present study show that most such communication is, in fact, methodologically deleterious. Excluding subjects who reported that they told others *only* that they were in an experiment and excluding those who said

---

[2]The results of the experiment per se are not pertinent to the present discussion; in general, Schachter's (1959) findings were successfully replicated.

that they talked *only* to fellow subjects, 47 subjects, or 65 percent, revealed that they had told one or more persons "what the research was about," either in general or in detail; 39 subjects, or 54 percent, told at least one other *within a week's time* of participation in the study. Subjects reported communicating experimentally *crucial* information about the study to 107 persons.

Table 1 provides a detailed breakdown of subjects' dissemination of experimentally crucial information by time elapsed after their participation and category of person told. Several general observations are in order. First, subjects talked to persons with a wide variety of relationships to them, from casual acquaintances to close relatives. However, by far the great majority of the persons who received information had more than a passing acquaintance with the subjects. Particularly surprising is the large number of relatives (27) who were told about the experiment (15 mothers, 8 fathers, 1 sister, 1 brother, 1 aunt, and 1 uncle).[3] Few classmates (5) and very few casual acquaintances (2) were informed; since most experiments probably draw from subject pools consisting of students in beginning classes, this finding must be regarded as methodologically comforting. Second, talking extended over an unexpectedly long time span, up to 31 days after the subject had participated in the experiment (it will be recalled that questionnaires were distributed three weeks after *all* subjects had been run and that one month passed between the first and last runs of the experiment). At least for these subjects, their experimental experiences proved to be a worthy topic of conversation—and recall—for a good period of time after their participation. Close relatives and friends in particular were told about the study long after its completion; many subjects reported that they talked to their parents and "hometown" friends during Thanksgiving vacation.

---

[3] It will be recalled that subjects were exclusively first-born or only children; many of them had no brothers or sisters.

TABLE 1

Number of People Receiving Experimentally Crucial* Information from Ex-subjects

Subject's Relation-ship to Person Told	Time Elapsed from Subject's Experimental Participation										
	Immediate-ly after	That night	1 day	2 days	3 days	4 days	5 days	6 days	7 days	7-31 days	Total days
Classmate, casual acquaintance	1	3	2	0	0	0	0	1	0	0	7
Date	2	5	1	2	1	1	1	1	2	2	18
Roommate	3	14	3	2	1	1	0	0	3	0	27
Friend	0	6	0	0	0	0	1	0	1	14	22
Boy friend, fiancé	2	0	0	1	0	1	0	0	2	0	6
Close relative	0	1	2	4	0	0	3	0	1	16	27
Total	8	29	8	9	2	3	5	2	9	32	107

*Subjects were classified as providing experimentally crucial information to others if they indicated on the questionnaire that they had told others either "in general" or "in detail" what the study was about (see text).

The extent of the methodological difficulty caused by subjects' dissemination of post-experimental information in this type of study cannot, of course, be precisely determined with these data. However, using this study as a guide, and given certain assumptions, the number of persons who typically *could* be informed later-run subjects may be grossly—and very conservatively—estimated. To be very sanguine, let it be supposed that in this study all subjects could have been run within one week's time. Let it be reasonably supposed, further, that subjects' parents or other close relatives could not have been student/subjects. Then, sometime during the one week the experiment would have taken place, 64 potential subjects would have been given experimentally crucial information by ex-subjects; 36 potential subjects would have been informed the same day that the talking subject participated. All 64 persons would have been given, in all likelihood, information about deceptions and the hypotheses of the study; 34 would have been given *detailed* reports.

Discussion

Several points should be considered in evaluating results from the present research and in thinking about post-experimental communications in general. First, the present experiment involved a major deception and both experimentally manipulated independent variables (fear of shock and "tested" task ability) appeared to have considerable experimental impact on the subjects. Thus this experiment cannot be considered representative of a number of other experiments in the social sciences, although it *is* clearly comparable to many. In any event, this experiment may have been more interesting and troubling than are others and may therefore have stimulated relatively more talking.

Second, the dependence of the study on self-reported talking in all probability resulted in a serious underestimation of the extent to which post-experimental communication occurred. In addition, the method employed here allows no measurement of the extent to which students informed by ex-subjects tell still others.[4] Higher order diffusions are also likely, particularly if a study is provocative, as was this one.

Third, the fact that subjects told an unexpectedly large number of non-students, friends and relatives about the experiment—sometime after their participation—has interesting implications for a common suggestion about improving experimental research. It is frequently maintained that non-student populations should be used as experimental subjects, if only to tap subject pools that are not likely to be suspicious of the experimenter or his cover story. To the extent that university students in other studies relate their experimental experiences to others in the manner subjects in the present study did, few completely naive subject populations may be left, particularly in the middle classes.

Fourth, the most economical and useful manner of handling the potentially damaging effects of subjects' post-experimental communications would undoubtedly involve determining which subjects had heard about an experiment before their participation in it. As the previous discussion has indicated, that may not be any easy task, although better methods can no doubt be devised when the determinants of subjects' lying are better understood (Wuebben, Straits, and Crowle, in preparation). However, it should be recognized that even if methods to identify truly uninformed subjects were developed, use of only such subjects in experiments would result in further problems. It is likely that uninformed subjects have both social and psychological characteristics which distinguish them from subjects to whom other people talk (Straits and Wuebben, 1973). These characteristics might interact with certain experimental treatments to produce seriously unrepresentative results.

---

[4] Two relatively minor points should be noted. First, some subjects may have talked to the same persons and thus fewer individuals than indicated may have received experimental information. Second, subjects may have continued talking *after* they completed their questionnaires. Although such extended talking could not have affected this study, it could well have contributed to generally held suspicions about the nature of social scientific experiments.

Finally, the small number of classmates who were told about the experiment by ex-subjects must be considered encouraging for those investigators, apparently the majority, who draw their subjects from beginning classes. (Of course a recipient who was identified as a "roommate" might also have been a classmate.) Further, the finding that the largest proportion of those who were told were persons with some sort of a "close" relationship to the subject suggests that subjects may indeed be true to the experimenter "in their fashion." That is, one may speculate that subjects by and large tell those who they realize will not be subjects in the future (e.g., parents), or whom they believe *they* can effectively swear to secrecy (e.g., roommates). Unfortunately, in the latter case subjects are probably as wrong in their presumptions as most experimenters have been.

11
Awareness, Learning, And The Beneficient Subject As Expert Witness

Leon H. Levy

There are certain issues in psychology for which it appears that even the most rigorous and behavioristically inclined researchers are apt to turn to their experimental subjects as expert witnesses. One such issue is the role of awareness in human learning (Adams, 1957). Beginning with Thorndike's (1932) assertion that learning can occur without awareness, and continuing through to the current controversy over the role of awareness and cognition in verbal conditioning (Spielberger, 1965), psychologists have based their positions in large part upon the verbal testimony of their subjects. Those who would dismiss awareness as a scientifically useful concept (Verplanck, 1962), no less than those who would embrace it (Dulany, 1962; Spielberger, 1962), have turned to their subjects' verbal reports in support of their positions. Farber (1963), for example, has said that awareness cannot be disregarded in the study of behavior and that one excellent approach is to "ask the subjects what they are doing or think they are doing and why

This study was supported in part by Grant MH 11081 from the National Institute of Mental Health, United States Public Health Service. The author wishes to express his thanks to Martha Henderson, Estelle Resnick, and Steve Barkley for their excellent performance in their respective roles in this experiment.

Reprinted with permission of author and publisher from *Journal of Personality and Social Psychology*, 6, no. 3 (1967): 365-70.

[p. 195] ." As straightforward as this approach might be, it is obviously not without its problems.

It seems to be generally accepted that awareness is a private event of which only the subject has knowledge: while the experimenter may gather data on learning via response frequencies, latencies, and the like, only the subject has access to data on awareness. Thus, to the extent that his verbal reports of awareness are taken as veridical or given the same weight as the experimenter's summary statistics, the subject may be said to be cast in the role of co-investigator or expert witness (Buck, 1961). This is a role which he has not formally played since the days of introspectionist psychology, and because so many crucial theoretical issues have been made to rest upon his testimony, it becomes a proper subject of investigation.

The present study was conducted within a verbal conditioning framework for both theoretical and methodological reasons. Verbal conditioning has come to occupy a focal position in theoretical controversies over the nature of complex human learning and psychotherapy (Krasner, 1958, 1962; Spielberger & Levin, 1962), and in the test of a variety of hypotheses in personality and psychotherapy (Williams, 1964). To a large degree, the issues hinge upon whether the learning curves are interpreted as manifesting the unconscious and automatic effects of reinforcements upon S-R contingencies, or whether they are a consequence of awareness and the hypotheses (Dulany, 1961) held by the subject as to what he should do in order to obtain reinforcement. While it has appeared that verbal conditioning is only found in those subjects who were inferred to be aware of the S-R reinforcement contingencies (Spielberger, 1965), this has not been true in all cases (Farber, 1963), and an element of ambiguity remains since (a) judgments of awareness have been shown to be dependent upon the thoroughness of the post-experimental interview (Levin, 1961), and (b) it is possible to argue that awareness may be a consequence of conditioning rather than a cause (Postman & Sassenrath, 1961). The present experiment attempts to reduce these ambiguities through experimental manipulation of awareness: it investigates the extent to which learning curves are a function of awareness.

Methodically, the use of verbal conditioning provides a convenient vehicle for the study of the subject in his role as expert witness. Orne (1962) has presented persuasive evidence for the effects of the "demand characteristics" of experiments on the subject's performance. Simply put, these are the effects of the subject's hypotheses or beliefs about the nature of the experiment and his attempt to be a "good subject" and provide the data sought for by the experimenter. But because not all subjects necessarily perform as they think the experimenter wishes them to (Farber, 1963), it seems reasonable to refer to those who do, or those who have been subjected to some experimental treatment which may be expected to increase the likelihood that they would, as "beneficent subjects." The verbal conditioning task permitted the author to manipulate awareness directly by either informing or not informing subjects how the experimenter wanted them to perform. Because of certain socio-cultural aspects of the experimental situation, to be described below, it seemed reasonable to assume that the informed subjects would also be beneficent. Thus it was possible to compare not only their performance in verbal conditioning as a function of awareness and beneficence, but also the quality of their testimony in the post-experimental awareness interview. If demand characteristics enter into the subjects' performance in the experiment proper, there seems to be no reason why they would not also affect their performance as expert witnesses in the post-experimental interview.

In summary, the purpose of this experiment was to contribute data relevant to the question of the role of awareness in verbal conditioning and also to study the behavior of subjects in post-experimental awareness interviews, where both awareness and demand characteristics have been experimentally manipulated.

METHOD

Subjects

The subjects were 32 male students enrolled in an introductory psychology course for which participation in four experiments was a requirement.

Stimulus Materials

A Taffel (1955) conditioning procedure was used for which 100 3 x 5-inch white index cards, each containing a past-tense verb and the pronouns *I, We, You, He, She,* and *They,* provided the stimuli. The verb was typed in the center of the card and the pronouns beneath it, in a different sequence from one card to the next.

Procedure

The subjects were randomly assigned in equal numbers according to a predetermined schedule to either an informed or an uninformed group. The experimental personnel consisted of a male undergraduate confederate, whose job it was to either inform or not inform each subject of what the experiment was all about; a female graduate student, who acted as the experimenter and whose physical endowments and manner were such as to leave little doubt concerning her ability to elicit beneficence from the typical male undergraduate; and an undergraduate female who conducted the post-conditioning interview.

Each subject was identified throughout the experiment by a code number based upon his order of arrival for the experiment. The schedule followed by the confederate which determined whether or not a subject was to be informed was not known either to the experimenter or to the interviewer. Thus each subject was run and interviewed blind so far as knowledge of which group he was in. Additionally, the interviewer had no knowledge of the subject's performance in verbal conditioning at the time that she conducted her awareness interview.

Upon arriving for the experiment each subject found the confederate sitting outside the laboratory and a vacant chair beside him. A sign by the laboratory door requested all subjects for the experiment to be seated until called by the experimenter. The confederate engaged in small talk with all subjects so that when the experimenter arrived to bring the subject into the lab she found them all engaged in conversation and could not determine which group they were in. For those subjects in the informed group, the confederate began his conversation with the following remarks delivered in a well-rehearsed, *entre-nous* fashion:

> "Are you waiting to be in the experiment 'words'? I just got through with it and I have to wait for a second part of something. I think the girl who is running it is doing it for her doctor's dissertation. Boy, I'll bet she's worried about getting the right results. It's a funny experiment. You have to sit there and make up sentences using these words she has on a card and it seems she wants you to make up sentences using *I* or *We* as the pronoun. I think I did pretty well once I caught on. Better not say that I told you about it."

In this way awareness was provided the informed group, and, given the aforementioned characteristics of the experimenter, it seemed likely that these subjects would also be beneficent.

Subjects were run individually by the experimenter, who gave them the conventional Taffel instructions to the effect that they were to make up a sentence for each card using the verb and one of the six pronouns beneath it, saying the first sentence that came to mind. The experimenter, who was separated from the subject by a small wooden partition resting on a table, presented the stimuli on a stimulus holder in front of the subject, recorded his pronoun choice, and, during the conditioning trials, reinforced each sentence beginning with *I* or *We* by saying "good." The first 20 sentences, which the subjects were told would be for practice, were used to determine the subject's operant level, and the remaining 80 constituted the conditioning trials. The experimenter knew that half of the subjects were in each group, and immediately after the subject left the room recorded her guess as to whether or not he had been informed.

Following completion of conditioning the experimenter thanked the subject for his cooperation, asked him not to tell anyone else about the experiment, and then led him into another room in the laboratory suite and introduced him to the interviewer who, she said, wished to ask him a few questions. The interviewer than administered a 12-question post-conditioning interview for awareness used by Spielberger and Levin (1962). The questions in this interview began in a nonleading way with "Did you usually give the first sentence that came to your mind?" and became increasingly direct and to the point, with the last question being "While going through the cards, did you think that her saying 'good' had anything to do with the words you chose to begin your sentences? What?" When awareness was judged on the basis of the subjects' answers to the entire interview, Spielberger and Levin found a highly significant difference in the number of conditioned responses between aware and unaware subjects, and no difference between unaware subjects and those in a non-reinforced control group. Our interest in using this interview was not only as a means of inferring awareness; by noting the question number on which the subject indicated awareness it seemed also to offer a way of investigating the effects of demand characteristics and beneficence upon the subject's candor.

If the subject reported awareness at any point during these 12 questions he was then asked to identify the trial block in which he first became aware. Finally, as the last question all subjects were asked: "Did you know anything about the experiment before you participated in it?" The interviewer recorded all answers verbatim and the early interviews were tape-recorded as a check on the interviewer's perfor-

mance. The interviewer proved so competent that it was not felt necessary to tape all of her interviews.

RESULTS

Interview Data and Detection of Beneficence

The experimenter's ability to identify which subjects had been informed and which had not was evaluted by comparing her judgments
against their actual treatment. She correctly identified 56 percent of
the informed subjects and 75 percent of the uninformed subjects, but
her overall hit rate of 66 percent was not any better than expected by
chance ($\chi^2 = 2.07$, $df = 1$). Hence, the experimenter was not able to
detect the beneficent subject on the basis of his performance alone.

A subject was classified as aware if any of his answers during the
post-conditioning interview could be taken as statements of the reinforcement contingency of "good" for sentences beginning with *I*
alone, with *We* alone, or with *I* or *We*. Subjects were classified without
knowledge of their pre-experimental treatment or their performance in
verbal conditioning. By definition it would be expected that a larger
proportion of the informed subjects would be aware than would the
uninformed. Actually, 81 percent of the informed subjects were classified as aware, compared to 44 percent of the uninformed subjects. Thus
the subjects' verbal reports did reflect their pre-experimental treatment
with some degree of accuracy ($\chi^2 = 3.33$, $df = 1$, $p < .05$), one-tailed).
There were no differences between the aware subjects in the two
groups, however, in the trial block which they designated as the one on
which they first became aware of the contingency (informed, $M = 2.2$;
uninformed, $M = 2.1$).

The number of questions it was necessary to ask in the post-
conditioning interview before the subject gave an answer from which
awareness might be inferred was taken as a measure of his readiness to
report awareness or his candor. While it might seem that it should take
relatively little persistence to elicit a report of awareness from an informed subject since he ostensibly came into the experiment with it,
considering the fact that he possesses guilty knowledge—the confederate asked him not to tell the experimenter that he had told him
about the experiment—it would seem reasonable to predict on the basis
of his possible conflict over this knowledge, as well as his beneficence
toward the experimenter, that he would be more reluctant to reveal
awareness as compared with an innocent uninformed subject. Giving

each aware subject a score based upon the number of questions asked before he revealed awareness, the mean for the 13 aware, informed subjects was 5.3 and for the 7 aware, uninformed subjects, 3.3. This difference was evaluated by a procedure suggested by Edwards (1960, pp. 106–7) for unequal n's and found to be statistically significant ($t = 2.02$, $p < .05$, one-tailed). Thus, as compared with the innocent subject, the beneficent subject appears less likely to give evidence revealing awareness unless pressed for it.

It will be recalled that the last question asked of all subjects was whether they had any knowledge of the experiment before taking part in it. Only 1 of the 16 informed subjects reported that he had been fully informed by the confederate, and 3 others only that the confederate had told them that they would have to make up sentences but nothing more. It is noteworthy that one of the partial reporters also said that he thought the interviewer might have known about the confederate—apparently he didn't want to be considered dishonest. Thus, 75 percent of the informed group denied any prior knowledge of the experiment, and *none* had spontaneously volunteered his knowledge to the experimenter during the experiment.

Verbal Conditioning

The 100 trials were divided into five blocks of 20 each. Because the groups were not found to differ significantly in their frequency of *I-We* responses during the operant period, all analyses included this period as the first block of trials and were based upon frequencies rather than difference scores. These data are presented in Figure 1 for all subjects in the informed and uninformed groups and separately for only the aware subjects in these groups.

An analysis of variance comparing frequency of *I-We* responses for all subjects in the informed and uninformed groups indicated that the informed group was superior to the uninformed group ($F = 6.06$, $df = 1/30$, $p < .05$). It also produced a significant main effect for trials ($F = 13.19$, $df = 4/120$, $p < .01$), but no significant interaction between groups and trials, confirming the impression gained from Figure 1 that both groups showed the same rate of increase in frequency and differed only in level. A similar analysis conducted only on the performance of the aware subjects in each group showed the informed subjects still tending to be superior to the uninformed subjects ($F = 3.56$, $df = 1/18$, $p < .10$), with a highly significant effect for trials ($F = 17.49$, $df = 4/72$,

$p < .01$), but again no significant Groups × Trials interaction. Thus, informed subjects inferred to be aware of the response-reinforcement contingency appear to differ from their uninformed counterparts only in their level of performance and not in the shape of their acquisition curve.

DISCUSSION

Because the rationale in so many human experiments assumes a naive subject to begin with, perhaps the most common operational thread running through human research is the request made by the experimenter just before the subject leaves the experiment that he not tell anyone about it. How often this request is honored has seen little investigation, but it seems unlikely, college students being what they

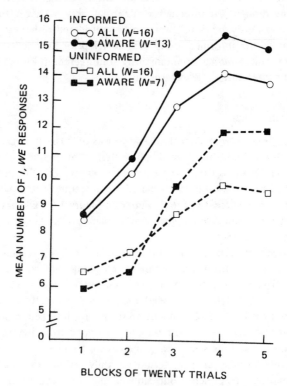

FIG. 1. Mean frequencies of *I-we* sentences in blocks of 20 each.

are, that it is anywhere near 100 percent. For this reason many experimenters also ask their subjects whether they knew anything about the experiment before taking part in it. It seems to be common practice to accept the subject's word on this. The data cast serious doubt on the validity of this practice.

For a variety of social psychological and other reasons, well discussed by Orne (1962) and others, the finding that 75 percent of the subjects in the present experiment did not give any indication that they had been told anything about it is not too surprising. But it is distressing. Given a beneficent subject, neither naiveté nor complete candor may be assumed.

These data strongly suggest that when subjects' verbal reports provide the evidential basis for hypothesis testing, demand characteristics may be expected to enter no less than when their performance, verbal or otherwise, is the source of data. For this reason studies in verbal conditioning, particularly of the Taffel type, must always be doubly suspect with respect to demand characteristics when the question is one of learning without awareness. Although more subjects in the informed than in the uninformed group indicated awareness during the post-conditioning interview, it required a larger number of questions on the average to elicit this indication from them. Indeed, had they been subjected to one of the briefer types of awareness interviews, not at all uncommon in verbal conditioning studies (Levin, 1961), less than half of the informed aware subjects would have been so classified.

By definition, awareness implies the ability to verbalize. But although awareness may be a necessary condition for verbalization, it is obviously not a sufficient one. Nevertheless, the present study should not be taken to mean either that no faith may be put in subjects' verbalizations or that awareness is beyond the reach of scientific investigation. (It was true that those subjects who were classified as unaware, in the informed as well as the uninformed group, showed very little change in performance as compared with aware subjects.) Rather, it demonstrates that these verbalizations, like any other form of behavior, cannot be adequately understood without knowledge of their antecedent conditions. Like any other hypothetical construct, the meaning of awareness resides in the nomological net of which it is a part (Cronbach & Meehl, 1955) and in the corresponding converging operations (Campbell & Fiske, 1959; Garner, Hake, & Eriksen, 1956) by which it is defined. But there is no intrinsic reason, as Dulany (1962), as well as the present experiment have shown, why the study of awareness need place the experimenter entirely at the mercy of his subjects' testimony, whether they be beneficent, innocent, expert, or otherwise. Converging operations are possible and the study cannot be based upon subject's verbal reports alone. For the present experiment makes it obvious that to rely upon the subject as an expert witness would be to betray as much naiveté on the part of the experimenter as that which he hopes exists in his subject; without corroborative, independent data the subject's verbal testimony possesses no greater (or lesser) validity than does an unstandardized test.

Given that a subject is aware of the reinforcement contingency or what the experimenter wishes him to do, as Dulany (1962) and Farber (1963) have observed, it does not necessarily follow that he will behave accordingly. The verbal conditioning data appear to be consistent with these observations. Although all of the informed subjects in the present experiment had been provided with information which would have permitted them to obtain 100 percent reinforcement from the first trial onward, none did. While the first block of unreinforced trials might have been confusing and account for part of this, the gain in *I-We* responses in the informed group during conditioning was of the same order as that for the uninformed group, only their level of responding was higher. Awareness, whether defined by directly informing subjects or by inference from interview protocols, appeared to be associated with the same kind of growth curve commonly taken as reflecting the continuous incremental effects or reinforcement upon habit strength. But to interpret these curves in this fashion seems obviously inappropriate. For this reason, the conditioning data of this experiment would seem to have important implications for the conceptualization of the processes involved in verbal conditioning.

Most generally, they tend to make suspect interpretations of verbal conditioning data within an operant conditioning framework. While it would certainly be gratuitous to argue that the curves obtained in the present study simply reflect the subjects' beneficent responses to the demand characteristics of the experiment, it would be just as unfounded to view them as representing the operation of the same principles of learning and conditioning as believed operative in rats and pigeons. And if this is true in the present experiment, it may well be true in others. Thus it seems obvious that the shape of a response curve plotted over trials is, by itself, a weak basis upon which to infer the nature of the underlying process.

The great similarity between the curves for the informed and uninformed groups, while startling, it not uninterpretable. That the pre-experimental treatment of informing or not informing subjects had an effect upon them is obvious from both the difference in height between the two curves, and the differences found in the number of aware subjects in each group and their readiness to admit awareness. However, when Dulany (1962) instructed subjects in the correct response and the reinforcement contingency their response rate increased abruptly; in the present experiment with essentially the same kind of information it did not. One possible explanation for this may be that in Dulany's experiment such an abrupt increase was socially sanctioned; the subject was acting upon legitimately obtained information. In the present experiment it is possible that the informed subjects were deterred from acting upon their knowledge and showing a similar abrupt increase in response frequency because of their fear that it would reveal their illicitly obtained information. Thus, one interpretation of the shape of the curve for the informed group is that it reflects the rate of change among the subjects in their decisions to act consistently with their knowledge in order to obtain reinforcement or to satisfy the experimenter. And if this is true for the informed group, it is also a plausible explanation for the similarly shaped curve produced by the uninformed group. Although their awareness was not based upon ill-gotten knowledge, when they obtained it during the conditioning series it may be expected to have varied from one subject to another just as when they decided to act upon it.

What this suggests, of course, is that the curves obtained in verbal conditioning studies may reflect the operation of cognitive and volitional processes, or hypotheses and intentions, as Dulany (1962) would have it, rather than the direct, automatic, and unconscious consequences of reinforcement. If this is the case, then it would seem to be misleading to speak of these studies as demonstrating verbal conditioning. They demonstrate the modification of verbal behavior, to be sure, but many of them may owe their data more to the beneficence of their subjects than to the potency of their theory or reinforcement. This is not to say that reinforcement is unimportant. It provides the subject with information; it tells him what to do, albeit in a most inefficient way, and he may do it if he wishes to. But if he does, the question remains whether he should be considered conditioned or beneficent.

12
Asch
Conformity Studies:
Conformity To The Experimenter
And/Or To The Group?

Gary I. Schulman*

A characteristic of the experimenter-subject relationship in almost all laboratory experiments is that the experimenter is an authority figure in position to observe and hence to evaluate the subject's behavior. The present study was designed to examine the effect of this characteristic in the Asch (1953) conformity situation. The Asch situation or modifications of it have been used in numerous studies to determine the relationship between independent variables (e.g., personality, status in the group, relative task competence) and the dependent variable, con-

The research reported in this paper was supported by a faculty research grant from the graduate school, Indiana University. The author is indebted to his students in Small Groups Analysis who as part of the requirement for this course took an active part in the pilot phase of the work; and in particular to Pamela Baird, Phyllis Greenfield, James Huber, and Ronald Jackson, and to Professor Sheldon Stryker for his many helpful suggestions in the preparation of this material for publication.

Reprinted with permission of author and publisher from *Sociometry*, 30, no. 1 (1967), pp. 26–40.

*References cited in this chapter may be found in the bibliography.

formity.[1] These studies have all been interpreted in terms of conformity to the group[2] despite the fact that there are three possible types of influence that may be operating.

In the Asch situation, the subject knows the unanimous, incorrect judgments of the other members of the group before he makes his own response. Thus he may give the same answer as the others because he takes their answers as evidence about reality (informational conformity to the group). The subject gives his response publicly, hence his response may be a function of concern with the evaluation of his behavior by the group (normative conformity to the group) and/or by the experimenter (normative conformity to the experimenter). [3]

This study seeks to determine the extent to which behavior observed in the Asch situation is a function of each of these three possible types of influence. It was predicted that the rate of conformity responses would be raised by informational influence and by normative conformity to the group; while it would be decreased by normative conformity to the experimenter.

METHOD

Experimental conditions were varied in terms of whether the experimenter and/or the group were perceived by the subject to be in a position to observe (evaluate) him. In all experimental conditions the following basic features of the Asch situation were employed: (a) the subjects were instructed that they were participating in a study of perceptual judgment, in which they were to match accurately the length of a given line with one of three lines, (b) correct judgments were easy to make, (c) before responding, the subject knew the judgment of other persons, and (d) on critical trials the judgments of the other persons were wrong and unanimous judgments.

---

[1] See Bartos (1958); Dittes and Kelley (1956); Kelley and Shapiro (1954); Moeller and Applezweig (1957); Crutchfield (1955); and Cohen, Mayer, Schulman, and Terry (1961).

[2] See for instance Homans (1961, ch. 16).

[3] The conceptual distinction between informational and normative conformity as applied to the Asch situation is attributable to Deutsch and Gerard (1955). However, they were unsuccessful in operationalizing this distinction. The distinction between group and experimenter normative conformity in the Asch situation was made by the present author.

The procedure differed from the classic Asch situation in the following ways: Each group was made up of four subjects, two males and two females who were not previously acquainted. Each believed that he or she was subject number four, the last to respond.[4] Live confederates were not used. The subjects indicated their answers by pressing a button on a panel, supposedly indicating the responses of persons one, two, and three, but the responses were in fact controlled by an assistant located in an adjoining room. Subjects were seated in cubicles which prevented them from seeing that everyone pressed a button when person number four was asked to respond.

The stimuli were slides projected on a screen for seven seconds at a distance of approximately eight feet. Subjects were asked to make their judgments after the slide was removed from the screen. The standard line was 11½ inches high, while the three lines from which subjects were to select its match were 9 inches, 11½ inches, and 9-11/16 inches high. All slides were identical except for the identifying letters which appeared under each of the three lines.

On thirty critical trials, the subject received information immediately prior to his response that persons 1, 2, and 3 had chosen the 9-11/16 line. There were four neutral trials: on trials 1 and 2, subjects received the information that persons 1, 2, and 3 had chosen the 11½ inch line, the correct answer; on trials 7 and 20, subjects received the information that persons 1, 2, and 3 had not been unanimous in their responses. Thus it was not possible to have, as Asch did, errors on critical trials in the direction of, but not identical to, that of the group. Subjects could choose the correct answer (11½ inches), the group's incorrect answer (9-11/16 inches), or an even more incorrect answer (9 inches).

Each of these differences might affect the observed rate of conformity responses. However, the basic features of the experimental situation have been replicated, and concern is not with absolute rates but with the comparison across the experimental conditions.

The Experimental Conditions

The four conditions and the manipulations to achieve them were:

---

[4] Immediately upon coming into the experimental room, subjects were told to take any of the four seats. They were then asked to pick slips of paper to determine their number. All were number 4.

I: Neither the experimenter nor the group is in a position to observe the subject, thus only informational influence is possible.

IG: The group, but not the experimenter, is in a position to observe the subject; thus both informational and group normative influence is possible.

IE: The experimenter, but not the group, is in a position to observe the subject; thus both informational and experimenter normative influence are possible.

IEG: Both the experimenter and the group are in a position to observe the subject; thus informational, experimenter normative, and group normative influence are possible.[5]

In the control condition, the perceptual task was performed without any knowledge of others' responses. This provides an indication of the rate of incorrect responses given the character of the subject population and the stimuli. No influence process is possible in the control condition.

The informational effect is indicated by comparing the control condition with condition I. The group normative effect is indicated by comparing condition I with condition IG, and by comparing condition IE with condition IEG. The experimenter normative effect is indicated by comparing condition I with condition IE, and by comparing condition IG with condition IEG.

When the subject was to believe that the group was in position to evaluate him, he was told that as each person responded, their responses would show on each of the other subjects' panels. When he was to believe that the group was not in position to evaluate him, he was told that the responses of 1, 2, and 3 would show on all subjects' panels as they responded, but that the response of the last person to respond (4) would not show on any of the other subjects' panels, since the last response set off an automatic clearing mechanism.

When the experimenter was to be in position to evaluate him, the subject was told that the experimenter had a panel from which he

---

[5] With male subjects and a three-man majority, Asch found, over twelve critical trials, an average of four responses identical to or in the direction of the confederates. In condition IEG for males, we find an average of 11.3 identical errors, and 17.3 for females, out of the thirty critical trials. We find that over all subjects the mean number of more extreme errors is only .42, and there are no significant differences by sex or condition. Thus, in presenting our data we will present the mean number of conformity responses (errors identical to the group).

would record each person's response on each trial. When the experimenter was not to be in position to evaluate him, the subject was told that the experimenter's panel would show nothing until all subjects had responded. Then, the responses would show on the experimenter's board but would be scrambled so that he could know only how many correct answers were given on each trial.

The remainder of the manipulation depended upon instructions upon sheets on which the subjects in all conditions recorded their responses *after* having pushed their buttons.

When both the experimenter and the group were to be in a position to evaluate the subject, they were instructed to put both their name and their number on the sheet, which would be collected by the experimenter at the end of the trials. They were told the experimenter would announce to the group the name, number, and individual score of each person at the end of the trials.

When the experimenter but not the group was to be in position to observe, they were instructed to put their name and number on the sheet, which would be collected by the experimenter at the end of the trials. The experimenter would write the number correct on these sheets, return them to each individual, and then re-collect them. They were told they would not be allowed to show their score to any of the other subjects so that the experimenter would be the only person (besides the subject) who would know his name, number, and score.

When the group but not the experimenter was to be in a position to observe, they were instructed that at the end of the trials the experimenter would give each subject a key and the subject would be required to record his score next to his name and number. The subjects would then have to exchange their sheet with each of the other three subjects. After the exchange, each subject would take his sheet with him without the experimenter's having seen them, so that only the group members would know the number, name and score of the subjects.

When neither the experimenter nor the group was to be in position to evaluate him, subjects were told that at the end of the trials the experimenter would give each a key from which each could determine his own score. They would not be allowed to show their score to any of the others, and the experimenter would not see these sheets.

Success of the Manipulation

At the end of the thirty-four slides, subjects were asked three questions in individual interviews: (1) Who knew when number 4 gave the same or a different answer than the others? (2) Who would know at the end of the session that you were number 4? (3) Who would know your individual score at the end of the session?

Giving one point for each correct response for the experimental condition intended, and computing a mean score for each condition, we find that the manipulation was reasonably successful. The lowest score was 2.00 for males in condition IG; the highest was 2.95 for females IE.[6]

Subjects

Undergraduate students in introductory sociology courses served as subjects. Most took part as a requirement of the course, others were volunteers. Each subject was randomly assigned to one of the conditions.

Experimenter

The same 28-year-old first-year male graduate student acted as experimenter for all conditions. He introduced himself as Dr. James, and gave the instructions from a standard script for the appropriate condition.

TABLE 1
Success in Creating Experimental Conditions:
Mean Number of Check Questions Answered Correctly.

Condition	Males		Females	
	Mean	N	Mean	N
IEG	2.26	23	2.52	21
IG	2.00	18	2.13	23
IE	2.82	24	2.95	21
I	2.52	23	2.38	21

Note: Maximum Score = 3.

RESULTS

Table 2 presents the data bearing on the occurrence of the three types of conformity influences.

[6] In order to minimize distortion of results due to differential success in creating conditions, the data were analyzed for all subjects in a condition, and for only those subjects who gave the correct response on at least two of the three check questions. The latter are presented only where relevant differences appear.

Informational Influence

Comparing the control condition with condition I, there is, as predicted, an increase in the mean conformity rate for both males and females. Informational influence raises the mean conformity rate for male subjects 6.4 (p = .02), and 14.5 (p < .001) for female subjects.

Normative Conformity to the Experimenter

There is no significant experimenter effect for females. Comparing conditions IG and IEG there is a mean conformity response rate *increase* of 1.6 (p = .48*), rather than the predicted decrease. Comparing females in conditions I and IE, there is an increase of 1.6 (p = .62*). For male subjects, the same comparisons yield decreases of 3.0 (p = .24) and 3.9 (p = .03), respectively. Given that the latter results are in the predicted direction in both independent tests (IG vs. IEG, and I vs. IE) the χ^2 procedure described by Edwards (1954) for determining a composite probability for independent tests was followed. The probability that both independent comparisons would be in the predicted direction due to chance is .01. Thus, for males there is, as predicted, an experimenter effect which decreases the conformity response rate.

TABLE 2
Mean Conformity Response Rate and Tests of Differences

Condition	Males		Females	
	Mean	N	Mean	N
IEG	11.3	23	17.3	21
IG	14.3	18	15.7	23
IE	6.6	24	16.1	21
I	10.5	23	14.5	21
Control	4.1	10	0.0	10
Experimenter				
IEG vs. IG	p = .24 } p = .01		p = .48*	
IE vs. I	p = .03		p = .62*	
Group				
IEG vs. IE	p = .03 } p = .04		p = .30 } p = .30	
IG vs. I	p = .18		p = .30	
Informational				
I vs. Control	p = .02		p < .001	

Note: Probability figures are 1-tailed using the Mann-Whitney Statistic U, except in the case of results in a direction other than predicted. For these the probabilities are 2-tailed and indicated by an asterisk (*).

Normative Conformity to the Group

There is no significant group normative effect for females. Comparing conditions I and IG there is an increase of 1.2 (p = .30) in the mean conformity response rate, and comparing conditions IE and IEG there is an increase of 1.2 (p = .30). The composite probability was not significant (p = .30). For males, there is, as predicted, a group normative effect that increases the mean rate of conformity responses. Comparing conditions I and IG, there is an increase of 3.8 (p = .18); and comparing conditions IE and IEG there is an increase of 4.7 (p = .03). The composite probability for these two independent tests was .04.

ASSUMPTIONS AND CONTROLS

These data indicate that, for males, behavior in the Asch situation reflects informational, group normative, and experimenter normative effects; while for females, behavior in the Asch situation reflects only informational influence.

The absence of experimenter and group effects for females was unexpected and strange since the females say, in post-session interviews, that (in the appropriate conditions) they thought about the experimenter's and the group's impression of them at least as much as did the males (see Table 3).

The prediction of a decrease in conformity responses due to the experimenter effect assumed that subjects would expect the experimenter's evaluation of them to be based primarily on whether they gave correct or incorrect answers. Thus, a decrease would be predicted only if subjects believed the nonconformity answer to be correct. An increase would be predicted if subjects believed the conformity answer to

TABLE 3
Subject's Report of Thinking About the Experimenter's and the Group's Reaction to Them (In Appropriate Conditions)

Question		Very fre- quently	A num- ber of times	A few times	Never	No re- sponse or not asked	N
. Had thoughts about	*Males*	2	3	23	17	2	47
"Dr. James' " reactions	*Females*	5	5	15	15	2	42
(conditions IE & IEG)							
. Had thoughts about	*Males*	3	4	22	12	0	41
the other three partici-	*Females*	6	13	15	10	0	44
pants' reactions							
(conditions IG & IEG)							

be correct, and no difference if subjects were uncertain as to which was correct.

Analysis of data from post-session interviews support the assumption as to the criteria the experimenter is expected to use (see Table 4). The assumption as to which response is believed to be correct is found to be valid only for males. Among males, 61 percent believed the non-conformity answer was correct, 15 percent were uncertain, and 24 percent believed that the conformity answer was correct. In contrast, among females the respective percentages were 35, 35 and 30.[7] Thus,

TABLE 4

Mean Evaluation Expected from Experimenter, and Tests of Differences Between Situations

Situation (experimenter knows that you:)	Females (N = 41)	Males (N = 45)
A) agreed with others, but have no idea which is correct	.44	.34
D) disagreed with others, but have no idea which is correct	+ .23	+ .49
AC) agreed with others, and you are correct	+1.22	+1.09
AI) agreed with others, and you are incorrect	-1.07	- .95
DC) disagreed with others, and you are correct	+2.05	+2.35
DI) disagreed with others, and you are incorrect	- .54	-1.13
Tests for Agreement		
A vs. D	p = .14	p = .18
DC vs. AC	p < .001	p < .001
DI vs. AI	p = .04	p = .18
Tests for Correctness		
A vs. AC	p = .002	p < .001
A vs. AI	p < .001	p < .001
D vs. DC	p < .001	p < .001
D vs. DI	p < .001	p < .001
DC vs. DI	p < .001	p < .001
AC vs. AI	p < .001	p < .001

Note: Responses tabled for subjects in conditions IEG and IE. The probabilities are 1-tailed based on the Mann Whitney statistic U. Mean scores were based on ratings ranging from +3 (extremely favorable) to -3 (extremely unfavorable). Two males and one female were not asked these questions due to interviewer error.

[7] Subjects were asked to bet in the interview as to the number of trials on which they gave the same or a different answer from the group. They were also asked to bet how many of each type of answer would turn out to be correct answers. Those who bet that the nonconformity answer was correct on 20 or more of the 30 critical trials were classified as believing the nonconformity answer

for females, any experimenter effect could not be seen with belief uncontrolled: a predicted decrease among the 35 percent who believe the nonconformity answer is correct would be balanced by a predicted increase among the 30 percent who believe the conformity answer is correct.

Controlling for Belief

For females who believe the nonconformity answer is correct, comparing conditions I and IE there is a predicted decrease of 5.18 ($p = .13$), and comparing conditions IG and IEG there is a decrease of 2.79 ($p = .38$). The composite probability for the two independent tests of experimenter effect is .19. When the data for only those who responded correctly on at least two of the three condition check questions are used—i.e., those for whom the experimental manipulations are most sure—there is a stronger experimenter effect (see Table 5).[8]

For females who believe that the conformity answer is correct, comparing conditions I and IE there is a predicted increase of 2.20 ($p = .11$); comparing conditions IG and IEG there is an increase of 3.25 ($p = .05$). The composite probability for the two independent tests of experimenter effect is .04. The data for only those who responded correctly on at least two of the three check questions shows a stronger experimenter effect in the I vs. IE comparison and a weaker effect in the IG vs. IEG comparison (see Table 5 and note 8).

For those females who are uncertain as to which answer is correct, no significant experimenter effect can be found in the I-IE, and IG-IEG comparisons.

---

was correct. Those who bet that the conformity answer was correct on 20 or more of the critical trials were classified as believing the conformity answer was correct. Remaining subjects were classified as uncertain, as all trials used identical stimuli.

[8] The data in Table 5 are for all subjects. However, in the following cases, relevant differences are found when the data are based only on subjects who gave the correct response for at least two of the three condition check questions:

(1) *For females who believe the nonconformity answer is correct,* I vs. IE shows a predicted decrease of 3.54, $p = .13$; IG vs. IEG a decrease of 5.06, $p = .10$ (composite $p = .07$). I vs. IG shows an increase of 3.72, $p = .10$; IE vs. IEG an increase of 2.20, $p = .07$ (composite $p = .04$).

(2) *For females who believe the conformity answer is correct,* I vs. IE shows a predicted increase of 4.90, $p = .09$; IG vs. IEG an increase of 1.33, $p = .30$ (composite $p = .13$).

TABLE 5
*Mean Conformity Rate Controlling for Belief as to Which Answer is Correct, and
Tests of Differences Between Conditions*

	Males					
	Nonconformity Correct		Uncertain		Conformity Correct	
Condition	Mean	N	Mean	N	Mean	N
IEG	4.53	15	18.00	1	25.00	7
IG	5.44	9	24.00	2	22.86	7
IE	2.41	17	13.50	4	21.33	3
I	4.54	13	13.67	6	25.00	4
Experimenter Effect						
IEG vs. IG	p = .43		p = .66*		p = .19	
IE vs. I	p = .03 } .07		p = .92*		p = .22*	
Group Effect						
IEG vs. IE	p = .05		p = .40		p = .19	
IG vs. I	p = .41 } .10		p = .07 } .14		p = .64*	
	Females					
IEG	4.43	7	19.50	6	26.87	8
IG	7.72	9	18.00	6	23.62	8
IE	1.60	5	18.18	11	26.40	5
I	6.78	9	17.57	7	24.20	5
Experimenter Effect						
IEG vs. IG.	p = .38		p = .94*		p = .05	
IE vs. I	p = .13 } .19		p = 1.00*		p = .11 } .04	
Group Effect						
IEG vs. IE	p = .05		p = .50		p = .31	
IG vs. I	p = .45 } .11		p = .42 } .55		p = .84*	

Note: The probabilities are 1-tailed using the Mann Whitney statistic U, except
when the data are not in the predicted direction in which case they are 2-tailed
and indicated by an asterisk (*). See, also, footnote 8.

For those males who believe the nonconformity answer is correct,
comparing conditions I and IE, there is a predicted decrease of 2.13
(p = .03); comparing conditions IG and IEG there is a decrease of .91
(p = .43). The composite probability for the two independent tests of
experimenter effect is .07.

For those males who believe the conformity answer is correct, the
data do not show a consistent effect due to the experimenter. Comparing conditions I and IE, there is, contrary to prediction, a decrease
of 3.67 (p = .22*). Comparing conditions IG and IEG, there is an increase of 2.14 (p = .19).

For those males who are uncertain as to which answer is correct, there is, as predicted, no significant effect due to the experimenter to be seen in the I-IE, and IG-IEG comparisons.

This analysis indicates that the conclusion that there is an experimenter effect for males, but not for females, must be reconsidered. For females, the absence of an experimenter influence when belief is not controlled is attributable to a balancing effect. For males, the significant decrease attributed to the experimenter when belief is not controlled, appears to be a function of (a) most males (61 percent) believing that the nonconformity answer is correct, and this belief category producing a significant decrease, and (b) a decrease due to the experimenter in three of the four comparisons in the two remaining belief categories.

One possible explanation for the consistency among males in the direction of experimenter effect across the belief categories might be that males are less willing than females to admit to the interviewer that they gave the conformity answer when they actually believed it was the wrong answer. If this is true, some proportion of those males otherwise classified should actually be in the "nonconformity correct" category. Then, the predicted increase among those who believe the conformity answer to be correct would be covered up; and the predicted decrease among those who believe the nonconformity answer is correct would be underestimated.

Partial support for this interpretation is found. A ratio of the number of conformity responses given over the number of trials on which the subject is willing to bet that the conformity answer was correct was computed for males and females who were classified as uncertain or believing that the conformity response was correct. A ratio greater than 1, implying that the subject gave more conformity responses than he thought correct, can be taken as an indication of willingness to admit influence to the interviewer. Among those classified as uncertain, there is a statistically significant difference ($p = .02$, 1-tailed Mann Whitney U) between the mean ratios for males (.90) and females (1.20), suggesting that some proportion of males classified as uncertain should be in the "nonconformity is correct" category and that the decrease observed in this category has been underestimated. Among those classified as believing the conformity answer was correct, there is no difference between males and females.

A similar analysis for group effect was made. This analysis shows that while there is a general consistency, as predicted, in the direction of an increase in conformity response rate due to the group, for both males and females, the only statistically significant increase is found among those who believe the "nonconformity answer correct."[9] It would seem that the findings of no significant group effect for females and a significant group effect for males when belief is not controlled was again due to the considerably larger proportion of the males, as compared to the females, in the "nonconformity is correct" belief category.

The prediction of an increase in conformity response rate due to the group was based on the assumptions that: (a) subjects would expect the group to evaluate them on both agreement-disagreement, and on whether they gave the correct or incorrect answer; and (b) at least during the task (before scores were reported or answer keys distributed) subjects would think that the group considers the answer the group gives unanimously to be the correct answer.

Data from the post-session interview confirms the first assumption (see Table 6), while there are no data relevant to the second assumption. The question thus arises as to why significant increases due to the group are found only among those who believe the nonconformity answer to be correct. To the extent that subjects believe that the group will evaluate them in terms of giving the correct or incorrect answer, one would expect the least increase among those who believe the nonconformity answer is correct.

A possible explanation exists. First, in the absence of the group's observation, the more a person believes that the conformity response is correct the higher is the rate of conformity responses. Thus, when group observability is introduced, there is a ceiling effect among those who believe that the conformity response is the correct answer. There is considerably more room for an increase among those who believe the nonconformity answer is correct. Second, subjects may expect that the group's evaluation of them will be affected more by what the group believes is the correct answer *during the task,* than what the subject believes the group will find out is the correct answer when scores are computed.

---

[9] Due to the probable misclassification of males in the "nonconformity is correct" category, as noted previously, and the large magnitude of increase observed among males categorized as uncertain, the increase observed for males in the "nonconformity is correct" category is probably underestimated.

CONCLUSIONS AND IMPLICATIONS

While behavior in the Asch situation has previously been interpreted as an indicator of conformity to the group, the data suggest that for both males and females the rate of conformity response in the Asch situation is a function of informational conformity, normative conformity to the experimenter, and normative conformity to the group.

The implications of these findings are twofold. They add to the growing body of research and comment indicating that we must consider the experimental situation itself as a social system containing expectations and role relationships between the experimenter and his subjects, which may affect the results obtained.[10]

Rosenthal has shown that an experimenter may unknowingly, and in some as yet unspecified way, bias results in the direction of the predic-

TABLE 6
Mean Evaluation Expected from the Group, and Tests of Differences Between Situations

Situation (The group knows that you:)	Females (N = 43)	Males (N = 40)
A) agreed with them, but have no idea which is correct	+ .80	+ .80
D) disagreed with them, but have no idea which is correct	- .68	- .35
AC) agreed with them, and you are correct	+1.23	+1.22
AI) agreed with them, and you are incorrect	+ .19	+ .32
DC) disagreed with them, and you are correct	.00	+ .27
DI) disagreed with them, and you are incorrect	- .56	-1.17
Tests for Agreement		
A vs. D	p < .001	p < .001
DC vs. AC	p < .001	p = .004
DI vs. AI	p < .001	p < .001
Tests for Correctness		
A vs. AC	p < .001	p < .001
A vs. AI	p < .001	p < .001
D vs. DC	p < .001	p = .07
D vs. DI	p < .001	p < .001
DC vs. DI	p = .033	p < .001
AC vs. AI	p < .001	p < .001

Note: (See note to Table 4). One male and one female were not asked these questions due to interviewer error.

[10] See Mills (1962) and Rosenthal (1963c).

tions. Mills has offered an explanation for some unexpected relationships observed between cohesiveness, task relevance, and rejection of a deviate; and he suggests that the results may be a function of systematic differences in the experimenter-subject relationship produced in the attempt to create the experimental variations in the independent variable.

To these experimenter effects, the present data add the indication that even when the experimenter-subject relationship is a constant, as it is in the classic Asch studies, that the nature of the experimenter-subject relationship is such that the dependent variable may be a function of this relationship.

Further, these results suggest that the interpretations placed upon results from studies which have used the Asch situation must be reconsidered. For instance, it has been found that persons of middle-status in a group give a higher rate of conformity responses than high-status persons. The interpretation has been that middle-status persons conform more to the group. However, the present data suggest an alternative interpretation. Perhaps middle- and high-status persons are equally influenced by concern with the group's evaluation of them, but high-status persons are more influenced than middle-status persons by concern with evaluations from authority figures (the experimenter). Given that the experimenter's effect is to reduce conformity responses among males (and the status-conformity findings cited were based on male subjects), it is possible that the high-status person gives few conformity responses in the Asch situation not because the group exerts less normative influence over him, but because the experimenter exerts more.[11]

[11] See Bartos (1958) and Homans (1961).

13
When
Dissonance Fails:
On Eliminating
Evaluation Apprehension
From Attitude Measurement

Milton J. Rosenberg

Certain studies that have been important in advancing the dissonance-theory explanation of attitude-change phenomena seem to be open to a particular kind of reinterpretation. After an explanatory discussion of some general considerations from which this reinterpretation derives we shall turn to an experiment that attempts to put it to a critical test.

Theorists from Thomas and Znaniecki (1918) to Lewin (1935) have contended that the person's "definition of the situation" is the ground from which behavior emerges and takes its direction. But psychologists have tended to miss the relevance of this nearly banal proposition as it might apply to the understanding of psychological research itself. For most human subjects psychological experiments are ambiguous situa-

This study was carried out while the author was a member of the Psychology Department at Ohio State University. It was supported by Contract 495 (24) with the Group Psychology Branch of the Office of Naval Research. The author is indebted to Frederick Weizmann for his assistance in executing the experiment and to David Glass and Irving Janis who raised a number of useful questions.

Reprinted with permission of author and publisher from *Journal of Personality and Social Psychology*, 1, no. 1 (1965), pp. 28–42.

tions, sometimes exhilarating, sometimes provocative of curiosity or anxiety; and all these forms of arousal are likely to set them searching for the possibly veiled meanings of the experimental situation. Just how the subject *does* define the situation, and thus how he is likely to behave in it, may often be affected by those differences in treatment manipulations or in instructions that distinguish one experimental condition from another. When such intercell differences in definition of the situation are not intended they may contaminate the design and lead to false confirmation, or for that matter to false disconfirmation, of hypotheses. Two separate ways in which this may happen will be explicated here.

Evaluation Apprehension as a Research Contaminant

It is proposed that the typical human subject approaches the typical psychological experiment with a preliminary expectation that the psychologist may undertake to evaluate his (the subject's) emotional adequacy, his mental health or lack of it. Members of the general public, including students in introductory psychology courses, have usually learned (despite our occasional efforts to persuade them otherwise) to attribute special abilities along these lines to those whose work is perceived as involving psychological interests and skills.[1] Even when the subject is convinced that his adjustment is not being directly studied he is likely to think that the experimenter is nevertheless bound to be sensitive to any behavior that bespeaks poor adjustment or immaturity.

In experiments the subject's initial suspicion that he may be exposing himself to evaluation will usually be confirmed or disconfirmed (as he perceives it) in the early stages of his encounter with the experimenter. Whenever it *is* confirmed, or to the extent that it is, the typical subject will be likely to experience *evaluation apprehension;* that is, an active, anxiety-toned concern that he win a positive evaluation from the experimenter, or at least that he provide no grounds for a negative one. Personality variables will have some bearing upon the extent to which

---

[1] As used in this paper the term "psychologist" is merely a convenient categorical simplification. It denotes anyone who "runs" subjects through an experimental or interview procedure and is perceived as being at least somewhat skilled at, and professionally interested in, figuring people out. For example, this is certainly the case when undergraduate subjects participate in a study conducted by an advanced psychology major or graduate student.

this pattern of apprehension develops. But equally important are various aspects of the experimental design such as the experimenter's explanatory "pitch," the types of measures used, and the experimental manipulations themselves.

Such factors may operate with equal potency across all cells of an experiment; but we shall focus upon the more troublesome situation in which treatment differences between experimental groups make for differential arousal and confirmation of evaluation apprehension. The particular difficulty with this state of affairs is that subjects in groups experiencing comparatively high levels of evaluation apprehension will be more prone than subjects in other groups to interpret the experimenter's instructions, explanations, and measures for what they may convey about the kinds of responses that will be considered healthy or unhealthy, mature or immature. In other words, they will develop *hypotheses* about how to win positive evaluation or to avoid negative evaluation. And usually the subjects in such an experimental group are enough alike in their perceptual reactions to the situation that there will be considerable similarity in the hypotheses at which they separately arrive. This similarity may, in turn, operate to systematically influence experimental responding in ways that foster false confirmation of the experimenter's predictions.

Let us consider one example of a situation in which some well-known findings might be accounted for in these terms. It seems quite conceivable that in certain dissonance experiments the use of surprisingly large monetary rewards for eliciting counterattitudinal arguments may seem quite strange to the subject, may suggest that he is being treated disingenuously. This in turn is likely to confirm initial expectations that evaluation is somehow being undertaken. As a result the typical subject, once exposed to this manipulation, may be aroused to a comparatively high level of evaluation apprehension; and, guided by the figural fact that an excessive reward has been offered, he may be led to hypothesize that the experimental situation is one in which his autonomy, his honesty, his resoluteness in resisting a special kind of bribe, are being tested. Thus, given the patterning of their initial expectations and the routinized cultural meanings of some of the main features of the experimental situation, most low-dissonance subjects may come to reason somewhat as follows: "They probably want to see whether getting paid so much will affect my own attitude, whether it will influence me, whether I am the kind of person whose views can be changed by buying him off."

The subject who has formulated such a subjective hypothesis about the real purpose of the experimental situation will be prone to resist giving evidence of attitude change; for to do so would, as he perceives it, convey something unattractive about himself, would lead to his being negatively evaluated by the experimenter. On the other hand, a similar hypothesis would be less likely to occur to the subject who is offered a smaller monetary reward and thus he would be less likely to resist giving evidence of attitude change.

Affect Toward the Experimenter as a Research Contaminant

Yet another and even simpler type of possible systematic bias should be noted. This involves the unsuspected affective consequences of designs which call for the experimenter to behave differently toward persons in different conditions of an experiment. Under certain circumstances such differences may generate further differences in how subjects feel toward the experimenter or toward his experiment; and these intercell affective differences too may have the final consequence of influencing experimental responses in ways which make for false confirmation of hypotheses. Thus, turning again to dissonance studies in which subjects are offered large rewards for the writing of counter-attitudinal essays, this manipulation, instead of creating low dissonance, may establish comparatively high arousal of the suspicion that one is being deceived; and this in turn may generate anger. A possible consequence is that the low-dissonance subject, provoked to hostility by the suspected duplicity, may find emotional release in refusing to show the response (attitude change) that he perceives the experimenter to be after.

Contaminant Control by Altered Replication

One way of checking upon the presence of these types of contamination is to ask the subject how he interpreted the purpose and meaning of the experiment. This will often be possible but it may sometimes involve one major hazard: such interviewing in itself can be open to the very kinds of contamination it seeks to disclose. Another approach is to conduct an altered replication of the original experiment, one in which we redesign those of its aspects that are presumed to have fostered the contaminating processes. Not only does such an approach enable application of the law of parsimony in interpreting the relation of data to theoretical claims, it also facilitates further study of the social psychology of the psychological experiment.[2] In pursuit of these goals much of this paper will report and discuss an altered replication of one important study that has been presented as confirming the prediction that counterattitudinal advocacy will generate greater attitude change when undertaken for a small reward than when undertaken for a large one. First it will be necessary to consider the background, design, and results of the original study upon which the present altered replication is based.

From the dissonance point of view counterattitudinal behavior, or even the commitment to undertake it, will lead to attitude change in inverse proportion to the strength and number of cognitions that could be used to justify such behavior (Brehm, 1960). Of the many conceivable types of counterattitudinal performance the one that has been most frequently studied both by dissonance theorists and others has been advocacy, in oral or written form, of an attitude position opposite to the subject's actual private attitude (Carlson, 1956; Culbertson, 1957; Janis & King, 1954; Kelman, 1953; Scott, 1957, 1959).

In most of the relevant dissonance studies the justification variable has been operationalized in one of three ways: subjects are given high or low choice in deciding whether to undertake counterattitudinal advocacy (for example, Cohen & Latané in Brehm & Cohen, 1962); they are told that their performances will be of great or little value for interested other parties (for example, Cohen, Brehm, & Fleming, 1958); or they are given or promised large or small monetary, or other, rewards (for example, Festinger & Carlsmith, 1959).

---

[2] For a programmatic statement that defines some outstanding prospects and problems in this area, see the useful article by Riecken (1962). In his comments on the subject's desire to "put his best foot forward" Riecken is speaking of something rather like the concept of "evaluation apprehension" that has been developed here and more briefly treated earlier (Rosenberg, 1961, 1963). However, for Riecken this is basically a source of "unintended variance" in data and the possibility that it will exert systematic influence making for false validations of hypotheses is not directly examined. Orne (1962) and Rosenthal (1963) have suggested other types of systematic bias. The former has argued that subjects are often motivated to help the experimenter "prove his hypothesis" while the latter has presented evidence that the experimenter's hypotheses or expectations are often indirectly communicated in ways that shape the subject's experimental responding. These views are not in conflict with, nor are they particularly close to, the interpretations offered here. More directly related are the studies on "social desirability" by Edwards (1957) and Crowne and Marlowe (1960). However, these investigators have been basically concerned with sources of invalidity in psychological testing rather than with systematic bias in experiments.

The study upon which the present paper is focused was conducted by Cohen and is one of the many recently reported by Brehm and Cohen (1962). Its general design was similar to earlier dissonance studies except that it used four levels of monetary reward, instead of the usual two. The prediction was that with this graded range of monetary rewards the resulting attitude change would be monotonically and inversely related to the size of the reward.

The subjects were Yale undergraduates. The issue concerned the actions of the New Haven police in a campus riot that had occurred a few weeks earlier. The experimenter, appearing at randomly chosen dormitory rooms, introduced himself as a "member of an Institute of Human Relations research team," ascertained by verbal inquiry that the subject disapproved of the actions of the police and asked him to write an essay in support of the actions of the police.[3] The request for the counterattitudinal essay was explained in this way:

> It has been shown that one of the best ways to get relevant arguments, on both sides of an issue, is to ask people to write essays favoring only one side. . . . What we really need now are some essays favoring the police side. I understand that you have very different views on the matter, but as you can see it's very interesting to know what kinds of arguments people bring up in their essays if they have different opinions about it.

The reward manipulation was then introduced by telling the subject that he would receive a particular sum for "writing the essay against your own position." Eight subjects were offered $ .50, six were offered $1, ten others were offered $5, six others were offered $10. The subject wrote his essay on a blank sheet headed "Why the New Haven Police Actions Were Justified," He was then told:

---

[3] It is not clear from the research report whether the experimenter actually referred to himself as a psychologist. But belonging to an "Institute of Human Relations research team" would have been sufficient to establish that he was some sort of psychologist or advanced psychological trainee who would be reporting back to a more senior colleague. This was because the "Institute of Human Relations" was the name of the building that housed the Yale psychology department; no other department that gave undergraduate courses was located there and the research organization for which it was named had long since ceased to exist. The experimenter also described himself as a "fellow student." This may have worked to further heighten the arousal of evaluation apprehension, since the Yale undergraduate culture places great emphasis upon the competititve show of maturity, sophistication, and "all around balance." It would probably be particularly important to the subject that the evaluation of him formed by a psychologically trained "fellow student" be a positive one.

Now that you have looked at some of the reasons for the actions of the New Haven police, we would like to get some of your reactions to the issue: *you may possibly want to look at the situation in the light of this.* So, would you please fill out this questionnaire.

The questionnaire on which the subject was invited to indicate approval of the New Haven police, if so inclined, began with this query: "Considering the circumstances, how justified do you think the New Haven police actions were in the recent riot?" An a priori 31-point scale was used with labels at every fifth point and ranging from "completely justified" to "not at all justified." Additional questionnaire items were used to check that the subject correctly perceived the amount of payment that he had been promised and that he had understood that he was to write a strong essay opposite to his own attitude. A control group was given the attitude questionnaire but received neither the manipulation nor the other measures.

It was found that the $5 and $10 groups did not differ significantly from the control group in expressed attitude toward the New Haven police. However, the subjects in the $.50 group were less negative toward the New Haven police than the $1 subjects ($p < .05$) who in turn were less negative than the $10 subjects ($p < .05$); and both the $.50 and $1 groups differed significantly from the control group.

Thus in the main the data appeared to confirm the original prediction. However, the point of view outlined above would suggest that in this study, as in others of similar design, the low-dissonance (high-reward) subjects would be more likely to suspect that the experimenter had some unrevealed purpose. The gross discrepancy between spending a few minutes writing an essay and the large sum offered, the fact that this large sum had not yet been delivered by the time the subject was handed the attitude questionnaire, the fact that he was virtually invited to show that he had become more positive toward the New Haven police: all these could have served to engender suspicion and thus to arouse evaluation apprehension and negative affect toward the experimenter. Either or both of these motivating states could probably be most efficiently reduced by the subject refusing to show anything but fairly strong disapproval of the New Haven police; for the subject who had come to believe that his autonomy in the face of a monetary lure was being assessed, remaining "anti-police" would demonstrate that he *had* autonomy; for the subject who perceived an indirect and disingenuous attempt to change his attitude and felt some reactive anger, holding fast to his original attitude could appear to be a relevant way of frustrating the experimenter.[4] Furthermore, with each *step* of increase in reward we could expect an increase in the proportion of subjects who had been brought to a motivating level of evaluation apprehension or affect arousal.

How can such an interpretation be tested? If it is correct it points to the importance of the fact that the experimenter conducts both the dissonance arousal and the attitude measurement. Evaluation apprehension and negative affect, if they exist, have been focused upon the experimenter; and it would be either to avoid his negative evaluation or to frustrate him, or both, that the high-reward subject would hold back (from the experimenter and possibly even from himself) any evidence of having been influenced by the essay he has just completed.

The most effective way then to eliminate the influence of the biasing factors would be to separate the dissonance-arousal phase of the experimenter from the attitude-measurement phase. The experiment should be organized so that it appears to the subject to be two separate, unrelated studies, conducted by investigators who have little or no relationship with each other and who are pursuing different research interests. In such a situation the evaluation apprehension and negative affect that are focused upon the dissonance-arousing experimenter would probably be lessened and more important, they would not govern the subject's responses to the attitude-measuring experimenter and to the information that he seeks from the subject.

---

[4] Some other reasons (see [3] for the first) why the experimenter calling himself a "fellow student" might have increased the potency of these biasing processes are worth noting here. Given the fact that the anti-police attitude was highly normative among Yale undergraduates at this time, many subjects would have been likely to, assume that the experimenter was also anti-police. Thus among the high-reward subjects who made this attribution to the experimenter any tendency to inhibit showing themselves capable of being "bought off" would be further strengthened by the expectation that the experimenter would personally disapprove of the subject's new attitude. On the other hand, if the experimenter was perceived, as he might have been by some subjects, to actually be pro-police, the fact that he was a "fellow student" would lead to his being seen as violating an important group standard; and this, particularly for high-reward subjects who might interpret the experimenter as trying to "buy them off" for the pro-police side, would have engendered even more anger toward the experimenter than would otherwise be the case. In turn this would have increased the likelihood that the high-reward subject would resist showing any change in the pro-police direction. Thus both the evaluation apprehension and affect arousal patterns of contamination might well have been intensified by the experimenter being perceived as a fellow student.

This was the main change introduced into the original design.[5] A second change was that the reward manipulation involved not only telling the subject that he would be paid a certain amount, but also the actual delivery of that amount to him immediately after he completed the essay. It was assumed that this change too would work to reduce the likelihood that the high-reward subjects would develop suspicions concerning the experimenter's possible duplicity and unrevealed purposes.

Adherence to the dissonance view would suggest that under these altered conditions the results would still show an inverse relationship between magnitude of reward and extent of attitude change. Indeed the significance of the dissonance-confirming relationship might be expected to increase; for now with each subject having actually received a monetary reward the cognitions concerning reasons for undertaking the counterattitudinal performance would be less variable within experimental groups than could have been the case in the original experiment.

However, the consistency theory developed by the present author (Rosenberg, 1956, 1960) suggests the opposite prediction. It holds that the most usual basis for attitude change is the establishment of new beliefs about the attitude object, beliefs that are inconsistent with the original affective orientation toward that object. In this view the significance of a reward received for writing a counterattitudinal essay (that is, for improvising or rehearsing inconsistency-generating cognitions) would be different from that claimed in dissonance theory: such a reward would, in proportion to its magnitude, be likely to have a positive effect both upon the development and the stabilization of the new cognitions. From this it would be predicted that with the removal of the biasing factors the degree of attitude change obtained after the subjects have written counterattitudinal essays will vary directly, rather than inversely, with the amount of reward. Thus the altered design outlined here may afford something approximating a critical test between this approach and the dissonance approach as regards their applicability to predicting the attitude-change effects of counterattitudinal advocacy.

[5] The author is aware of only one dissonance study in which some attempt was made to separate counterattitudinal advocacy from subsequent attitude measurement; this is the experiment by Festinger and Carlsmith (1959). However, the degree of separation may well have been insufficient. That experiment did not involve, as did the present one, disguising the two phases as two different studies conducted in two different departments. Furthermore, the dependent variable was not change in a previously stable social attitude but rather a momentary rating of how much the subject liked or disliked an experiment just completed.

METHOD

Attitude Issue and Subjects

To replicate as closely as possible, except for the major changes that distinguish the present study from its model, the author sought an issue comparable to "the actions of the New Haven police." Late in 1961 the Ohio State University football team, having won the Big Ten championship, received an invitation to the Rose Bowl. Concerned with the extent to which its reputation as the "football capital of the world" weakened OSU's academic reputation and performance, the faculty council of the University voted to reject the invitation and thereby engendered, both in the student body and the surrounding community, a sense of incredulous outrage. This, through the promptings of local news media, was rapidly turned toward active protest. The immediate result was a riot in which a large crowd of undergraduates (estimates varied between one to three thousand) stormed through University buildings shouting pro-Rose Bowl and anti-faculty slogans. The more longlasting result was the stabilization among the undergraduates of an attitude of disapproval toward any limitation upon Rose Bowl participation. This attitude remained salient during the following year and even in the face of the fact that during that year the faculty council, by a close vote, reversed its original decision. In general, interested students felt that future faculty interference with participation in Bowl games continued to be a real possibility.

With a pilot questionnaire administered early in 1963 it was confirmed that opposition to a Rose Bowl ban remained a consensual position among the undergraduate body; more than 94 percent of the sample indicated strong disapproval toward any restoration of the ban in the future. Upon completion of this pilot study a new group of male subjects was recruited from sections of introductory psychology for participation in the present study. In all, fifty-one subjects were finally used. Ten were randomly assigned to each of three experimental conditions and twenty-one to a control condition.

Dissonance Arousal

As each experimental subject arrived at the author's office he found him busily engaged either in writing or in a conversation with another "student." The experimenter then told the subject:

"I'm sorry, but I'm running late on my schedule today and I'll have to keep you waiting for about fifteen or twenty minutes. Is that all right?"

Most subjects simply said it was, though a few expressed concern about getting to their next class on time. All of the latter, when assured that the work the experimenter wanted them to do would take no more than twenty minutes, accepted the situation with equanimity. The experimenter then said:

"Oh, I've just thought of something; while you are waiting you could participate in another little experiment that some graduate student in education is doing."

The experimenter explained that he had had a call the previous day from the "graduate student" who needed volunteers in a hurry for

"some sort of study he's doing—I don't know what it's about exactly except that it has to do with attitudes and that's why he called me, because my research is in a similar area as you'll see later. Of course he can't give you any credit [the usual research credit point used to keep up experimental participation rates in introductory psychology courses] but I gather they have some research funds and that they are paying people instead. So if you care to go down there, you can."

All but three subjects indicated that they did want to participate in the other study. (The three who did not were eliminated from the experiment.) With some show of effort and uncertainty the experimenter then recalled the name of the education graduate student and the room, actually located in the education department, where he could be found.

Upon reporting to the "education graduate student" the subject received an explanation modeled word-for-word upon that used in the earlier experiment reported by Brehm and Cohen. Also, as in that experiment, it was determined by verbal inquiry that the subject held an attitude position opposite to the one he was to argue for in the essay. Subjects were randomly assigned to one of three reward conditions ($.50, $1, $5), and the amount that each subject was to receive was made clear to him before he undertook to write an essay on why the OSU football team should not be allowed to participate in the Rose Bowl. After the subject had completed the essay he was *paid* the amount that he had been promised, then thanked for his participation and dismissed. He then returned to the experimenter's office and, under the guise of participating in another study, his attitudes toward the Rose Bowl ban and toward various other issues were ascertained.

Attitude Measurement

This phase of the study began with the experimenter telling the subject that the study for which his participation had originally been solicited was a continuing survey on student attitudes "that I run every semester as a sort of Gallup poll to keep a check on opinion patterns on different University issues." (The experimenter, of course, did not know at this point which of the three magnitudes of reward the subject had received for writing the essay.) The subject then filled out an attitude questionnaire dealing with eight different issues. One of these read, "How would you feel if it were decided that from now on the OSU football team would not be allowed to participate in the Rose Bowl?" Following the procedure in the earlier study the subject responded on a 31-point graphic scale, marked at every fifth point by these labels: I think this decision would be not justified at all; very little justified; little justified; slightly justified; rather justified (instead of "quite justified" as in the earlier study); very justified; completely justified.

The same scale form was used with the other seven issues. One of these dealt with the area of varsity athletics and read, "How would you feel if it were decided that the University would no longer give any athletic scholarships?" This issue was included to provide another and more indirect test of the attitude-change consequences of writing the anti–Rose Bowl essay under varying conditions of reward. The other six issues dealt with nonathletic matters such as dormitory regulations, University admission policies, library rules, etc.

When the subject had completed this questionnaire he was asked what he thought the experiment was really about. His responses during a period of subsequent inquiry were transcribed and these were to be analyzed for the extent to which they reflected any suspicion that the two experiments were actually related to one another. The subject then filled out a follow-up questionnaire. The first item asked, "While you were filling out the opinion questionnaire, did it occur to you that there might be some connection between this experiment and the one you worked on in the education department?" After he had answered this item the subject was told that in fact there had been "a connection between the two experiments" and that it would all be explained after he completed the questionnaire. The subject then proceeded to answer the other questions, which asked how strong an essay he had agreed to write, how strong an essay he did write, how free he had felt in his decision to write the essay, how getting paid for the essay had made him feel, etc. Each of the questions was answered by choosing one of a number of alternative positions.

The experimenter then told the subject about the nature (but not the purpose) of the deception that had been used and proceeded to engage him in an interview designed to elicit further evidence of any doubts or suspicions that the subject might have felt during the experiment. The experimenter then explained the actual purpose of the experiment, commenting both upon its basic hypothesis and its design, and then answered all of the subject's questions. Before the subject was thanked and dismissed he was urged not to speak of the experiment to any fellow students during the remainder of the academic semester. All subjects promised to comply with this request.

In distinction to the experimental subjects, each of the control subjects, upon reporting for his appointment, was merely told that the experimenter was conducting "a sort of Gallup poll on University issues" and then filled out the attitude questionnaire.

RESULTS

In all, sixty-two subjects were originally run through the experiment. Eleven were discarded from the final analysis because on one basis or another they failed to meet necessary conditions that had been specified in advance. Six subjects (two originally assigned to the control condition and four to the experimental conditions) were rejected because post-experimental questioning revealed that they were members of varsity athletic teams. It had been decided that persons in this category would not be used since their pro–Rose Bowl attitudes could be assumed to be considerably stronger, more firmly anchored, than those of other students. Two other subjects, originally assigned to experimental groups, were discarded from the analysis because they evidenced virtually complete and spontaneous insight into the deception that had been employed. One other subject was discarded because he reported, on the post-experimental questionnaire, that he had been asked to write a "weak" rather than a "strong" essay. Two additional experimental subjects were discarded because they impressed both the experimenter and his assistant as showing psychotic tendencies. However, when the analysis reported below is repeated with the last three rejected subjects *included,* the findings are in no wise altered.

Except for the manipulated independent variable, other factors that might influence attitudinal response appear to have remained constant across experimental groups. Thus on the post-experimental question-naire the subjects in the three experimental groups do not differ in their perceptions as to how strong an essay they were asked to write or actually did write; nor do they differ in their self-reports on how free they felt to refuse. From the post-experimental interview data it appears that though a few subjects were surprised to find the Rose Bowl situation featured in the "two different experiments," the groups were equally lacking in insight both as regards the deception that was used and as regards the real purpose of the experiment.[6]

It will be remembered that the measurement phase of the present study consisted of a questionnaire concerned with eight different Uni-versity issues. On the six issues concerning matters unrelated to athletic policy, and thus not subjected to manipulation through the essay-writing procedure, statistical analysis reveals no overall differences and no differences between any specific groups taken two at a time.

On the main matter of experimental interest, whether attitude change on the Rose Bowl and athletic-scholarship issues varies directly or inversely with the magnitude of monetary reward, the data reviewed below reveal that the former is the case; that is, the prediction drawn from a consistency-theory interpretation appears to be confirmed and the opposite prediction based upon dissonance theory appears thereby to be disconfirmed.

Scoring the 31-point attitude scale from 1.0 (for the banning of Rose Bowl participation would be "not justified at all") through 1.2,

---

[6] It has been already suggested that in interviews, as in experiments, subjects' responses may often be influenced by their private interpretations of the situa-tion. Thus the post-experimental data collected in this study cannot necessarily be taken at simple face value. But there is at least one important consideration (probably relevant whenever the credibility of an experimental deception is being assessed) that suggests that the subjects were not holding back evidence of having discerned the true design of the experiment or of having doubted the explanations that were given them. Experienced experimenters will probably agree that college student subjects usually desire to represent themselves as sophisticated and as not easily misled. Thus when the post-experimental interview situation is a permissive one the subjects are likely to disclose, rather than withhold, promptings toward insight. *Yet none of the present subjects revealed any such insights when, after completion of the experiment, they were asked, "What do you think the experi-*

1.4 .. to 6.8, 7.0 (banning Rose Bowl participation would be "completely justified") we find the following mean scores: 1.45 for the control group, 2.24 for the $.50 reward group, 2.32 for the $1 reward group, and 3.24 for the $5 reward group. The attitude score ranges are 1-3 for the control group, 1-4 for the $.50 group, 1-5 for the $1 group, and 2-6 for the $5 group.

The significance of the reward variable in its influence upon attitude toward a Rose Bowl ban was assessed by computing the Kruskal-Wallis one-way analysis of variance from the ranked scores of all groups. H which is distributed as chi square, equals 17.89 and has a chance probability of less than .001 (see Table 1). In addition to this overall confirmation of the original prediction it is desirable to test the significance of differences between the specific groups.

Analysis by the Mann-Whitney rank sum test (computing z; see Mosteller & Bush, 1954) reveals that there is no significant difference between the $.50 and $1 groups. Accordingly, in some of the additional analyses these two groups were combined. As Table 1 indicates the combined $.50-$1 group is significantly more favorable toward banning Rose Bowl participation than is the control group ($p < .015$) and significantly less favorable than the $5 group ($p < .02$). When the $.50 and $1 groups are analyzed separately each is found to be significantly different from both the control and $5 conditions (see Table 1). As would be expected the difference between the control and $5 groups is of very large significance ($p < .0001$).

Thus the only deviation from the original prediction in this set of findings is the absence of a significant difference between the $.50 and $1 groups. Since these groups do differ as predicted from both the control and $5 groups, respectively, it might be conjectured that the

---

ment was really about?" Later on when *told* by the experimenter that the "two experiments" were really one, or still later when the full explanation was given, only a few subjects (two or three per group) claimed to have had suspicions suggestive of what had now been revealed. However, in their attitudinal responses on the two athletic issues these subjects do not differ from others in their groups (that is, they are not clustered in the low, middle, or high portions of the within-group attitude score rankings). Thus it seems likely that most of these particular subjects were exaggerating, and some perhaps were even imagining, their earlier doubts and in so doing were seeking positive evaluation from the experimenter after they had been shown capable of being "taken in." As intended, then, the procedures of the present experiment seem to have achieved their basic purpose which was to avoid, or at least to minimize, the kind of suspicion and disturbing confusion that tends to activate such biasing processes as affect arousal and evaluation apprehension.

$.50 difference between them does not generate a large enough *subjective* difference in the magnitude of payment. However, the alternative possibility that even this small magnitude of difference in reward does have some subtler influence upon attitude is suggested by the additional data regarding the issue of abandoning the policy of giving athletic scholarships.

This issue was used as a second test of the basic hypothesis. The expectation was that attitude change on the Rose Bowl issue should tend to *generalize* toward a similar issue, one that suggests another way of de-emphasizing the role of varsity sports in university life. It would of course be expected that the group differences would be of lesser magnitude on this issue than on the Rose Bowl issue since the latter served as the actual topic for the counterattitudinal essay.

Analysis of the subjects' responses on the athletic-scholarship issue reveals again a pattern of findings that supports the original hypothesis. Responding on a 31-point scale from 1.0 to 7.0 (with higher scores indicating greater approval for "abandoning athletic scholarships"), the groups yield the following mean scores: 2.28 for the control group, 2.26 for the $.50 group, 3.04 for the $1 group, and 3.88 for the $5 group. The score ranges are 1–7 for the control group, 1–4.8 for the $.50 group, 1–6 for the $1 group, and 1.2–7 for the $5 group.

TABLE 1
Group Means and Differences Between Groups
on Attitude Toward the Rose Bowl Ban

Group	M	Group Differences[a]			
		$.50	$1	$.50 and $1	$5
Control	1.45	$z = 1.97$, $p < .03$	$z = 1.80$, $p < .04$	$z = 2.31$, $p < .015$	$z = 3.93$, $p < .0001$
$.50	2.24		$z = .11$		$z = 1.77$, $p < .04$
$1	2.32				$z = 1.81$, $p < .04$
$.50 and $1	2.28				$z = 2.11$, $p < .02$
$5	3.24				

Note.—Overall difference between groups as assessed by Kruskal-Wallis test: $H = 17.89, p < .001$.
[a]Tested by Mann-Whitney z, one-tailed.

Application of the Kruskal-Wallis test indicates a significant main effect ($H = 14.50$, $p < .005$); thus the extent to which the writing of the essay affects an attitude *related* to the topic of the essay is shown to be a positive monotonic function of the amount of reward.

Analysis of the differences between the specific groups as reported in Table 2 clarifies certain interesting details. While the mean attitude scores of the control and $.50 groups are virtually identical, there is a slight and insignificant trend ($p < .20$) toward a greater concentration of extreme negative scores in the control group. The difference between the control and $1 groups comes closer to an acceptable probability level ($p < .10$) reflecting the greater differences in means (control = 2.28, $1 = 3.04$) reported above.

As predicted, the control and $.50 groups do show significantly less approval of abandoning athletic scholarships than does the $5 group; $p < .01$ in both cases. When the control and $.50 groups are combined, the difference from the $5 group has a probability of less than .005, as compared to less than .08 when the difference between the combined group and the $1 group is assessed. The $1 group clearly stands in an intermediate position. While its mean attitude score reflects greater endorsement of the anti-athletic scholarship view than does the $.50 group and less endorsement than the $5 group, neither of these differ-

TABLE 2

Group Means and Differences Between Groups on Attitude Toward Ending Athletic Scholarships

Group	M	Group Differences[a]		
		$.50	$1	$5
Control	2.28	$z = .95$ $p < .20$	$z = 1.33$, $p < .10$	$z = 2.45$, $p < .01$
$.50	2.26		$z = 1.09$, $p < .15$	$z = 2.36$, $p < .01$
Control and $.50	2.27		$z = 1.44$, $p < .08$	$z = 2.67$, $p < .005$
$1	3.04			$z = 1.24$, $p < .12$
$5	3.88			

Note.—Overall difference between groups as assessed by Kruskal-Wallis test: $H = 14.50$, $p < .005$
[a] Tested by Mann-Whitney z, one-tailed.

ences ($p < .15$ and $p < .12$, respectively) reaches significance.

Thus in comparison to the $.50 group the $1 group is less clearly differentiated from the $5 group and more clearly differentiated from the control group. From this it is apparent that the difference in size of reward between the $.50 and $1 groups does have some influence upon the extent to which the writing of the essay affected the subjects' attitudes on a related issue; and that influence too is consistent with the prediction that attitude change following counterattitudinal performance will be a *positive* function of the degree of reward received for such performance.

A question of considerable interest is why the difference between the $.50 and $1 groups shows up more clearly on a related issue rather than on the issue with which the essay was directly concerned. One possible interpretation emerges when we recall that the $.50 group does differ significantly from the control group on the Rose Bowl issue but does not show such a difference on the athletic-scholarship issue. With this small amount of reward there may be a minimal likelihood that the induced attitude change will generalize to a similar issue; with the somewhat larger reward of $1 a somewhat stronger tendency toward generalization may be operative.

On the basis of the findings that have so far been presented, the following conclusion seems warranted: when the design of the original study reported by Brehm and Cohen is altered so as to eliminate aspects that were likely to have generated evaluation apprehension and unsuspected affect arousal, the prediction that guided the present study is confirmed and the original dissonance prediction is disconfirmed.

DISCUSSION

This paper has combined two purposes: to present some propositions about how subjects' perceptions of experimental situations may affect their experimental performances; and, on this basis, to report an experimental re-examination of the dissonance-theory interpretation of attitude change due to counterattitudinal advocacy.

As regards the first purpose, the confirmation of the predictions in the present study lends support to the original propositions about evaluation apprehension and affect arousal; for it was in part on the basis of those propositions that the experimental predictions were formulated. However, more direct investigation of these contaminating processes is possible and desirable. For example, in two recent studies the author has, by intention rather than by inadvertence, supplied cues to the subjects about types of responding that might connote maturity and immaturity. In one of these studies some subjects were led to believe that mature persons like strangers more than immature people do, while other subjects were led to believe the opposite. In a second study some subjects were led to believe that mature people perform well on dull arithmetic tasks while others were led to believe that immature people do better at such tasks. The results of these studies, to be reported elsewhere, strongly demonstrate the power of evaluation apprehension in controlling experimental responding.

However, it is necessary that we go beyond such demonstration studies if these contaminating processes are to be better understood and thus more effectively controlled. A number of questions remain to be investigated. Do such personality variables as passivity, low self-esteem, and the need for social approval predict to the likelihood that evaluation apprehension will be aroused in the experimental situation? Does evaluation apprehension, once aroused, interact with experimenter bias (see Rosenthal, 1963) in a way that guides the subject in his hypothesizing about the kinds of responding that will win approval? Will exposure to psychological perspectives, as in the introductory courses from which so many subjects are drawn, tend to heighten the likelihood of experiencing evaluation apprehension in the experimental situation? Is there a minority of subjects who seek *negative* evaluation for masochistic purposes or as a way of asking for help, and will this affect their experimental responding? Can the presence of evaluation apprehension be uncovered by post-experimental inquiry? Comparable questions about the arousal of aggressive and other contaminating affective states could just as readily be formulated. Indeed it would seem desirable in further studies to attempt an operational separation of the two types of contamination that have been stressed in this paper.

In general the recently developed interest in investigating the experimenter-subject interaction as a source of bias in psychological research is a long-needed innovation. The work of Orne (1962), Riecken (1962), Rosenthal (1963c) and others has provided a most useful beginning. To the list of research contaminating processes that they have investigated might well be added those that have been discussed here.

As regards the second major focus of this paper, do the present findings call the validity of dissonance theory into question? Recently there have been reported many challenging studies testing that theory's pertinence not only to attitude change but also to perceptual and motivational processes and even to learning phenomena.[7] Thus the present study, taken alone, cannot be interpreted as challenging the general theory as such. However, it does seem to indicate that, at least in its account of the attitude-change consequences of counterattitudinal advocacy, dissonance theory has been overextended.

In the author's view the kind of counterattitudinal performance that best fits the dissonance paradigm is a simple overt act that directly violates one's private attitude (for example, eating or agreeing to eat a disliked food; expressing approval of a disliked proposal or candidate; merely *committing* oneself to develop counterattitudinal arguments; etc.). But when a person actually *does* elaborate a set of arguments opposite to his own attitude, the dissonance he experiences is probably of much wider scope than dissonance analysis would have it; it encompasses considerably more than merely realizing that he has argued against his own position. The broader pattern of inconsistency that he encounters is that between the content and apparent plausibility, on the one hand, of the new arguments that he has developed and, on the other hand, his original affective judgment of the attitude object.

Thus the subject who opposes the Rose Bowl ban and then argues in favor of it may come up with some good arguments (for example, "If we ban going to the Rose Bowl we will improve our reputation as a serious University . . . we will draw better students," etc.). In so doing he may become convinced of the validity of those arguments. This will produce intra-attitudinal inconsistency; that is, the newly established beliefs relating the Rose Bowl ban to positive ends and values will be inconsistent with the original negative affect toward the ban.

As was suggested earlier, the author's theoretical model (Rosenberg, 1956, 1960) takes this sort of inconsistency to be a basic condition for the occurrence of attitude change. It will be useful to show how this alternative model may be applied to interpreting the process of counterattitudinal advocacy. From this standpoint attitudes normally are stable, affective-cognitive structures and feature considerable internal

---

[7] For example, and despite the fact that the author has found it possible to reinterpret one of the experiments reported by them, the work of Brehm and Cohen (1962) does seem to establish the relevance of the dissonance approach to the study of certain aspects of motivation and does so with considerable inventiveness and concern for methodological issues. Similarly the work of Lawrence and Festinger (1962) has opened a very interesting new line of inquiry on some problems in the psychology of learning.

consistency. It is assumed that the production of *inconsistency* through change in either the affective or cognitive component (the latter being more usual and likely) will, if it transcends the individual's tolerance limits, motivate further symbolic activity. This may lead either to the restoration of the original attitude or, if this line of defense is not available, to its reorganization in the opposite direction.

For the sequence that begins with cognitive alterations what is required is that the new cognitions be sufficiently internalized and difficult to reverse; then the most likely outcome will be for the affective disposition toward the attitude object to move in the direction consistent with the newly established cognitions. Thus attitude change in its conventional sense will have occurred.

In this context a basic question is: what will render the new, inconsistency-generating cognitions sufficiently internalized and difficult to reverse? Many variables could have this influence; but in the present study the necessary suggestion would be that the most important is the amount of reward expected and received for *developing* such cognitions. Putting this another way it may be hypothesized that the demonstrated influence of the magnitude of payment upon ultimate attitude change is mediated through its effects upon the cognitive processes that are activated during the essay-writing task.

Broadly speaking, two separate kinds of mediation are easily conceivable: the *expectation* of payment for counterattitudinal advocacy may operate as an incentive and thus affect the quality of the arguments advanced in support of the new cognitions; the *receipt* of payment may operate as a reinforcement that further fosters the internalization of the counterattitudinal cognitions; and of course the scope of these two processes would be expected to vary as a function of the actual amount of payment.

A subsidiary analysis of the essays themselves tends to support and clarify this view. One unequivocal finding is that the $.50 and $1 groups differ in the actual number of words per essay, the latter group writing the longer ones ($p < .05$).[8] However, the $1 and $5 groups do not show any such difference. Considering that the $.50 and $1 groups do not differ on the Rose Bowl issue while the $1 and $5 groups do, sheer verbal productivity does not seem to mediate the main effect.

---

[8] All probability estimates reported in this discussion are based on a one-tailed interpretation of the Mann-Whitney statistic; in each case it was possible to make a unidirectional prediction about the attitude-change effects of the mediational variable under study.

Furthermore, separate analyses within each of the three experimental groups reveal absolutely no relationship between essay length and the post-essay attitude toward the Rose Bowl ban.

But do the essays vary in quality, in the actual *persuasiveness* with which they are written; and if so, does this relate to the post-essay attitude score? Two judges, working without knowledge of the different reward conditions and using a 5-point scale, rated all the essays for their basic persuasiveness. As part of their instructions they were asked to ignore the length of essays "because a long one may often be less persuasive than a short one." The interjudge reliability of these ratings proved quite adequate: for 80 percent of the essays the two ratings were either identical or within 1 point of each other.

Six of the twenty subjects in the combined $.50 and $1 group had persuasiveness scores that were lower (1 and 1.5, based on the pooled ratings of the two judges) than any that occurred in the $5 group. Four of these six subjects also had extreme negative attitudes. A comparable finding is obtained when we split the $.50–$1 group into approximately equal low persuasiveness and high persuasiveness halves. Those who wrote comparatively unpersuasive essays show significantly more attitudinal negativism toward the Rose Bowl ban than those who wrote comparatively persuasive essays ($p < .03$). When the same sort of analysis is separately performed with the $.50 and $1 groups, respectively, similar findings are obtained with borderline significance ($p < .10$ in both instances). On the other hand, within the high-reward group a division of the subjects into those who got the five lowest (though not as low as the comparable subjects in the low-reward group) and the five highest persuasiveness ratings does not yield any corresponding difference in attitudes toward the Rose Bowl ban.

An exactly similar finding is obtained when we use as the estimate of persuasiveness not the judges' ratings but the subjects' own post-experimental judgments of "how strong" their essays actually were. In the combined low-reward group those below the median in their self-ratings are less favorable to the Rose Bowl ban than those above the median ($p < .05$). Again, no such effect is discovered in the high-reward group.

From these findings it may be concluded that one mediating source of the overall difference between the low- and high-reward groups is that some of the subjects in the former group were insufficiently motivated by the small reward that had been promised them: in consequence they wrote insufficiently developed essays, essays that were essentially unpersuasive to themselves. Thus it would seem appropriate to conclude that the overall positive relationship between reward and attitude-change reflects the operation of an incentive or effort variable.

However, our analysis need not stop at this point. While some low-reward subjects wrote essays that are rated as extremely low on persuasiveness, others did not. Thus it is possible to match the low- and high-reward groups on this factor and by so doing we can test for the presence of some other process that may also play a role in mediating the overall relationship between reward and attitude-change. This was done by simply excluding from the analysis those low-reward subjects who got extremely low ratings (1 and 1.5) on the 5-point persuasiveness scale. With persuasiveness thus equalized (actually the mean persuasiveness score is then slightly *higher* for the remaining low-reward subjects than for the high-reward subjects) the high-reward group *still* shows significantly greater acceptance of the Rose Bowl ban ($p < .05$) and also of the proposal that athletic scholarships be abandoned ($p < .05$). These last findings do thus seem to confirm the expectation that, in addition to the incentive effect of variations in promised reward, there is yet another factor that contributes to the positive relationship between reward and attitude change. It would seem reasonable to interpret this other factor as based not upon the *promise* of reward but rather upon its *receipt;* thus our original conjecture that a reinforcement dynamic may be operative seems, on these grounds, to be rendered more plausible.

The use here of the term reinforcement should not, of course, be taken as referring solely to the kinds of relationships emphasized in conventional models of instrumental learning. In the present study the $5 payment, once received, could have increased the habit strength of the improvised counterattitudinal cognitions by directly increasing their attractiveness and credibility. Similarly, working for an expected large reward could have made the essay-writing a more ego-involving task and thus could have sensitized the subject to pay closer attention to the persuasive worth of his own arguments or to find greater merit in them. Furthermore, the amount of payment may also have affected the very clarity with which the new counterattitudinal arguments were remembered after the essay-writing session.

In this discussion we have attempted to state, and also to present some additional data in support of, a consistency theory view of how counterattitudinal advocacy produces attitude change. That view can be summarized in the following set of propositions: the counterattitudinal

improvisation establishes new cognitions that are inconsistent with the
original attitudinal affect; the extent to which the affective judgment of
the object will move toward the content of these new cognitions will
depend upon the degree of affective-cognitive inconsistency they generate; this in turn will depend upon the strength and stability of the new
cognitions; the strength and stability of the new cognitions are influenced, among other things, by the degree of reward received for their
improvisation—and this is probably due both to the promised reward
operating as an incentive and the received reward as a reinforcement; in
consequence, when counterattitudinal advocacy is investigated in a way
that circumvents certain biasing factors it will be found, as in the
present study, that it produces attitude change in proportion to the
magnitude of the reward for such advocacy.

Turning again to dissonance theory and shifting from its approach to
one type of attitude change to its approach toward attitude change
generally, the author would venture the judgment that dissonance research in this area has been complicated by certain difficult methodological and interpretive issues. Thus, as Chapanis and Chapanis (1964)
have noted, it is common to many of these studies that they do not
investigate the subject's personal reactions to the dissonance-arousing
situation, that the magnitudes of attitude change are often quite small
and that often a rather large number of subjects is, for one or another
theory-based reason, eliminated from analysis. To this must be added
the present demonstration that, in experiments on counterattitudinal
advocacy, certain data-biasing processes may be invoked to account for
reported findings. Indeed, since dissonance studies on other types of
attitude change also place some, but not other, subjects in highly puz-
zling and unexpected situations, it should be recognized that in these
studies as well biased contamination may often affect the results obtained. In the light of all these points it would seem desirable to undertake an empirical re-examination of some of the major studies that have
been offered as confirming the dissonance analysis of attitude change.
In the opinion of the present author the consequence of such re-
examination would not be the disconfirmation of the dissonance view
of attitude processes but the discovery that its generality is of somewhat smaller scope that its advocates have estimated and that certain
kinds of attitude change are better predicted and accounted for by
other theories.

Part Four
CONCLUSION

14
A Discussion
Of Problems
And Solutions

Two seemingly contradictory themes are prominent in the preceding essays and reprinted articles. First, we maintain that experimentation is a primary method for testing causal hypotheses. Second, it is clear that experimentation has important limitations as a means for hypothesis testing since experimental paradigms are frequently subject to plausible alternative explanations of the observed results, as demonstrated by the work on the "social psychology of experiments."

In this concluding essay we will first show that the two themes are not in contradiction since *logically* it is impossible to directly verify a causal hypothesis. That is, theories and hypotheses may be disproved, but not proved by empirical research. The scientific enterprise is thus seen as a process of disproving inadequate theories and of eliminating alternatives that make problematic the proper inference of a causal relationship. However, we maintain that the experimental method is an important tool for eliminating alternatives to inferences of cause-effect relationships. The work on the "social psychology of the experiment," then, will be seen not as a rejection of the logic of the experimental method but as a healthy recognition that modifications may be needed. The second part of this essay focuses on ways to cope with these recently realized problems of experimentation.

RIVAL HYPOTHESES
AND THE EXPERIMENTAL METHOD

A simple analogy should demonstrate why theoretical statements are not directly provable. Suppose absent-minded Conrad, a frequent traveler between Bombay and Los Angeles, awakes to find himself in an airplane that has just landed at one of the two cities. Conrad momentarily cannot remember to which city he was flying, but the sight of an elephant near an airfreight terminal leads him to conclude that it is Bombay. Conrad's conclusion, while probably correct, nevertheless rests upon an invalid argument:

India is inhabited by elephants

The unknown country contains an elephant

Therefore the country is India

The flaw in this argument is that there are reasonable explanations for the elephants's presence other than the country being India. For example, Conrad may well have observed a zoo-bound elephant at the Los Angeles Airport.

The above logical fallacy, that of "affirming the consequent," is an important limitation on the scientific enterprise. We may start with a theory, for example, which logically implies certain empirical consequences A and B. If A and B are unconfirmed by an empirical test, the credibility of our theory is in jeopardy. But if on the other hand A and B are confirmed, the theory is not "proven" for there may exist reasonable alternative explanations (rival hypotheses) for the findings A and B. Thus, theories can never be directly verified.

Since theories are not logically provable, the key to the

advancement of a science involves rigorous repeated attempts to disprove theories by finding consequences (predictions) of them that are empirically false. In the ideal scientific enterprise, then, the weaker theories would be excluded over time in a Darwinian fashion. As Campbell has said:

> Thus the only process available for establishing a scientific theory is one of "eliminating plausible rival hypotheses." Since these are never enumerable in advance, or at all, and since these are usually quite particular and require quite unique modes of elimination, this is inevitably a rather unsatisfactory and inconclusive procedure. But the logical analysis of our predicament as scientific knowers, from Hume to Popper, convinces us that this is the best we can do, that this is our labor of Hercules, if not our task of Sisyphus. (Campbell, 1969, pp. 354–55.)

In the same sense that we cannot prove a theory, we cannot directly prove a causal hypothesis. However, in order to test a theory, we may need to know whether there is a *cause-effect* relationship between the variables. The experimental method is a set of procedures designed to maximize the probability of correctly inferring that observed covariation between our variables represents a cause-effect relationship.

The work on the "social psychology of experiments" has shown, however, that the likelihood of making false causal inferences may be considerably higher than commonly believed by many experimenters. Two general classes of problems in traditional experimental design may be identified. The first are related to previously unrecognized "nuisance" variables, such as experimenter bias, which in principle may be handled by additional control groups or other practical methodological procedures. Experimenter bias, for example, may be managed through such means as mechanical delivery systems (audio or videotapes), double-blind designs, or experimenter expectancy control groups.

The second, and more troublesome, class of problems arise from features intrinsic to the experiment as a social situation, such as the subject's awareness that the experimenter is observing his behavior. Since we lack a theory of the experiment as a social situation, methodological approaches for coping with problems arising from intrinsic features of social experiments are problematic. The need for a theory of the experiment as a social occasion becomes evident in the following discussion.

INTRINSIC FEATURES OF EXPERIMENTS

The Nature of the Problem

An invariant feature of all situations recognized as a study by the subject is the fact that the subject knows that the experimenter has created the situation for the purpose of making observations of the subject's behavior. It is within this context that subjects respond to experimental stimuli and construct their own definitions of the situation. Both internal and external validity may be threatened—sometimes in very subtle ways—by this pervasive feature of experiments. Let us briefly consider two of the ways in which awareness of observation may affect experimental results (see Campbell, 1969, pp. 358–63 for an expanded discussion).

Awareness of being observed may *interact* with independent variables and thus affect internal validity. Subjects in different experimental conditions necessarily are exposed to different stimuli to create variation in the intended independent variable. This intended variation may have the *un*-intended consequence of differentiating treatment groups in terms of a number of factors related to being observed: (a) the *salience* of the experimenter, (b) perception of *what it is* that the experimenter is observing, (c) perception of how the experimenter will *evaluate* given behaviors, (d) perception of what behavior the experimenter *expects* or hypothesizes. Thus, for example, Rosenberg (1965, reprinted in this book) holds that when small as opposed to large monetary inducements are given for counterattitudinal advocacy, it is not cognitive dissonance which is affected but rather the subjects' definition of the situation, i.e., subjects given large inducements may believe their honesty is being observed (evaluated) and behave accordingly. While Rosenberg emphasizes the subject's concern with not performing in a way which would lead the experimenter to a negative evaluation of the subject's psychological adjustment, it should be recognized that the problems raised would persist even if we assumed other motivations on the subject's part. For instance, assume that the subject is motivated to give responses which are true and honest. The subject may "overcorrect" his behavior in an attempt not to let his awareness of the experimenter's observation focus influence his behavior.

External validity may also be jeopardized by the fact that subjects are aware that the experiment has been designed for the purpose of the experimenter's observing their behavior. In this sense, problems are raised even if observability is constant across all experimental conditions, i.e., does not interact with the independent variable. To take a by now familiar example, in the Asch paradigm, giving the same answers as the confederates has been taken as an indicator of "conformity *to the group.*" Schulman's (1967) study suggests that the number of subjects' answers that are the same as those of the confederates' may reflect the degree of the subjects' concern with the experimenter's (observer's) evaluation. Questions are thus raised concerning the inferences about conformity *to the group* which can be drawn from data obtained within the social context of the experiment. Perhaps the results from studies using the Asch paradigm only hold for situations in which there is a reference figure comparable to the experimenter. Similar questions of external validity may be raised about any number of causal relationships that have been "established" within the social context of the laboratory experiment.

Several solutions have been proposed to the problems raised by subjects' awareness of being observed and other aspects of subjects' definitions of the experimental situation. We will discuss several of these strategies in turn and comment on some of their major limitations.

The Creation of Control Groups
for Suspected Confounding Factors

An experiment which is well designed consists of a set of procedures which, if properly executed, make it unlikely that there exists an alternative to the presumed causal relationship between independent and dependent variables. The history of attempting to apply the experimental method to the study of human behavior has involved the creation of various kinds of control groups to eliminate specific factors believed to introduce plausible alternative hypotheses.

The basic question that the social psychology of the experiment forces us to face is: "Is the nature of the alternative hypotheses generated by the features of the experiment as a social occasion such that the traditional solution of creating control groups will allow us to choose between these alternatives and the hypothesized causal relationship between the independent and dependent variables?"

For the traditional solution to be useful three conditions must be met:

1. The extraneous or confounding factor and its hypothesized effect upon the results must be clearly *specified* before the control can be created.
2. The extraneous or confounding factor must be manipulable.
3. One must be willing to assume that the control condition itself does not introduce extraneous or confounding factors equal to or greater than the factor for which it is intended to control.

For some of the problems that have been raised by the social psychology of the experiment, the traditional control group strategy may work. For instance, the problem of experimenter bias is such that the three foregoing conditions are met and one is able to compare the results from experimenters who have, based upon a random process, been led to expect different results. However, the problems raised by demand characteristics, for example, do not meet these three conditions. As we have seen, the demand characteristic formulation is very general. The subject's behavior may be a function of the definition of the situation he constructs, using both information he brings with him and cues available in the experiment. There is no a priori specification of what we should control.

It must be recognized that there is always an infinite number of possible alternative explanations for any set of data. One kind of response to this fact of life is to say, in effect, that we need be concerned only when a reasonable, a probable, a *specific* alternative can be formulated. This position suggests a pragmatic traditional control groups procedure in which (1) an experiment is done, (2) persons who feel that the results reflect confounding factors must be able to *specify* what those factors were and perform an experiment adding control groups relevant to that specific hypotheses, (3) the "new" experiment then has the same status as the original, and those who would argue that these results were a function of confounding factors would be required to specify them and perform an experiment relevant to that hypothesis, and so on until a consensus was reached by the parties to the controversy.

The obvious limitation to this pragmatic approach revolves about the lengthy period of time involved, and it clearly would be less desirable than a standard methodological procedure for detecting or eliminating the influence of confounding extraneous factors. The following suggestions are attempts to provide such procedures.

Multiple Manipulations and Indicators

As a general method of controlling extraneous and confounding factors, Campbell and others (Campbell and Fiske, 1959; Webb et. al., 1966; Campbell, 1969) propose increasing the variety of empirical procedures brought to bear upon a causal hypothesis, either by employing multiple measures of conceptual variables within an experiment or by replicating

the hypothesis with altered methods in different experimental settings. Within a single experiment, for example, one
might include differing methods of manipulating or measuring the efficacy of the independent variable and multiple
indicators of the dependent variable. To the extent that the
means of manipulating the independent variable and the indicators of the dependent variable are varied, it is felt that
each will introduce *different* extraneous factors. If the results
(the relationship between the independent and dependent
variable) hold up despite the diversity of extraneous factors,
one's confidence in the validity of the observed relationship
should be high (*see* Costner, 1971, for a causal-model procedure for interpreting the results of multi-measurement experiments).

This approach has merit but its application to the problems raised by "demand characteristics" involves a basic
underlying assumption: the probability that the different
means of manipulating the independent variable and of
measuring the dependent variable will introduce varied artifacts is significantly greater than the probability that all of
the variations will be subject to common artifacts derived
from the features common to all experiments as a type of
social situation. Lacking a theory of the experiment as a
social system we have no principled means by which to judge
the validity of this assumption, but we would be more willing
tentatively to accept this assumption the greater the contrast
in the methods employed.

Disguised Experiments

The most obvious and direct solution to the problems associated with subjects' awareness of being in an experiment is
to conduct the experiment in such a way that subjects do not
know that they are being experimented with. This is most
easily accomplished by employing a "natural" (non-
laboratory) setting.

An interesting example of this approach is Evan and
Zelditch's (1961) work on bureaucratic authority. Based on

Weber's theory of bureaucratic authority, the experiment was designed to study the effect of varying "authority of knowledge" while holding "authority of office" constant. Evan and Zelditch's experiment differed from the typical laboratory experiment in that subjects were in the "subject role" only from the experimenter's perspective. Subjects believed they had been hired to code questionnaires as part-time employees of National Social Survey, Inc. It is undoubtedly the case that subjects were aware that their performance (for instance, speed and number of errors in coding) was being observed and evaluated. However, the important point is that the observation did not take place in a context in which the subject was aware that his behavior was being observed in terms of whether it was affected by factors about which the observer had some hypotheses.

In this study the researchers were able to establish theoretically relevant conditions, standardize stimuli, record and measure behavior, and effect random assignment of subjects to experimental conditions just as in the typical laboratory experiment. However, it should be noted that they were able to do this because the social situation from the subjects' point of view involved an employer-employee relationship. In our culture employers enjoy a considerable degree of control over employees. Thus, Evan and Zelditch were able to achieve considerable experimental control (e.g., "subjects" worked alone and communicated only with the "supervisor" and only by phone) because employers can legitimately specify (some) working conditions for employees.

It must of course be recognized that while the "employer-employee" cover story holds considerable promise for avoiding the problems of awareness of experimentation, its utility may be limited to a certain class of theoretical questions. The use of the disguised experiment strategy may in general be limited by the extent to which there are situations in our culture which allow the degree of control possible in the employer-employee or experimenter-subject relationship. While we see a growing number of ingenious and valuable experiments using the natural setting approach (Lefkowitz, Blake, and Mouton, 1955; Doob and Gross, 1968; Abelson and Miller, 1967; and Jung, 1959), we must recognize that to the extent to which one cannot control the entry of other persons and events into the "experimental" scene, limitations are placed upon implementing the experimental model. Unavailability of "natural" or unobtrusive measures for some variables places further limitations on what can be studied in disguised experiments. And finally, when subjects do not realize that they are being experimented with, numerous ethical problems emerge (e.g., Kelman, 1967).

Observability Controls

The natural situation approach has as its basic strategy eliminating from the subject's definition of the situation the idea that his behavior will be observed in terms of some purposive design on the part of the researcher. Rosenberg's work on cognitive dissonance suggests another strategy in which the systematic effect of observability on the relationship between the independent and the dependent variable is eliminated. In the "observability" control strategy, the subject is led to psychologically dissociate the events which, from the experimenter's perspective, constitute the manipulation of the independent variable from the events which constitute observations relevant to the dependent variable. This is achieved by presenting what are in fact the independent and dependent variable phases of the study, in different locations. Subjects are led to believe that they are participating in two totally unrelated studies being conducted by research personnel who will not be in communication with one another and who are pursuing completely independent research interests.

While this approach has promise, one difficulty with it is in determining whether or not the psychological dissociation has in fact been achieved. In Rosenberg's study, subjects, in post-experiment interviews, gave no indication that they were aware of a connection between the two "experiments." However, work on admission of prior knowledge about experiments clearly indicates the low degree of confidence that can be placed in subjects' denial of awareness. Confidence in the achievement of psychological dissociation would, of course, increase with an increase in time between phases of a study. However, as time separation increases, the occurrence of intervening events also increases the likelihood that only relationships not subject to decay over time, or relationships of extremely high power, will be successfully observed.

In addition, it is questionable to assume that if subjects are unaware of the connection between "study 1" and "study 2," unintended effects of awareness of observation will be thereby eliminated. For example, if in "study 1" a subject who receives $20 as opposed to $1 for counterattitudinal advocacy is likely to develop relatively high concern with what the experimenter "is up to," the differential level of concern with the experimenter in "study 1" may carry over to "study 2" and thus may affect the relationship between the independent and dependent variables.

Schulman's work on conformity suggests a variant of the Observability Control strategy. Schulman's study had some conditions in which the experimenter could (ostensibly) know only what the group's performance was, and other conditions in which the experimenter could know what each individual had done. Such variations in observability are, of course, only useful in designs where the experimenter can plausibly be interested either in a group performance or an individual performance. This strategy also runs into difficulty in convincing (and determining that you have convinced) subjects that their individual behavior cannot be observed by the experimenter.

Quasi-Controls

Orne (1962, 1969) suggests that one method of dealing with "demand characteristics" and their effects on subjects' definitions of the experimental situation is through the use of "quasi-controls." According to Orne (1969, p. 159), a quasi-control subject is "outside of the usual experimenter-subject relationship ... the experimenter redefines the interaction ... to make him [the subject] a co-investigator instead of a manipulated object." Orne suggests three ways in which quasi-controls may be created. First, subjects may be interviewed at different points in the sequence of activities that comprise the experiment. For example, some subjects may be asked what they think of the situation after initial instructions have been delivered, others after the manipulation, and so forth. In this way, the investigator may learn what hypotheses are suggested to subjects by various features of the experimental situation. Second, quasi-control subjects may be exposed to a description of everything a "real" subject experiences during an experiment, but such quasi-control subjects are not actually put through the experiment; it is only described to them. At the conclusion of the description, quasi-control subjects may be asked to respond to measures of the dependent variable *as if* they had really been subjects. Comparison of experimental and quasi-experimental data may then be made with the purpose of discovering how demand characteristics affect behavior relevant to the dependent variable. Finally, experimenters might be exposed both to real subjects and to subjects who are fully informed about the experiment (as in the second technique above) but who are instructed to act as if they were naive subjects. If some subtle "demand characteristics" are operative, simulating subjects might thereby be led to produce results similar to those of real subjects; whether or not the experimenter was able to distinguish the simulating from the real subjects might also be of interest.

Orne (1969) holds that if the behavior of real subjects and quasi-control subjects reveals the same relationship between "independent" and dependent variables, then the study's design was such that the experimental results *may* be a function of the social system features of the experiment *qua* experiment. Only when role-playing or simulating subjects yield *different* results from real subjects can one be relatively comfortable that experimental findings represent the effects of the experimental treatments rather than the effects of demand characteristics. However, Orne is very careful to emphasize the difficulty of making strong inferences on the basis of data from quasi-control subjects:

> Quasi-control procedures tend to maximally elicit the subject's responses to demand characteristics. As a result, the behavior seen with quasi-control subjects may include responses to aspects of the demand characteristics which for the real subjects are essentially inert. All that possibly can be determined with quasi-controls is what could be salient demand characteristics in the situation; whether the subjects actually respond to those same demand characteristics cannot be confirmed (Orne, 1969, p. 173).

Unfortunately, it may be contended that data from quasi-control subjects may have even less utility than Orne believes. The basic notion informing quasi-control procedures is that of the investigator redefining the role relationship between himself/herself and the subject so that the subject sees himself as a co-investigator whose task is to provide the experimenter with information about demand characteristics as they affect the subject's perceptions. It is assumed that subjects will accept such a definition of their relationship to the experimenter and will, as a result, provide him with full, accurate information about the experiment. The tenability of this assumption must be considered questionable. For example, in a study by Schulman and Freed (1970), all subjects were informed (by a confederate) that the experiment for which they were waiting had to do with verbal conditioning and that the experimenter expected them, as the experiment progressed, to use the words "I" and "we" increasingly in the sentences they made up. After the experiment, some subjects were given a standard post-experimental interview designed to assess awareness of reinforcement and prior knowledge about the experiment. Other subjects, however, were told before the interview that the experimenter was merely pretesting his procedures in the study in which they had participated. They were strongly urged to give him *any* information which might enable him to improve the study. It was found that the subjects in the pre-test introduction to the interview condition were *not* more likely to admit either awareness of reinforcement or prior knowledge about the study. If anything, they were less honest in their reports than the subjects not invited to redefine their role relationship in the direction of co-investigator.

Of course, great caution must be exercised in drawing any general conclusions about quasi-control data on the basis of a single study. However, we suspect that the relationship between subject and experimenter in our culture is such that it cannot be easily redefined. Subjects may find it very difficult—on the initiative of the experimenter—to define their role in the study as that of co-investigator and then carry out behaviors appropriate to their changed status. However, such considerations apply primarily to quasi-control techniques which involve direct questioning of the subject; quasi-controls who are simply asked to respond to measures of the dependent variable apparently can perform their task easily. But a close examination of the nature of demand characteristics suggests problems with this technique as well.

In Orne's formulation, a subject's behavior in an experiment is in part determined by his definition of the experimental situation and that definition, in turn, is said to be determined by two classes of variables, (a) the manipulated independent variables, and (b) demand characteristics which "include scuttlebutt about the experiment, its setting, implicit and explicit instructions, the person of the experimenter, subtle cues provided by him or her, and, of particular importance, the experimental procedure itself." (Orne, 1969, p. 146) All of these factors must be considered significant because together they from the *complex* of cues which will determine how subjects perceive the experiment. A change in *any single cue* might totally alter subjects' definition of the situation. But if we accept this reasoning, what is the status of data from quasi-control subjects for whom at least two vital features of the situation are different from those faced by real subjects? The quasi-controls (a) are not subjected to the experimental manipulation and (b) are responding to measures of the dependent variable *as if* they had been in the experiment, i.e., their "real" behavior is not being observed. Differences between quasi-control results and the real experimental data may themselves be a function of "demand characteristics." Given our present state of ignorance about the experiment as a social system, the logic of demand characteristics suggests that any systematic change in the stimuli presented to subjects may alter the subjects' definition of the experimental situation in unintended ways and quasi-control procedures as described by Orne do not represent a solution to this problem.

Situated Identities

In an interesting extension of the quasi-control approach, Alexander and Knight (1971) propose a situated identities procedure that concentrates on the self-presentational aspect of demand characteristics. They exposed "observer subjects" to a tape-recorded description of one of four experimental conditions based on previous insufficient justification dissonance experiments. The "observer subjects" are asked to estimate the dependent-variable response (a task-liking measure) of a "real subject" described in the tape recording. Alexander and Knight find that this produces results comparable to those obtained in the series of actual experiments. Then, after having been exposed to a simulation of the experiment and told how the "real subject" responded to the task-liking measure, the "observer subjects" are asked to use an adjective checklist to give their impression of what kind of person the "real subject" is. Alexander and Knight find: (1) the "real subject" receives the most favorable evaluations when he is described as having given the response the "observer subject" expected (which is also the response actually found in previous real experiments); (2) the adjectives which the "observer subjects" select as most relevant for describing the "real subject" differ systematically across the experimental conditions.

Alexander and Knight assume that the evaluative criteria used by "observer subjects" are similar to the evaluative criteria real subjects use on themselves in a real experiment. Thus they argue that they have shown *empirically* that the intended independent variable manipulation created systematic differences in the self-presentational meaning of dependent variable behavior and have provided an *empirical* demonstration of self-presentation (or, to use their term, situated-identities) as an alternative to dissonance or incentive as the variable accounting for the results of these experiments. Presumably it is the socially shared situational meanings created by each condition of the insufficient justification dissonance experiment, rather than the intended independent variable manipulation, that explains subject behavior.

Alexander and Knight base their procedure on the assumption that subjects in real experiments would be even more conscious of the situated-identities implied by the behavior alternatives among which they must choose than are "observer subjects." This assumption is questionable, particularly when the procedure with "observer subjects" explicitly directs them to report what kind of person the real subject is; attention should be directed to developing less direct means of getting this kind of information. In this sense the Alexander and Knight proposal is subject to criticisms similar to those made earlier about Orne's quasi-control procedures.

In commenting on Alexander and Knight's proposal it is also important to note that it is directed to testing for self-presentation artifacts which, recalling Orne's more general concept of demand characteristics, is only one potential source of artifacts, although probably a major one. For instance, the "good subject" idea suggests that subjects may seek to help the experimenter achieve the results they think he wants. Perhaps the situated-identities procedure can be broadened to allow inferences about other sources of artifacts not only by gathering data on the self-evaluative dimension, but by asking "observer subjects" to indicate what other evaluative dimensions they think the experimenter will use.

SUMMARY

The experimental method has long been a favored research strategy in the social sciences because it is ideally suited to eliminating alternative explanations to inferences of cause-effect relationships. The work in the "social psychology of the experiment" demonstrates, however, that the probability of making false causal inferences from any single experiment may be considerably higher than formerly recognized. The source of the problem is located in the features of the experiment as a social occasion.

Attempts to solve the problem are primarily hampered by three factors: (1) the lack of a well-defined theory of the experiment which would specify the sources of artifacts in any particular experiment or in specific classes of experiments, (2) difficulties in accurately tapping subjects' definition of the situation, (3) the fact that any *single* manipulated control intended to handle a specific source of artifact may introduce extraneous and confounding factors equal to or greater than the factor for which the control condition was created.

Given this state of affairs, it is tempting to hold that the experimental method is not applicable to the study of human behavior. In contrast to this position, we see the work on the social psychology of the experiment as representative of a healthy process in which we are beginning to recognize sources of confounding elements that are a threat to both the internal and external validity of experiments using human subjects. We also see the beginning of the development of a variety of procedures for addressing these problems—traditional control groups, multi-methods, disguised experiments, observability controls, quasi-controls, and the situated-identities procedure.

While each of the proposals in its own way may be inadequate as a general strategy, it is important to point out
that in some contexts one or another of the suggested procedures may be useful in detecting or ruling out plausible
alternatives to the causal hypothesis one wishes to test.
Secondly, although each in its own right may be defective,
each results in increased variation in the social features of the
context in which one's observations take place. This should
increase the chance of novel or serendipitous findings that
can be related to the social features of experiments. It is
quite likely that such a data base is a necessary step for the
development of a theory of the experiment as a social occasion.

Given the element of uncertainty introduced by considerations of the social psychology of the experiment, it would
seem wise to require that when a hypothesis is regarded as
important it be systematically tested in a series of altered
replications and that the variations discussed earlier be candi-
dates for inclusion in such a set of replications. However,
while the work documenting the problems uncovered in the
social psychology of the experiment is widely known, and
the logical utility of altered replications is in principle widely
accepted, its use is rather rare. In part, then, it would seem
that a solution to the problems raised by the social nature of
experiments with human subjects involves recognition of the
factors which presently act as barriers to the intensified im-
plementation of an altered replication strategy.

Certainly one of those factors must be the structure of
rewards for researchers in human behavior. That is, prestige,
academic rank, and money are less likely to be bestowed for
the often laborious and "uninteresting" work represented in
replication than for new, exciting, and "innovative" studies;
new institutional structures will be required to produce
changes in this state of affairs.

As a final comment, we should note that we do *not* believe
that, even given its "problems," the experimental method
should be regarded as a method subject to the same kinds of

limitations as other research strategies. Although studies in the social psychology of the experimental situation have shown that there is often greater ambiguity about the nature of the variables operating in a given relationship than researchers had previously supposed, it remains true that the experiment provides greater certainty about time-ordering of variables and control of known extraneous factors than any other kind of research. Furthermore, the randomization feature of experiments gives one increased confidence that an observed relationship between the *operations* that constitute the independent variable and the *operations* that constitute the measure of the dependent variable, is a causal one. Whatever the variable *in fact* manipulated and whatever the variable *in fact* measured in an experiment, their observed *relationship* will not (within the limits of chance) be spuriously produced by unknown factors. Thus, given comparable data obtained in experimental and non-experimental research and given an equal degree of certainty (or uncertainty) about the fit between the operational measures used and the theoretical concepts of interest, the experimental research procedure is less likely to lead to a false inference of a causal relationship.

For these reasons the experimental method remains a primary tool for testing proposed causal hypotheses.

Bibliography

Abelson, R.P. and J.C. Miller.
   1967   "Negative persuasion via personal insult." *Journal of Experimental and Social Psychology* 3:321-333.

Adair, J.G. and J. Epstein.
   1967   "Verbal cues in the mediation of experimenter bias." Paper presented at the meeting of the Midwestern Psychological Association held in Chicago, May.

Adams, J.K.
   1957   "Laboratory studies of behavior without awareness." *Psychological Bulletin* 54:383-405.

Alden, Priscilla, and A.L. Benton.
   1951   "Relationship of sex of examiner to incidence of Rorschach responses with sexual content." *Journal of Projective Techniques* 15 (June):231-234.

Alexander, C. Norman Jr. and Gordon W. Knight.
   1971   "Situated Identities and Social Psychological Experimentation." *Sociometry* 34 (March):65-82.

Alexander, C. Norman Jr., Lynne G. Zucker and Charles L. Brody.
   1970   "Experimental expectations and autokinetic experiences: consistency theories and judgmental convergence." *Sociometry* 33 (March):108-122.

Anderson, Hilton L. and Bruce W. Tuckman.
   1969   "Rule-breaking behavior and acquiescence response bias." *Perceptual and Motor Skills* 28 (April):598.

Argyris, C.
   1958   "Creating effective relationships in organizations." *Human Organization* 17 (Spring):34-40.

Argyris, C.
   1962   *Interpersonal Competence and Organizational Effectiveness.*
          Homewood, Illinois: Irwin.

Argyris, C.
   1964   *Integrating the Individual and the Organization.* New York:
          Wiley.

Argyris, C.
   1965   *Organization and Innovation.* Homewood, Illinois: Irwin.

Argyris, C.
   1966   "Interpersonal barriers to decision making." *Harvard Busi-
          ness Review* 44 (2):84-97.

Argyris, C.
   1967   "Today's problems with tomorrow's organizations." *Journal
          of Management Studies* 4 (1):31-55.

Argyris, C.
   1968   "Some unintended consequences of rigorous research."
          Psychological Bulletin 70 (September):185-197.

Aronson, E.
   1966   "Avoidance of inter-subject communication." *Psychological
          Reports* 19:238.

Aronson, E. and J.M. Carlsmith.
   1962   "Performance expectancy as a determinant of actual per-
          formance." *Journal of Abnormal and Social Psychology* 65
          (September):178-182.

Aronson, E. and J.M. Carlsmith.
   1968   "Experimentation in social psychology." Pp. 1-79 in Gard-
          ner Lindzey and Elliot Aronson (eds.), *The Handbook of
          Social Psychology* (Second Edition), Volume 2. Reading,
          Massachuseets: Addison-Wesley.

Aronson, E., J.M. Carlsmith, and J.M. Darley.
   1963   "The effects of expectancy on volunteering for an un-
          pleasant experience." *Journal of Abnormal and Social
          Psychology* 66:220-224.

As, A., J.W. O'Hara, and M.P. Munger.
   1962   "The measurement of subjective experiences presumably re-
          lated to hypnotic susceptibility." *Scandinavian Journal of
          Psychology* 3 (January):47-64.

Asch, S.E.
   1952   *Social Psychology.* New York: Prentice-Hall.

Asch, S.E.
   1953   "Effects of group pressure upon the modification and distor-
          tion of judgments." Pp. 189-213 in D. Cartwright and A.

Zander (eds.), *Group Dynamics.* Evanston, Illinois: Row, Peterson and Company.

Back, K.W., T.C. Hood, and M.L. Brehm.
1964   "The subject role in small group experiments." *Social Forces* 43 (December):181-187.

Baer, Paul E. and Marxus J. Fuhrer.
1969   "Cognitive factors in differential conditioning of the GSR: use of a reaction time task as the UCS with normals and schizophrenics." *Journal of Abnormal Psychology* 74 (August):544-552.

Barber, T.X.
1965   "Measuring 'hypnotic-like' suggestibility with and without 'hypnotic induction'; psychometric properties, norms, and variables influencing response to the Barber Suggestibility Scale (BSS)." *Psychological Reports* 16:809-844.

Barber, T.X.
1969   "Invalid arguments, postmortem analyses, and the experimenter bias effect." *Journal of Consulting and Clinical Psychology* 33 (1):11-14.

Barber, T.X. and D.S. Calverley.
1964a   "Effect of E's tone of voice on 'hypnotic-like' suggestibility." *Psychological Reports* 15 (August):139-144.

Barber, T.X. and D.S. Calverley.
1964b   "Toward a theory of hypnotic behavior: effects on suggestibility of defining the situation as hypnosis and defining response to suggestions as easy." *Journal of Abnormal and Social Psychology* 68 (June):585-592.

Barber, T.X., D.S. Calverley, A. Forgione, J.D. McPeake, J.F. Chaves, and B. Bowen.
1966   "Five attempts to replicate the experimenter bias effect." Harding, Mass.: Medfield Foundation. (Mimeo).

Barber, T.X., D.S. Calverley, A. Forgione, J.D. McPeake, J.F. Chaves, and B. Bowen.
1969   "Five attempts to replicate the experimenter bias effect." *Journal of Consulting and Clinical Psychology* 33 (February):1-6.

Barber, T.X. and M.J. Silver.
1968a   "Fact, fiction, and the experimenter bias effect." *Psychological Bulletin Monograph Supplement* 70:1-29.

Barber, T.X. and M.J. Silver.
1968b   "Pitfalls in data analysis and interpretation: a reply to Rosenthal." *Psychological Bulletin Monograph Supplement* 70 (December):48-62.

Barker, R.G. (ed.)
    1963   *Stream of Behavior.* New York: Appleton-Century-Crofts.

Barker, R.G., and P.V. Gump.
    1964   *Big School, Small School.* Stanford, California: Stanford Press.

Barker, R.G. and H.F. Wright.
    1955   *Midwest and Its Children.* Evanston, Illinois: Row, Peterson.

Barnard, P.G.
    1968   "Interaction effects among certain experimenter and subject characteristics on a projective test." *Journal of Consulting and Clinical Psychology* 32:514-521.

Barron, F.
    1965   "Some studies of creativity at the Institute of Personality Assessment and Research." Pp. 118-119 in A. Steiner (ed.), *The Creative Organization.* Chicago: University of Chicago Press.

Bartos, O.J.
    1958   "Leadership, conformity, and originality." Unpublished paper presented at American Sociological Society meeting.

Bateson, G., D.D. Jackson, J. Haley, and J. Weakland.
    1956   "Toward a theory of schizophrenia." *Behavioral Science* 1:251-264.

Baughman, E.E.
    1951   "Rorschach scores as a function of examiner difference." *Journal of Projective Techniques* 15 (June):243-249.

Bean, W.B.
    1959   "The ethics of experimentation on human beings." Pp. 76-84 in S.O. Waife and A.P. Shapiro (eds.), *The Clinical Evaluation of New Drugs.* New York: Hoeber-Harper.

Becker, H.G.
    1968   "Experimenter expectancy, experience, and status as factors in observational data." Unpublished master's thesis, University of Saskatchewan.

Bell, C.R.
    1961   "Psychological versus sociological variables in studies of volunteer bias in surveys." *Journal of Applied Psychology* 45 (April):80-85.

Bell, C.R.
    1962   "Personality characteristics of volunteers for psychological studies." *British Journal of Social and Clinical Psychology* 1 (June):81-95.

Bell, Donald R., and Donald L. McManis.
1968 "Perceptual differences of Ss classified as reward seekers and punishment avoiders." *Perceptual and Motor Skills* 27 (August):51-56.

Belson, W.A.
1960 "Volunteer bias in test-room groups." *Public Opinion Quarterly* 24:115-126.

Bem, Daryl J.
1967 "Self-perception: an alternative interpretation of cognitive dissonance phenomena." *Psychological Review* 74 (May):183-200.

Benney, M., D. Riesman, and S.A. Star.
1956 "Age and sex in the interview." *American Journal of Sociology* 62 (September):143-152.

Bennis, W.
1966 *Changing Organizations.* New York: McGraw-Hill.

Berelson, B.R., P.F. Lazarsfeld, and W.N. McPhee.
1954 *Voting: A Study of Opinion Formation in a Presidential Campaign.* Chicago: University of Chicago Press.

Berger, D.
1954 "Examiner influence on the Rorschach." *Journal of Clinical Psychology* 10 (July):245-248.

Berkowitz, L., Sharon B. Klanderman and Richard Harris.
1964 "Effects of experimenter awareness and sex of subject and experimenter on reactions to dependency relationship." *Sociometry* 27 (September):327-337.

Berkowitz, Hershel.
1964 "Effects of prior experimenter-subject relationships on reinforced reaction time of schizophrenics and normals." *Journal of Abnormal and Social Psychology* 69 (November):522-530.

Bernstein, A.S.
1965 "Race and examiner as significant influences on basal skin impedance." *Journal of Personality and Social Psychology* 1 (April):346-349.

Bernstein, L.
1956 "The examiner as an inhibiting factor in clinical testing." *Journal of Consulting Psychology* 20 (August):287-290.

Binder, A., D. McConnell, and Nancy A. Sjoholm.
1957 "Verbal conditioning as a function of experimenter characteristics." *Journal of Abnormal and Social Psychology* 55 (November): 309-314.

Birney, R.C.
1958   "The achievement motive and task performance: a replication." *Journal of Abnormal and Social Psychology* 56:133-135.

Blake, R., H. Berkowitz, R. Bellamy, and J. Mouton.
1956   "Volunteering as an avoidance act." *Journal of Abnormal and Social Psychology* 53 (September):154-156.

Blake, R.R., and J.W. Brehm.
1954   "The use of tape recording to simulate a group atmosphere." *Journal of Abnormal and Social Psychology* 49:311-313.

Blalock, Jr., H.M.
1961   *Causal Inferences in Nonexperimental Research.* Chapel Hill: The University of North Carolina Press.

Blankenship, A.B.
1940   "The effect of the interviewer upon the response in a public opinion poll." *Journal of Consulting Psychology* 4 (July-August):134-136.

Boring, E.G.
1950   *A History of Experimental Psychology* (Second Edition). New York: Appleton-Century-Crofts.

Boucher, R.G. and E.R. Hilgard.
1962   "Volunteer bias in hypnotic experimentation." *American Journal of Clinical Hypnosis* 5:49-51.

Bowers, Kenneth S. and J. Barnard Gilmore.
1969   "Subjective report and credibility: an inquiry involving hypnotic hallucinations." *Journal of Abnormal Psychology* 74 (August):443-451.

Braden, Marcia, and Elaine Walster.
1964   "The effect of anticipated dissonance on pre-decision behavior." Pp. 145-151 in L. Festinger (ed.), *Conflict, Decision, and Dissonance.* Stanford, California: Stanford University Press.

Brady, J.P., E.E. Levitt, and B. Lubin.
1961   "Expressed fear of hypnosis and volunteering behavior." *Journal of Nervous and Mental Disease* 133 (September):216-217.

Breer, P.E., and E.A. Locke.
1965   *Task Experience as a Source of Attitudes.* Homewood, Illinois: Dorsey Press.

Brehm, J.W.
1960   "A dissonance analysis of attitude-discrepant behavior." Pp. 164-197 in M.J. Rosenberg, C.I. Hovland, W.J. McGuire,

R.P. Abelson, and J.W. Brehm (eds.), *Attitude Organization and Change*. New Haven: Yale University Press.

Brehm, J.W. and A.R. Cohen.
1962   *Explorations in Cognitive Dissonance*. New York: Wiley.

Brightbill, R. and H.S. Zamansky.
1963   "The conceptual space of good and poor hypnotic subjects: a preliminary exploration." *International Journal of Clinical and Experimental Hypnosis* 11:112-121.

Brock, T.C. and G. Becker.
1965   "Birth order and subject recruitment." *Journal of Social Psychology* 65 (February):63-66.

Brock, T.C. and L.A. Becker.
1966   " 'Debriefing' and susceptibility to subsequent experimental manipulation." *Journal of Experimental Social Psychology* 2 (July):314-323.

Brogden, W.J.
1962   "The experimenter as a factor in animal conditioning." *Psychological Reports* 11 (August):239-242.

Brower, Daniel.
1948   "The role of incentive in psychological research." *Journal of General Psychology* 39 (July):145-147.

Brunswik, E.
1947   *Systematic and Representative Design of Psychological Experiments, With Results in Physical and Social Perception*. (Syllabus Series, Number 304) Berkeley: University of California Press.

Brunswik, E.
1956   *Perception and the Representative Design of Psychological Experiments*. Berkeley: University of California Press.

Bryan, James H. and E. Lichtenstein.
1966   "Effects of subject and experimenter attitudes in verbal conditioning." *Journal of Personality and Social Psychology* 3 (February):182-189.

Buck, Roger.
1961   "Comments on Buchwald's 'verbal utterances as data.' " Pp. 468-472 in H. Feigl and G. Maxwell (eds.), *Current Issues in the Philosophy of Science*. New York: Holt, Rinehart and Winston.

Burchinal, Lee G.
1960   "Personality characteristics and sample bias." *Journal of Applied Psychology* 44 (June):172-174.

Burdick, E.
  1957   *The Ninth Wave.* New York: Dell.

Burnham, J.R.
  1968   "Effects of experimenter's expectancies on children's ability to learn to swim." Unpublished master's thesis, Purdue University.

Byrne, Donn, John Lamberth, John Palmer and Oliver London.
  1969   "Sequential effects as a function of explicit and implicit interpolated attraction responses." *Journal of Personality and Social Psychology* 13 (September):70-78.

Campbell, Donald T.
  1957   "Factors relevant to the validity of experiments in social settings." *Psychological Bulletin* 54 (July):297-312.

Campbell, Donald T.
  1969   "Prospective: Artifact and Control." Pp. 351-382 in Robert Rosenthal and Ralph L. Rosnow (eds.), *Artifact in Behavioral Research.* New York: Academic Press.

Campbell, Donald T. and D.W. Fiske.
  1959   "Convergent and discriminant validation by the multitrait-multi-method matrix." *Psychological Bulletin* 56 (March): 81-105.

Campbell, Donald T. and Julian C. Stanley.
  1963   *Experimental and Quasi-Experimental Designs for Research.* Chicago: Rand-McNally.

Capra, P.C. and J.E. Dittes.
  1962   "Birth order as a selective factor among volunteer subjects." *Journal of Abnormal and Social Psychology* 64 (April):302.

Carlsmith, J.M. and E. Aronson.
  1963   "Some hedonic consequences of the confirmation and disconfirmation of expectancies." *Journal of Abnormal and Social Psychology* 66 (February):151-156.

Carlson, E.R.
  1956   "Attitude change through modification of attitude structure." *Journal of Abnormal and Social Psychology* 52 (March):256-261.

Carlson, J.A. and B.R. Hergenhahn.
  1968   "Use of tape-recorded instructions and a visual screen to reduce experimenter bias." Unpublished manuscript, Hamline University.

Carlson, R.
  1971   "Where is the person in personality research?" *Psychological Bulletin,* 75:203-219.

Carr, John E.
  1969   "Instructional set and social desirability scale values." *Psychological Reports* 24 (February):277-278.

Cartwright, D.
  1942   "The effect of interruption, completion and failure upon the attractiveness of activities." *Journal of Experimental Psychology* 31 (July):1-16.

Cataldo, J.F., I. Silverman, and J.M. Brown.
  1967   "Demand characteristics associated with semantic differential ratings of nouns and verbs." *Educational and Psychological Measurement* 27 (Spring):83-87.

Cattell, R.B.
  1964   "Validity and reliability: A proposed more basic set of concepts." *Journal of Educational Psychology* 55 (February): 1-22.

Cattell, R.B. (ed.).
  1966   *Handbook of Multivariate Experimental Psychology.* Chicago: Rand-McNally.

Chapanis, Natalie P. and A.C. Chapanis.
  1964   "Cognitive dissonance: Five years later." *Psychological Bulletin* 61 (January):1-22.

Chapman, Loren J., Jean P. Chapman, and Terry Brelje.
  1969   "Influence of the experimenter on pupillary dilation to sexually provocative pictures." *Journal of Abnormal Psychology* 74 (June):396-400.

Christie, Richard
  1951   "Experimental naivete and experiential naivete." *Psychological Bulletin* 48 (July):327-339.

Cicourel, Aaron V.
  1964   *Method and Measurement in Sociology.* New York: Free Press of Glencoe.

Cieutat, V.J.
  1965   "Examiner differences with the Stanford-Binet I.Q." *Perceptual and Motor Skills* 20:317-318.

Cieutat, V.J. and G.L. Flick.
  1967   "Examiner differences among Stanford-Binet items." *Psychological Reports* 2 (October):613-622.

Claiborn, W.L.
   1968   "An investigation of the relationship between teacher expec-
          tancy, teacher behavior, and pupil performance." Unpub-
          lished doctoral dissertation, Syracuse University.

Clausen, Aage R.
  1968-69 "Response validity in surveys." *Public Opinion Quarterly* 32
          (Winter):588-606.

Coffin, T.E.
   1941   "Some conditions of suggestion and suggestibility." *Psycho-
          logical Monographs* 53, No. 4 (Whole No. 241).

Cohen, A.R., J.W. Brehm, and W.H. Fleming.
   1958   "Attitude change and justification for compliance." *Journal
          of Abnormal and Social Psychology* 56 (March):276-278.

Cohen, B.P., T.F. Mayer, G.I. Schulman, and C. Terry.
   1961   "Relative competence and conformity." Informal report
          under National Science Grant G9030, Department of Sociol-
          ogy, Stanford University.

Cohen, Morris R., and Ernest Nagel.
   1934   *An Introduction to Logic and Scientific Method.* New York:
          Harcourt, Brace, Inc.

Conn, L.K., C.N. Edwards, R. Rosenthal, and D. Crowne.
   1968   "Perception of emotion and response to teachers' expec-
          tancy by elementary school children." *Psychological Reports*
          22 (February):27-34.

Conroy, G.I. and J.R. Morris.
   1968   "Psychological health among volunteers, non-volunteers, and
          no shows." Reprint: mimeo.

Cook, Peggy.
   1958   "Authoritarian or acquiescent: some behavioral differences."
          American Psychologist 338 (Abstract).

Cook, Thomas D., James R. Bean, Bobby J. Calder, Robert Frey,
   Martin L. Krovetz, and Stephen R. Riesman.
   1970   "Demand characteristics and three conceptions of the fre-
          quently deceived subject." Journal of Personality and Social
          Psychology 14 (March):185-194.

Cook, S.W. and Claire Selltiz.
   1964   "A multiple-indicator approach to attitude measurement."
          Psychological Bulletin 62 (July):36-55.

Cooper, J., L. Eisenberg, J. Robert, and B.S. Dohrenwend.
   1967   "The effect of experimenter expectancy and preparatory
          effort on belief in the probable occurrence of future events."
          Journal of Social Psychology 71:221-226.

Cooper, Eunice, and Marie Jahoda.
  1947   "The evasion of propaganda: how prejudiced people respond
         to anti-prejudice propaganda." *Journal of Psychology*
         23:15-25.

Cordaro, L. and J.R. Ison.
  1963   "Psychology of the scientist: X observer bias in classical con-
         ditioning of the planarian." *Psychological Reports* 13
         (December):787-789.

Costner, Herbert L.
  1971   "Utilizing causal models to discover flaws in experiments."
         Sociometry 34:398-410.

Couch, A. and K. Keniston.
  1960   "Yeasayers and naysayers: agreeing response set as a person-
         ality variable." *Journal of Abnormal and Social Psychology*
         60:151-174.

Cowan, G. and S.S. Komorita.
  1968   "Awareness and attitude change." Reprint: ditto.

Crespi, L.P.
  1946   "The cheater problem in polling." *Public Opinion Quarterly*
         9:431-445.

Criswell, Joan H.
  1958   "The psychologist as perceiver." Pp. 95-109 in R. Tagiuri
         and L. Petrullo (eds.), *Person Perception and Interpersonal
         Behavior.* Stanford: Stanford University Press.

Cronbach, L.J. and P.E. Meehl.
  1955   "Construct validity in psychological tests." *Psychological
         Bulletin* 52:281-302.

Crowne, D.P. and D. Marlowe.
  1960   "A new scale of social desirability independent of psycho-
         pathology." *Journal of Consulting Psychology* 24:349-354.

Crowne, D.P. and D. Marlowe.
  1964   *The Approval Motive.* New York: Wiley.

Crowne, D.P. and B.R. Strickland.
  1961   "The conditioning of verbal behavior as a function of the
         need for social approval." *Journal of Abnormal and Social
         Psychology* 63 (September):395-401.

Crutchfield, R.S.
  1955   "Conformity and character." *American Psychologist* 10
         (May):191-198.

Culbertson, F.M.
  1957   "Modification of an emotionally held attitude through role

playing." *Journal of Abnormal and Social Psychology* 54:230-233.

Curtis, H.S. and E.B. Wolf.
1951   "Influence of sex of examiner on the prediction of sex responses on the Rorschach." *American Psychologist* 6 (August):345-346.

Cutler, R.L.
1958   "Countertransference effects in psychotherapy." *Journal of Consulting Psychology* 22 (October):349-356.

Damaser, Esther C., R.E. Shor, and M.T. Orne
1963   "Physiological effects during hypnotically-requested emotions." *Psychosomatic Medicine* 25:334-343.

Dana, Jean M. and Richard H. Dana.
1969a   "Experimenter bias and the WAIS." *Perceptual and Motor Skills* 28 (June):694.

Dana, Jean M. and Richard H. Dana.
1969b   "Experimenter bias or task bias?" *Perceptual and Motor Skills* 29 (August):8.

Davis, J.
1930   "Study of 163 outstanding communist leaders." *Proceedings of the American Sociological Society* 24:42-55.

Denner, Bruce.
1967   "Informers and their influence on the handling of illicit information." Read at 39th annual meeting of the Midwestern Psychology Association: Chicago, Illinois.

Deutsch, M. and H.B. Gerard.
1955   "A study of normative and informational social influences upon individual judgment." *Journal of Abnormal and Social Psychology* 51 (November):629-636.

Dittes, James E. and Paul C. Capra.
1961   "Birth order and vulnerability to differences in acceptance." *American Psychologist* 16 (July):358 (Abstract).

Dittes, James E. and H.H. Kelley.
1956   "Effects of different conditions of acceptance on conformity to group norms." *Journal of Abnormal and Social Psychology* 53 (July):100-107.

Dohrenwend, Barbara Snell, John Colombotos and Bruce P. Dohrenwend.
1968   "Social distance and interviewer effect." *Public Opinion Quarterly* 32 (Fall):410-422.

Doob, A.N. and A.E. Gross.
1968 "Status of frustrator as an inhibitor of hornhonking responses." *Journal of Social Psychology* 76:213-218.

Doob, L.W.
1948 *Public Opinion and Propaganda.* New York: Holt.

Dua, J.K.
1969 "Decrements in human instrumental performance due to response competition and fear extinction." *Journal of Experimental Psychology* 81 (September):547-556.

Dulany, D.E.
1961 "Hypotheses and habits in verbal 'operant conditioning.' "
Journal of Abnormal and Social Psychology 63 (September):
251-263.

Dulany, D.E.
1962 "The place of hypotheses and intentions: an analysis of
verbal control in verbal conditioning." Pp. 102-129 in
C. Eriksen (ed.), *Behavior and Awareness—A Symposium of
Research and Interpretation.* Durham, N.C.: Duke University
Press.

Duncan, S. Jr., Milton J. Rosenberg and Jonathan Finkelstein.
1969 "The paralanguage of experimenter bias." *Sociometry* 32
(June):207-219.

Duncan, S. and R. Rosenthal.
1968 "Vocal emphasis in experimenters' instruction reading as unintended determinant of subjects' responses." *Language and
Speech* 11 (January-March):20-26.

Edgerton, H.A., S.H. Britt, and R.D. Norman.
1947 "Objective differences among various types of respondents
to a mailed questionnaire." *American Sociological Review*
12 (August):435-444.

Edwards, A.L.
1954 "Experiments: their planning and execution." In G. Lindzey
(ed.), *Handbook of Social Psychology.* Reading, Massachusetts: Addison-Wesley.

Edwards, A.L.
1957 *The Social Desirability Variable in Personality Assessment
and Research.* NewYork: Dryden Press.

Edwards, A.L.
1960 *Experimental Design in Psychological Research.* New York:
Rinehart.

Edwards, Allen L.
  1954   *Statistical Methods for the Behavioral Sciences.* New York: Rinehart and Company, Inc.

Edwards, C.N.
  1968   "Characteristics of volunteers and nonvolunteers for a sleep and hypnotic experiment." *American Journal of Clinical Hypnosis* 11:26-29.

Ekman, P.
  1965   "Differential communication of affect by head and body cues." *Journal of Personality and Social Psychology* 2: 726-735.

Ekman, P. and W.W. Friesen.
  1960   "Status and personality of the experimenter as a determinant of verbal conditioning." *American Psychologist* 15 (July):430.

Ellson, D.G., R.C. Davis, I.J. Saltzman, and C.J. Burke.
  1952   "A report on research on detection of deception." (Contract N 6onr-18011 with Office of Naval Research). Bloomington, Indiana: Department of Psychology, Indiana University.

Entwisle, D.R.
  1961   "Interactive effects of pretesting." *Educational and Psychological Measurement* 21 (Autumn):607-620.

Evan, W.E. and Morris Zelditch, Jr.
  1961   "Experiment on bureaucratic authorities." *American Sociological Review* 26 (6):883-893.

Farber, I.E.
  1963   "The things people say to themselves." *American Psychologist* 18:185-197.

Ferber, R. and H.G. Wales.
  1952   "Detection and correction of interviewer bias." *Public Opinion Quarterly* 16 (Spring):107-127.

Ferguson, Donald C. and Arnold H. Buss.
  1960   "Operant conditioning of hostile verbs in relation to experimenter and subject characteristics." *Journal of Consulting Psychology* 24 (August):324-327.

Festinger, L.
  1954   "A theory of social comparison processes." *Human Relations* 7:117-140.

Festinger, L.
  1964   "Behavioral support for opinion change." *Public Opinion Quarterly* 28:404-417.

Festinger, L. and J.M. Carlsmith.
  1959   "Cognitive consequences of forced compliance." *Journal of Abnormal and Social Psychology* 58:203-210.

Festinger, L. and N. Maccoby.
1964 "On resistance to persuasive communications." *Journal of Abnormal and Social Psychology* 68 (April):359-366.

Filer, R.N.
1952 "The Clinician's personality and his case reports." *American Psychologist* 7 (May):336.

Fillenbaum, S.
1966 "Prior deception and subsequent experimental performance: the 'faithful' subject." *Journal of Personality and Social Psychology* 4 (November):532-537.

Fisher, S., J.O. Cole, K. Rickels, and E.H. Uhlenhoth.
1964 "Drug-set interaction: the effect of expectations on drug response in outpatients." Pp. 149-156 in P.B. Bradley, F. Flugel, and P. Hoch (eds.), *Neuropsychopharmacology* 3. New York: Elseuier.

Fode, K.L.
1967 "The effects of experimenters' anxiety, and subjects' anxiety, social desirability and sex, on experimenter out-come-bias." Unpublished doctoral dissertation, University of North Dakota.

Frank, J.D.
1944 "Experimental studies of personal pressure and resistance: I. Experimental production of resistance." *Journal of General Psychology* 30:23-41.

Freedman, J.L.
1965 "Long-term behavioral effects of cognitive dissonance." *Journal of Experimental Social Psychology* 1:145-155.

Freedman, J.L. and D.O. Sears.
1965 "Selective exposure." Pp. 57-97 in L. Berkowitz (ed.), *Advances in Experimental Social Psychology*. Volume 2. New York: Academic.

French, J.R.P., Jr.
1956 "A formal theory of social power." *Psychological Review* 63 (May):181-194.

Frey, A.H. and W.C. Becker.
1958 "Some personality correlates of subjects who fail to appear for experimental appointments." *Journal of Consulting Psychology* 22 (June):164.

Friedman, N.
1964 "The psychological experiment as a social interaction." Unpublished doctoral dissertation, Harvard University.

Friedman, N.
1967 *The Social Nature of Psychological Research: the Psycho-*

logical Experiment as Social Interaction. New York: Basic
Books.

Friedman, N., D. Kurland, and R. Rosenthal.
    1965   "Experimenter behavior as an unintended determinant of
        experimental results." *Journal of Projective Techniques* 29
        (December):479-490.

Friedman, P.
    1942   "A second experiment on interviewer bias." *Sociometry*
        5:378-381.

Gall, M. and G.A. Mendelsohn.
    1967   "Effects of facilitating techniques and subject-experimenter
        interaction on creative problem solving." *Journal of Person-*
        ality and Social Psychology 5:211-216.

Gaudet, Hazel and E.C. Wilson.
    1940   "Who escapes the personal investigator?" *Journal of Applied*
        Psychology 24 (December):773-777.

Garfield, S.L. and D.C. Affleck.
    1960   "Therapists' judgments concerning patients considered for
        psycho-therapy." *American Psychologist* 15 (July):414.

Garfinkel, Harold.
    1967   *Studies in Ethnomethodology.* Englewood Cliffs, New
        Jersey: Prentice-Hall.

Garner, W.R., H.W. Hake, and C.W. Eriksen.
    1956   "Operationism and the concept of perception." *Psycho-*
        logical Review 63:149-159.

Gibby, R.G.
    1952   "Examiner influence on the Rorschach inquiry." *Journal of*
        Consulting Psychology 16 (December):449-455.

Gibby, R.G., D.R. Miller, and E.L. Walker.
    1953   "The examiner's influence on the Rorschach protocol."
        Journal of Consulting Psychology 17 (December):425-428.

Glass, John F. and Harry H. Frankiel.
    1968   "The influence of subjects on the researcher: a problem in
        observing social interaction." *The Pacific Sociological*
        Review 11 (Fall):75-80.

Goffman, E.
    1959   *The Presentation of Self in Everyday Life.* New York:
        Doubleday.

Goldberg, S.C.
    1954   "Three situational determinants of conformity to social
        norms." *Journal of Abnormal and Social Psychology* 49
        (July):325-329.

Goldblatt, R.A. and R.A. Schackner.
1968   "Categorizing emotion depicted in facial expressions and
        reaction to the experimental situation as a function of ex-
        perimenter friendliness." Paper presented at the meeting of
        the Eastern Psychological Association (April): Washington.

Golding, Stephen L. and Edward Lichtenstein.
1970   "Confession of awareness and prior knowledge of deception
        as a function of interview set and approval motivation."
        Journal of Personality and Social Psychology 14 (March):
        213-223.

Goldman-Eisler, Frieda.
1958   "Speech analysis and mental processes." *Language and
        Speech* 1:59-75.

Goldstein, A.P.
1962   *Therapist-patient Expectancies in Psychotherapy.* New
        York: Macmillan.

Gordon, L.V. and M.A. Durea.
1948   "The effect of discouragement on the revised Stanford-Binet
        Scale." *Journal of Genetic Psychology* 73:201-207.

Gosnell, H.F.
1927   *Getting Out the Vote: An Experiment in the Stimulation of
        Voting.* Chicago: University of Chicago Press.

Greenberg, Martin S.
1967   "Role playing: an alternative to deception?" *Journal of Per-
        sonality and Social Psychology* 7 (October):152-157.

Greene, Edward B.
1937   "Abnormal adjustments to experimental situations." *Psycho-
        logical Bulletin* 34 (November):747-748. (Abstract)

Guest, L.
1947   "A study of interviewer competence." *International Journal
        of Opinion and Attitude Research* 1:17-30.

Gustafson, L.A. and M.T. Orne.
1963   "Effects of heightened motivation on the detection of de-
        ception." *Journal of Applied Psychology* 47 (December):
        408-411.

Gustafson, L.A. and M.T. Orne.
1965   "Effects of perceived role and role success on the detection
        of deception." *Journal of Applied Psychology* 49
        (December):412-417.

Gustav, Alice.
1962   "Students' attitudes toward compulsory participation in ex-
        periments." *Journal of Psychology* 53 (January):119-125.

Haas, Harold I. and Martin L. Maehr.
  1965   "Two experiments on the concept of self and the reaction of
          others." *Journal of Personality and Social Psychology* 1
          (January):100-105.

Haase, W.
  1964   "The role of socioeconomic class in examiner bias." Pp.
          241-247 in F. Riessman, J. Cohen, and A. Pearl (eds.), *Mental Health of the Poor.* New York: The Free Press of
          Glencoe.

Hall, E.T.
  1966   *The   Hidden   Dimension.*   Garden   City,   New   York:
          Doubleday.

Harari, C. and J. Chwast.
  1959   "Class bias in psychodiagnosis of delinquents." *American
          Psychologist* 14:377-378.

Hargreaves, W.A. and J.A. Starkweather.
  1963   "Recognition of speaker identity." *Language and Speech* 6
          (2):63-67.

Harrington, G.M.
  1967   "Psychology of the scientist: XXVII Experimental bias:
          Occam's razor versus Pascal's wager." *Psychological Reports*
          21:527-528.

Harrington, G.M. and L.H. Ingraham.
  1967   "Experimenter bias and tails of Pascal." *Psychological
          Reports* 21:513-516.

Harvey, O.J. and W.F. Clapp.
  1965   "Hope, expectancy, and reactions to the unexpected."
          Journal of Personality and Social Psychology 2 (July):45-52.

Hefferline, R.F.
  1962   "Learning theory and clinical psychology—an eventual
          symbiosis?" Pp. 97-138 in A.J. Bachrach (ed.), *Experimental
          Foundations of Clinical Psychology.* New York: Basic
          Books, Inc.

Heller, K., R.A. Myers, and L. Vikan-Kline.
  1963   "Interviewer behavior as a function of standardized client
          roles." *Journal of Consulting Psychology* 27 (April):
          117-122.

Hendrick, C., B. Wallace and J. Tappenbeck.
  1968   "Effect of cognitive set on color perception." *Journal of
          Personality and Social Psychology* 10:34-37.

Hetherington, Mavis, and Leonard E. Ross.
  1963   "Effect of sex of subject, sex of experimenter, and reinforce-
          ment condition on serial verbal learning." *Journal of Experimental Psychology* 65 (June):572-575.

Hildum, D.C. and R.W. Brown.
  1956 "Verbal reinforcement and interviewer bias." *Journal of Abnormal and Social Psychology* 53 (July):108-111.

Himelstein, Philip.
  1956 "Taylor scale characteristics of volunteers and nonvolunteers for psychological experiments." *Journal of Abnormal and Social Psychology* 52 (January):138-139.

Hoffman, L.R. and N.R.F. Maier.
  1964 "Valence in the adoption of solutions by problem-solving groups: concept, method, and results." *Journal of Abnormal and Social Psychology* 69:264-271.

Holmes, D.S.
  1967 "Amount of experience in experiments as a determinant of performance in later experiments." *Journal of Personality and Social Psychology* 7 (December):403-407.

Holmes, David S. and Alan S. Appelbaum.
  1970 "Nature of prior experimental experience as a determinant of performance in a subsequent experiment." *Journal of Personality and Social Psychology* 14:195-202.

Homans, George C.
  1961 *Social Behavior, Its Elementary Forms.* New York: Harcourt, Brace, and World, Inc.

Honigfeld, G.
  1964 "Non-specific factors in treatment. I: Review of placebo reactions and placebo reactors." *Diseases of the Nervous System* 25:145-156.

Hood, T.C.
  1963 "The volunteer subject: patterns of self-presentation and the decision to participate in social psychological experiments." Unpublished master's thesis, Duke University.

Hood, T.C. and K.W. Back.
  1967 "Patterns of self-disclosure and the volunteer: the decision to participate in small groups experiments." Paper read at Southern Sociological Society (April): Atlanta.

Horowitz, I.A.
  1969 "Effects of volunteering, fear arousal and number of communications on attitude change." *Journal of Personality and Social Psychology* 11 (January):34-37.

Hovland, C.I.
  1954 "Effects of the mass media of communication." Pp. 1062-1103 in G. Lindzey (ed.), *Handbook of Social Psychology II.* Cambridge, Massachusetts: Addison-Wesley.

Hovland, C.I.
1959   "Reconciling conflicting results derived from experimental
        and survey studies of attitude change." *American Psychologist* 14:8-17.

Hovland, C.I., O.J. Harvey, and M. Sherif.
1957   "Assimilation and contrast effects in reactions to communication and attitude change." *Journal of Abnormal and
        Social Psychology* 55:244-252.

Hovland, C.I., I.L. Janis, and H.H. Kelley.
1953   *Communication and Persuasion.* New Haven: Yale University
        Press.

Hovland, C.I., A.A. Lumsdaine, and F.D. Sheffield.
1949   *Experiments on Mass Communication.* Princeton: Princeton
        University Press.

Hovland, C.I., W. Mandell, Enid H. Campbell, T. Brock. A.S. Luchins,
A.R. Cohen, W.J. McGuire, I.L. Janis, Rosalind L. Feierabend, and
N.H. Anderson.
1957   *The Order of Presentation in Persuasion.* New Haven: Yale
        University Press.

Hovland, C.I. and H.A. Pritzker.
1957   "Extent of opinion change as a function of amount of
        change advocated." *Journal of Abnormal and Social Psychology* 54:257-261.

Hovland, C.I. and W. Weiss.
1951   "The influence of source credibility on communication
        effectiveness." *Public Opinion Quarterly* 15:635-650.

Howe, Edmund S.
1960   "Quantitative motivational differences between volunteers
        and nonvolunteers for a psychological experiment." *Journal
        of Applied Psychology* 44:115-120.

Hume, David.
1951   "An inquiry concerning human understanding," (1748). Reprinted in D.C. Yalden-Thomson (ed.) *Theory of Knowledge.* Edinburgh: Nelson.

Hyman, Herbert.
1966   "Problems in the collection of opinion-research data." Pp.
        21-27 in C.W. Backman and P.F. Secord (eds.), *Problems in
        Social Psychology: Selected Readings.* New York: McGraw-Hill.

Hyman, H.H., W.J. Cobb, J.J. Feldman, C.W. Hart, and C.H. Stember.
1954   *Interviewing In Social Research.* Chicago: University of Chicago Press.

Ingraham, L.H. and G.M. Harrington.
1966   "Psychology of the scientist: XVI. Experience of E as a variable in reducing experimenter bias." *Psychological Reports* 19 (2):455-461.

Ismir, A.A.
1962   "The effects of prior knowledge of the Thematic Apperception Test on test performance." *Psychological Record* 12 (April): 157-164.

Jackson, C.W. and J.C. Pollard.
1966   "Some nondeprivation variables which influence the 'effects' of experimental sensory deprivation." *Journal of Abnormal Psychology* 71 (October):383-388.

Janis, I.L. and J.B. Gilmore.
1965   "The influence of incentive conditions on the success of role playing in modifying attitudes." *Journal of Personality and Social Psychology* 1:17-27.

Janis, I.L., C.I. Hovland, P.B. Field, Harriet Linton, Elaine Graham, A.R. Cohen, D. Rife, R.P. Abelson, G.S. Lesser, and B.T. King.
1959   *Personality and Persuasibility*. New Haven: Yale University Press.

Janis, I.L. and B.T. King.
1954   "The influence of role playing on opinion change." *Journal of Abnormal and Social Psychology* 49:211-218.

Jones, E.E. and J.W. Thibaut.
1958   "Interaction goals as bases of inference in interpersonal perception." Pp. 151-178 in R. Tagiuri and L. Petrullo (eds.), *Person Perception and Interpersonal Behavior*. Stanford, California: Stanford University Press.

Jourard, S.M.
1968   "Project replication: experimenter-subject acquaintance and outcome in psychological research." Reprint: mimeo.

Jung, A.F.
1959   "Price variations among automobile dealers in Chicago, Illinois." *Journal of Business* 32:315-326.

Kahn, R.L. and C.F. Cannell.
1957   *The Dynamics of Interviewing: Theory, Technique and Cases*. New York: Wiley and Sons.

Kanfer, F.H.
1958   "Verbal conditioning: reinforcement schedules and experimenter influence." *Psychological Reports* 4 (September): 443-452.

Kanfer, F.H. and S.C. Karas.
  1959   "Prior experimenter-subject interaction and verbal condi-
          tioning." *Psychological Reports* 5 (June):345-353.

Katz, E. and P.F. Lazarsfeld.
  1955   *Personal Influence; the Part Played by People in the Flow of
          Mass Communications.* Glencoe, Ill.: Free Press.

Katz, I., S.O. Roberts, and J.M. Robinson.
  1965   "Effects of task difficulty, race of administrator, and in-
          struction on digit-symbol performance of Negroes." *Journal
          of Personality and Social Psychology* 2 (July):53-59.

Katz, R.
  1964   "Body language: a study in unintentional communication."
          Unpublished Doctoral Dissertation, Harvard University.

Keisner, R.H.
  1968   "Debriefing and responsiveness to overt experimenter expec-
          tancy cues." Reprint: mimeo.

Kelley, H.H. and M.M. Shapiro.
  1954   "An experiment on conformity to group norms when con-
          formity is detrimental to group achievement." *American
          Sociological Review* 19 (September):667-677.

Kelly, E. Lowell, Catherine Cox Miles and Lewis M. Terman.
  1936   "Ability to influence one's score on a typical paper-and-
          pencil test of personality." *Character and Personality* 4
          (March):206-215.

Kelman, H.C.
  1953   "Attitude change as a function of response restriction."
          Human Relations 6:185-214.

Kelman, H.C.
  1958   "Compliance, identification, and internalization: three proc-
          esses of attitude change." *Journal of Conflict Resolution*
          2:51-60.

Kelman, H.C.
  1967   "Human use of human subjects; the problem of deception in
          social psychological experiments." *Psychological Bulletin*
          67:1-11.

Kelman, H.C. and C.I. Hovland.
  1953   " 'Reinstatement' of the communicator in delayed measure-
          ment of opinion change." *Journal of Abnormal and Social
          Psychology* 48: 327-335.

Kendall, Patricia L. and P.F. Lazarsfeld.
  1950   "Problems of survey analysis." Pp. 133-196 in R.K. Merton
          and P.F. Lazarsfeld (eds.), *Continuities in Social Research:*

Studies in the Scope and Method of "The American Soldier." Glencoe, Ill.: Free Press.

Kendall, Patricia and Paul F. Lazarsfeld.
1966 "Problems of survey analysis." Pp. 28-33 in C.W. Backman and P.F. Secord (eds.), *Problems in Social Psychology: Selected Readings.* New York: McGraw-Hill.

Kiesler, C.
1967 "Group pressure and conformity." In J. Mills (ed.), *Advanced Experimental Social Psychology.* New York: Macmillan.

Kintz, B.L., D.J. Delprato, D.R. Mettee, C.E. Persons and R.H. Schappe.
1965a "The experimenter as a discriminative stimulus in a T-maze." *Psychological Record* 15:449-454.

Kintz, B.L., D.J. Delprato, D.R. Mettee, C.E. Persons, and R.H. Schappe.
1965b "The experimenter effect." *Psychological Bulletin* 63 (April):223-232.

Klapper, J.T.
1949 *The effects of Mass Media.* New York: Columbia University Bureau of Applied Social Research.

Koenig, Karl P. and David del Castillo.
1969 "False feedback and longevity of the conditioned GSR during extinction: some implications for aversion therapy." *Journal of Abnormal Psychology* 74 (August): 505-510.

Krasner, L.
1958 "Studies of the conditioning of verbal behavior." *Psychological Bulletin* 55 (May):148-171.

Krasner, L.
1962 "The therapist as a social reinforcement machine." Pp. 61-94 in H.H. Strupp and L. Luborsky (eds.), *Research in Psychotherapy.* Volume 2. Washington, D.C.: American Psychological Association.

Krasner, L., L.P. Ullman, R.L. Weiss, and B.J. Collins.
1961 "Responsivity to verbal conditioning as a function of three different examiners." *Journal of Clinical Psychology* 17 (October):411-415.

Kroger, R.O.
1967 "The effects of role demands and test-cue properties upon personality-test performance." *Journal of Consulting Psychology* 31 (June):304-312.

Krout, M.H.
    1954   "An experimental attempt to determine the significance of
            unconscious manual symbolic movements." *Journal of Gene-
            ral Psychology* 51:121-152.

Kruglov, L.P. and H.H. Davidson.
    1953   "The willingness to be interviewed: a selective factor in
            sampling." *Journal of Social Psychology* 38:39-47.

Lana, R.E.
    1959a   "Pretest-treatment interaction effects in attitudinal studies."
            Psychological Bulletin 56 (July):293-300.

Lana, R.E.
    1959b   "A further investigation of the pretest-treatment interaction
            effect." *Journal of Applied Psychology* 43:421-422.

Lana, R.E.
    1964a   "Existing familiarity and order of presentation of persuasive
            communications." *Psychological Reports* 15 (November):
            607-610.

Lana, R.E.
    1964b   "The influence of the pretest on order effects in persuasive
            communications." *Journal of Abnormal and Social
            Psychology* 69 (September):337-341.

Lana, R.E.
    1964c   "Three theoretical interpretations of order effects in per-
            suasive communications." *Psychological Bulletin* 61 (April):
            314-320.

Lana, R.E.
    1966   "Inhibitory effects of a pretest on opinion change." *Educa-
            tional and Psychological Measurement* 26 (Spring):139-150.

Lana, R.E. and D.J. King.
    1960   "Learning factors as determiners of pretest sensitization."
            Journal of Applied Psychology 44:189-191.

Lana, R.E. and R.L. Rosnow.
    1963   "Subject awareness and order effects in persuasive communi-
            cations." *Psychological Reports* 12 (April):523-529.

Lana, R.E. and R.L. Rosnow.
    1968   "Effects of pre-test treatment interval on opinion change."
            Reprint: *Psychological Reports* 22.

Larson, R.F. and W.R. Catton, Jr.
    1959   "Can the mail-back bias contribute to a study's validity?"
            American Sociological Review 24:243-245.

Lasagna, L. and J.M. von Felsinger.
    1954   "The volunteer subject in research." *Science* 120:359-361.

Laszlo, J.P. and R. Rosenthal.
  1967 "Subject dogmatism, experimenter status and experimenter expectancy effects." Cambridge, Mass: Harvard University, Department of Social Relations (mimeo).

Lawrence, D.H. and L. Festinger.
  1962 *Deterrents and Reinforcement; The Psychology of Insufficient Reward.* Stanford: Stanford University Press.

Lazarsfeld, P.F., B. Berelson, and Hazel Gaudet.
  1948 *The People's Choice.* New York: Columbia University Press.

Lefkowitz, M., R.R. Blake, and J.S. Mouton.
  1955 "Status factors in pedestrian violation of traffic signals." *Journal of Abnormal and Social Psychology* 51:704-706.

Leik, Robert K.
  1965 "Irrelevant aspects of stooge behavior: implications for leadership studies and experimental methodology." *Sociometry* 28 (September):259-271.

Leipold, W.D. and R.L. James.
  1962 "Characteristics of shows and no-shows in a psychological experiment." *Psychological Reports* 11 (August):171-174.

Leventhal, H. and Patricia Niles.
  1964 "A field experiment on fear arousal with data on the validity of questionnaire measures." *Journal of Personality* 32:459-479.

Levin, S.M.
  1961 "The effects of awareness on verbal conditioning." *Journal of Experimental Psychology* 61:67-75.

Levitt, E.E., B. Lubin, and M. Zuckerman.
  1962 "The effect of incentives on volunteering for an hypnosis experiment." *International Journal of Clinical and Experimental Hypnosis* 10:39-41.

Levitt, E.E., B. Lubin, and J.P. Brady.
  1962 "The effect of the pseudo volunteer on studies of volunteers for psychology experiments." *Journal of Applied Psychology* 46 (February):72-75.

Levitt, E.E., B. Lubin, and M. Zuckerman.
  1959 "Note on the attitude toward hypnosis of volunteers and nonvolunteers for an hypnosis experiment." *Psychological Reports* 5:712.

Levy, L.H.
  1967 "Awareness, learning, and the beneficent subject as expert witness." *Journal of Personality and Social Psychology* 6 (July):365-370.

Levy, L.H.
1969 "Reflections on replications and the experimenter bias effect." *Journal of Consulting and Clinical Psychology* 33 (February):15-17.

Levy, L.H. and T.B. Orr.
1959 "The social psychology of Rorschach validity research." *Journal of Abnormal and Social Psychology* 58 (January): 79-83.

Lewin, K.
1935 *Dynamic Theory of Personality*. New York: McGraw-Hill.

Lichtenstein, E.
1968a "Admission of prior information about deceptive experimental procedures." Unpublished manuscript. University of Oregon.

Lichtenstein, E.
1968b "Please don't talk to anyone about this experiment: disclosure of deception by debriefed subjects." Unpublished manuscript. University of Oregon.

Lichtenstein, E.
1970 "Please don't talk to anyone about this experiment: disclosure of deception by debriefed subjects." *Psychological Reports*, 26:485-486.

Lindzey, Gardner.
1951 "A note on interviewer bias." *Journal of Applied Psychology* 35 (June):182-184.

Lipset, S.M., P.F. Lazarsfeld, A.H. Barton, and J. Linz.
1954 "The psychology of voting: an analysis of political behavior." Pp. 1124-1175 in G. Lindzey (ed.), *Handbook of Social Psychology*, volume 2. Addison-Wesley.

Locke, Edwin A. and J.F. Brugan.
1968 "Goal setting as a determinant of the effect of knowledge of score on performance." *The American Journal of Psychology* 81 (September):398-406.

Locke, H.J.
1954 "Are volunteer interviewees representative?" *Social Problems* 1:143-146.

London, P.
1961 "Subject characteristics in hypnosis research: Part I. A survey of experience, interest, and opinion." *International Journal of Clinical and Experimental Hypnosis* 9:151-161.

London, P., L.M. Cooper, and H.J. Johnson.
1962 "Subject characteristics in hypnosis research. II. Attitudes towards hypnosis, volunteer status, and personality mea-

sures. III. Some correlates of hypnotic susceptibility." *International Journal of Clinical and Experimental Hypnosis* 10:13-21.

London, P. and M. Fuhrer.
1961   "Hypnosis, motivation, and performance." *Journal of Personality* 29 (September):321-333.

Lorge, Irving.
1937   "Gen-like: halo or reality." *Psychological Bulletin* 34 (October):545-546.

Lowin, A. and M.M. Ingraham.
1968   "On lasting effects of deceptions." Reprint: Xerox.

Lowin, A., J.A. Walsh, D.M. Klieger, and B.E. Sandler.
1968   "Are there any lasting effects of deceptive manipulation." Reprint: Xerox.

Lubin, B., J.P. Brady, and E.E. Levitt.
1962   "A comparison of personality characteristics of volunteers and nonvolunteers for hypnosis experiments." *Journal of Clinical Psychology* 18:341-343.

Lubin, B., E.E. Levitt, and M. Zuckerman.
1962   "Some personality differences between responders and nonresponders to a survey questionnaire." *Journal of Consulting Psychology* 26:192.

Luft, T.
1953   "Interaction and projection." *Journal of Projective Techniques* 17:489-492.

Lyons, J.
1964   "On the psychology of the psychological experiment." In C. Scheerer (ed.), *Cognitions: Theory, Research, Promise.* New York: Harper and Row.

McClintock, Charles G.
1969   "Instrumentation in social psychology." *American Psychologist* 24 (March):283-286.

McDavid, J.W.
1965   "Approval-seeking motivation and the volunteer subject." *Journal of Personality and Social Psychology* 2 (July): 115-117.

McFall, R.M.
1965   "Unintentional communication: the effect of congruence and incongruence between subject and experimenter constructions." Unpublished doctoral dissertation, Ohio State University.

McGinnies, E. and Elaine Donelson.
1963   "Knowledge of experimenter's intent and attitude change

under induced compliance." *Department of Psychology,* University of Maryland.

McGuigan, F.J.
  1963 "The experimenter: a neglected stimulus object." *Psychological Bulletin* 60 (July):421-428.

McGuire, W.J.
  1960 "A syllogistic analysis of cognitive relationships." Pp. 65-111 in M.J. Rosenberg and C.I. Hovland (eds.), *Attitude Organization and Attitude Change.* New Haven: Yale University Press.

McGuire, W.J.
  1964 "Inducing resistance to persuasion: some contemporary approaches." Pp. 191-229 in L. Berkowitz (ed.), *Advances in Experimental Social Psychology.* Volume 1. New York: Academic Press.

McGuire, W.J.
  1967 "Some impending reorientations in social psychology: some thoughts provoked by Kenneth Ring." *Journal of Experimental Social Psychology* 3:124-239.

McGuire, W.J.
  1968 "Personality and susceptibility to social influence." In E.F. Borgatta and W.W. Lambert (eds.), *Handbook of Personality Theory and Research.* Chicago: Rand McNally.

Maccoby, Eleanor E.
  1956 "Pitfalls in the analysis of panel data: a research note on some technical aspects of voting." *American Journal of Sociology* 61 (January):359-362.

Mahl, G.F.
  1956 "Disturbances and silences in the patient's speech in psychotherapy." *Journal of Abnormal and Social Psychology* 53:1-15.

Marcia, J.E.
  1961 "Hypothesis-making, need for social approval, and their effects on unconscious experimenter bias." Unpublished master's thesis, Ohio State University.

Marine, E.L.
  1929 "The effect of familiarity with the examiner upon Stanford-Binet test performance." New York: Bureau of Publications, Teachers College, Columbia University.

Marmer, Roberta S.
  1967 "The effects of volunteer status on dissonance reduction." Unpublished master's thesis, Boston University.

Martin, R.M. and F.L. Marcuse.
1957 "Characteristics of volunteers and nonvolunteers for hypnosis." *International Journal of Clinical and Experimental Hypnosis* 5:176-180.

Martin, R.M. and F.L. Marcuse.
1958 "Characteristics of volunteers and nonvolunteers in psychological experimentation." *Journal of Consulting Psychology* 22:475-479.

Marwit, S.J. and J.E. Marcia.
1967 "Tester bias and response to projective instruments." *Journal of Consulting Psychology* 31:253-258.

Masling, Joseph.
1957 "Effects of warm and cold interaction on the interpretation of a projective protocol." *Journal of Projective Techniques* 21 (December):377-383.

Masling, Joseph.
1959 "The effects of warm and cold interaction on the administration and scoring of an intelligence test." *Journal of Consulting Psychology* 23 (August):336-341.

Masling, Joseph.
1960 "The influence of situational and interpersonal variables in projective testing." *Psychological Bulletin* 57 (January): 65-85.

Masling, Joseph.
1965 "Differential indoctrination of examiners and Rorschach responses." *Journal of Consulting Psychology* 29 (June): 198-201.

Masling, Joseph.
1966 "Role-related behavior of the subject and psychologist and its effects upon psychological data." Pp. 67-103 in D. Levine (ed.), *Nebraska Symposium on Motivation*. Lincoln, Nebraska: University of Nebraska Press.

Matarazzo, J.D., G. Saslow, and E.N. Pareis.
1960 "Verbal conditioning of two response classes: some methodological considerations." *Journal of Abnormal and Social Psychology* 61 (September):190-206.

Mausner, Bernard.
1953 "Studies in social interaction: III. Effect of variation in one partner's prestige on the interaction of observer pairs." *Journal of Applied Psychology* 37 (October):391-393.

Mausner, Bernard.
1954 "The effect of prior reinforcement on the interaction of observer pairs." *Journal of Abnormal and Social Psychology* 49:65-68.

Meehl, P.E.
    1965   "The creative individual: why it is hard to identify him." Pp.
            25-34 in G.A. Steiner (ed.), *The Creative Organization*. Chi-
            cago: University of Chicago Press.

Mefferd, Roy B. Jr., Betty A. Wieland, Donald G. Greenstein, and Peter
    K. Leppman.
    1968   "Effects of pretraining and instructions on validity of per-
            ceptual reports by inexperienced observers." *Perceptual and
            Motor Skills* 27 (December):1003-1006.

Merton, R.K.
    1968   *Social Theory and Social Structure*. (Enlarged Edition). New
            York: Free Press.

Milan, J.R.
    1954   "Examiner influences on the Thematic Apperception Test
            stories. *Journal of Projective Techniques* 18 (June):221-226.

Milgram, S.
    1965   "Some conditions of obedience and disobedience to
            authority." *Human Relations* 18:57-76.

Milgram, S., L. Mann, and Susan Harter.
    1965   "The lost-letter technique: a tool of social research." *Public
            Opinion Quarterly* 29:437-438.

Miller, Arthur G. and Henry L. Minton.
    1969   "Machiavellianism, internal-external control, and the viola-
            tions of experimental instructions." *The Psychological
            Record* 19 (July):369-380.

Miller, N.
    1965   "Defaming and agreeing with the communicator as a func-
            tion of communication extremity, emotional arousal, and
            evaluative set." Paper presented at Eastern Psychology Asso-
            ciation.

Miller, Samuel.
    1966   "Psychology experiments without subjects' consent."
            Science 152 (April):15.

Mills, Judson.
    1969   *Experimental Social Psychology*. New York: Macmillan.

Mills, T.M.
    1962   "A sleeper variable in small groups research: the experi-
            menter." *Pacific Sociology Review* 5:21-28.

Milmoe, S., R. Rosenthal, H.T. Blane, M.E. Chafetz, and I. Wolf.
    1967   "The doctor's voice: postdictor of successful referral of alco-
            holic patients." *Journal of Abnormal Psychology* 72:78-84.

Mintz, N.
    1957   "On the psychology of aesthetics and architecture." Un-
            published manuscript, Brandeis University.

Moeller G. and M.H. Applezweig.
1957   "A motivational factor in conformity." *Journal of Abnormal and Social Psychology* 55 (January):114-120.

Morris, C.G.
1966   "Task effects on group interaction." *Journal of Personality and Social Psychology* 4 (November):545-554.

Mosteller, F. and R.R. Bush.
1954   "Selected quantitative techniques." Pp. 289-334 in G. Lindzey (ed.), *Handbook of Social Psychology. Volume 1, Theory and Method.* Cambridge, Mass.: Addison-Wesley.

Neher, A.
1967   "Probability pyramiding, research error, and the need for independent replication." *Psychological Record* 17:257-262.

Newman, M.
1956   "Personality differences between volunteers and non-volunteers for psychological investigations." (Doctoral Dissertation, New York University School of Education) Ann Arbor, Michigan: University Microfilms, No. 19, 999.

Newman, Richard, Jay Katz, and Robert Rubenstein.
1960   "The experimental situation as a determinant of hypnotic dreams." *Psychiatry* 23 (February):63-73.

Ora, J.P., Jr.
1965   "Characteristics of the volunteer for psychological investigations." Technical Report, No. 27, (November) Vanderbilt University, Contract Nonr 2 149 (03).

Ora, J.P., Jr.
1966   "Personality characteristics of college freshman volunteers for psychological experiments." Unpublished master's thesis, Vanderbilt University.

Orne, M.T.
1959a   "The demand characteristics of an experimental design and their implications." Paper read at American Psychological Association, Cincinnati.

Orne, M.T.
1959b   "The nature of hypnosis: artifact and essence." *Journal of Abnormal and Social Psychology* 58 (May):277-299.

Orne, M.T.
1962   "On the social psychology of the psychological experiment: with particular reference to demand characteristics and their implications." *American Psychologist* 17 (November): 776-783.

Orne, M.T.
1969   "Demand characteristics and the concept of quasi-controls."

Pp. 147-179 in Robert Rosenthal and Ralph L. Rosnow (eds.), *Artifact in Behavioral Research.* New York: Academic Press.

Orne, M.T. and F.J. Evans.
1965   "Social control in the psychological experiment: antisocial behavior and hypnosis." *Journal of Personality and Social Psychology* 1 (March):189-200.

Orne, M.T. and F.J. Evans.
1966   "Inadvertent termination of hypnosis on hypnotized and simulating subjects." *International Journal of Clinical and Experimental Hypnosis* 14:61-78.

Orne, M.T. and K.E. Scheibe.
1964   "The contribution of nondeprivation factors in the production of sensory deprivation effects: the psychology of the 'panic button.' " *Journal of Abnormal and Social Psychology* 68:3-13.

Orne, M.T., P.W. Sheehan, and F.J. Evans.
1968   "Occurrence of posthypnotic behavior outside the experimental setting." *Journal of Personality and Social Psychology* 9:189-196.

Page, M.M. and A.R. Lumia.
1968   "Cooperation with demand characteristics and the bimodal distribution of verbal conditioning data." *Psychonomic Science* 12:243-244.

Pan, Ju-Shu.
1951   "Social characteristics of respondents and nonrespondents in a questionnaire study of later maturity." *Journal of Applied Psychology* 35 (April):120-121.

Perlin, S., W. Pollin, and R.N. Butler.
1958   "The experimental subject: I. The psychiatric evaluation and selection of a volunteer population." *American Medical Association Archives of Neurology and Psychiatry* 80:65-70.

Persinger, G.W.
1963   "The effect of acquaintanceship on the mediation of experimenter bias." Unpublished master's thesis, University of North Dakota.

Pflugratn, J.
1962   "Examiner influence in a group testing situation with particular reference to examiner bias." Unpublished master's thesis, University of North Dakota.

Pfungst, O.
1911   *Clever Hans (the horse of Mr. von Osten): A Contribution to Experimental, Animal, and Human Psychology.* (Translated by C.L. Rahn) New York: Holt.

Pierce, A.H.
    1908   "The subconscious again." *Journal of Philosophy, Psychology, and Scientific Methods* 5:264-271.

Pittenger, R.E., C.F. Hockett, and J.J. Danehy.
    1960   *The First Five Minutes: A Sample of Microscopic Interview Analysis.* Ithaca, New York: Paul Martineau.

Pollin, W. and S. Perlin.
    1958   "Psychiatric evaluation of 'normal control' volunteers." *American Journal of Psychiatry* 115:129-133.

Poor, D.
    1967   "The social psychology of questionnaires." Unpublished bachelor's thesis, Harvard University.

Postman, L. and J.M. Sassenrath.
    1961   "The automatic action of verbal rewards and punishments." *Journal of General Psychology* 65:109-136.

Raffetto, A.M.
            "Experimenter effects on subjects' reported hallucinatory experiences under visual and auditory deprivation." San Francisco State College: Reprint.

Reece, M.M. and R.N. Whitman.
    1962   "Expressive movements, warmth, and verbal reinforcement." *Journal of Abnormal and Social Psychology* 64 (March): 234-236.

Reuss, C.F.
    1943   "Differences between persons responding and not responding to a mailed questionnaire." *American Sociological Review* 8 (August): 433-438.

Rice, S.A.
    1929   "Contagious bias in the interview: a methodological note." *American Journal of Sociology* 35 (November):420-423.

Richards, T.W.
    1960   "Personality of subjects who volunteer for research on a drug (mescaline)." *Journal of Projective Techniques* 24 (December):424-428.

Riecken, H.W. (Chairman)
    1954   "Narrowing the gap between field studies and laboratory experiments in social psychology: a statement by the summer seminar." *Items of the Social Science Research Council* 8:37-42.

Riecken, H.W.
    1958   "A program for research on experiments in social psychology." Paper read at Behavioral Sciences Conference, University of Mexico.

Riecken, H.W.
  1962 "A program for research on experiments in social
         psychology." Pp. 25-41 in N.F. Washburne (ed.), *Decisions,
         Values, and Groups.* Volume 2. New York: Pergamon Press.

Riggs, Margaret M. and W. Kaess.
  1955 "Personality differences between volunteers and non-
         volunteers." *Journal of Psychology* 40 (October):229-245.

Ring, K.
  1967 "Experimental social psychology: some sober questions
         about some frivolous values." *Journal of Experimental
         Social Psychology* 3 (April):113-123.

Ringuette, E.L. and T. Kennedy.
  1966 "An experimental study of the double bind hypothesis."
         Journal of Abnormal Psychology 71:136-141.

Robins, Lee N.
  1963 "The reluctant respondent." *Public Opinion Quarterly*
         27:276-286.

Robinson, D. and S. Rohde.
  1946 "Two experiments with an anti-Semitism poll." *Journal of
         Abnormal and Social Psychology* 41 (April):136-144.

Rokeach, M.R., R. Zemach and Gwendolyn Norrell.
  1966 "The pledge to secrecy: a method to assess violations." Un-
         published manuscript, Michigan State University.

Rorer, L.G.
  1965 "The great response-style myth." *Psychological Bulletin*
         63:129-156.

Rosen, Ephraim.
  1951 "Differences between volunteers and non-volunteers for
         psychological studies." *Journal of Applied Psychology* 35
         (June):185-193.

Rosenbaum, M.
  1956 "The effect of stimulus and background factors on the
         volunteering response." *Journal of Abnormal and Social
         Psychology* 53 (July):118-121.

Rosenbaum, M. and R.R. Blake.
  1955 "Volunteering as a function of field structure." *Journal of
         Abnormal and Social Psychology* 50 (March):193-196.

Rosenberg, M.J.
  1956 "Cognitive structure and attitudinal affect." *Journal of Ab-
         normal and Social Psychology* 53:367-372.

Rosenberg, M.J.
  1960 "An analysis of affective-cognitive consistency." Pp. 15-64
         in M.J. Rosenberg, C.I. Hovland, W.J. McGuire, R.P. Abel-

son, and J.W. Brehm (ed.), *Attitude Organization and Change.* New Haven: Yale University Press.

Rosenberg, M.J.
1961 *A Research Program on Consistency and Change in Social Attitudes.* Columbus: Ohio State University.

Rosenberg, M.J.
1963 "Simulated man and the humanistic criticism." Pp. 113-124 in S.S. Tomkins and S.J. Messick (eds.), *Computer Simulation of Personality.* New York: John Wiley and Sons, Inc.

Rosenberg, M.J.
1965 "When dissonance fails: on eliminating evaluation apprehension from attitude measurement." *Journal of Personality and Social Psychology* 1 (January):28-42.

Rosenberg, M.J.
1966 "Some limits of dissonance: toward a differential view of counterattitudinal performance." Pp. 135-170 in S. Feldman (ed.), *Cognitive Consistency: Motivational Antecedents and Behavioral Consequents.* New York: Academic Press.

Rosenberg, M.J.
1969 "The conditions and consequences of evaluation apprehension." Pp. 280-349 in Robert Rosenthal and Ralph L. Rosnow (eds.), *Artifact in Behavioral Research.* New York: Academic Press.

Rosenberg, Morris.
1968 *The Logic of Survey Analysis.* New York: Basic Books.

Rosenblatt, P.C. and J.M. Hicks.
1966 "Pretesting, forewarning, and persuasion." Read at the 38th annual meeting of the Midwestern Psychology Association.

Rosenfield, Howard M. and Donald M. Baer.
1969 "Unnoticed verbal conditioning of an aware experimenter by a more aware subject; the double agent effect." *Psychological Review* 76 (July):425-432.

Rosenhan, D.
1967 "On the social psychology of hypnosis research." Pp. 481-510 in J.E. Gordon (ed.), *Handbook of Clinical and Experimental Hypnosis.* New York: MacMillan.

Rosenthal, D. and J.O. Frank.
1956 "Psychotherapy and the placebo effect." *Psychological Bulletin* 53:294-302.

Rosenthal, R.
1958a "Note on the fallible E." *Psychological Reports* 4 (December):662.

Rosenthal, R.
  1958b "Projection, excitement, and unconscious experimenter bias." *American Psychologist* 13:345-346 (Abstract).

Rosenthal, R.
  1961   "On the social psychology of the psychological experiment: with particular reference to experimenter bias." Paper read at the American Psychological Association, New York.

Rosenthal, R.
  1963a "Experimenter attributes as determinants of subjects' responses." *Journal of Projective Techniques and Personality Assessment* 27 (September):324-331.

Rosenthal, R.
  1963b "Experimenter modeling effects as determinants of subject's responses." *Journal of Projective Techniques and Personality Assessment* 27 (December):467-471.

Rosenthal, R.
  1963c "On the social psychology of the psychological experiment: the experimenter's hypothesis as unintended determinant of experimental results." *American Scientist* 51 (June): 268-283.

Rosenthal, R.
  1964a "Experimenter outcome-orientation and the results of the psychological experiment." *Psychological Bulletin* 61:405-412.

Rosenthal, R.
  1964b "The effect of the experimenter on the results of psychological research." Pp. 79-114 in B.A. Maher (ed.), *Progress in Experimental Personality Research.* Volume 1. New York: Academic Press.

Rosenthal, R.
  1965   "The volunteer subject." *Human Relations* 18 (November): 389-406.

Rosenthal, R.
  1966   *Experimenter Effects in Behavioral Research.* New York: Appleton-Century-Crofts.

Rosenthal, R.
  1967a "Covert communication in the psychological experiment." *Psychological Bulletin* 67:356-367.

Rosenthal, R.
  1967b "The eternal triangle: investigators, data, and the hypotheses called null." Harvard University, Department of Social Relations.

Rosenthal, R.
  1967c "Psychology of the scientist: XXIII. Experimenter expec-

tancy, experimenter experience, and Pascal's Wager."
Psychological Reports 20:619-622.

Rosenthal, R.
1968   "Experimenter expectancy and the reassuring nature of the
        null hypothesis decision procedure." *Psychological Bulletin*
        70 (December):30-47.

Rosenthal, R.
1969a   "Interpersonal expectations: effects of the experimenter's
        hypothesis." Pp. 182-277 in Robert Rosenthal and Ralph L.
        Rosnow (eds.), *Artifact in Behavioral Research*. New York:
        Academic Press.

Rosenthal, R.
1969b   "On not so replicated experiments and not so null results."
        Journal of Consulting and Clinical Psychology 33:7-10.

Rosenthal, Robert
1969c   "Unintended effects of the clinician in clinical interaction: a
        taxonomy and a review of clinician expectancy effects."
        Australian Journal of Psychology 21 (April):1-20.

Rosenthal, Robert and K.L. Fode.
1963a   "The effect of experimenter bias on the performance of the
        albino rat." *Behavioral Science* 8:183-189.

Rosenthal, R. and K.L. Fode.
1963b   "Psychology of the scientist: V. Three experiments in ex-
        perimenter bias." *Psychological Reports* 12 (April):491-511.

Rosenthal, R., K.L. Fode, C.J. Friedman and L. Vikan-Kline.
1960   "Subjects' perception of their experimenter under condi-
        tions of experimenter bias." *Perceptual and Motor Skills* 11
        (December):325-331.

Rosenthal, R., K.L. Fode, L. Vikan-Kline, and G.W. Persinger.
1964   "Verbal conditioning: mediator of experimenter expectancy
        effects." *Psychological Reports* 14 (February):71-74.

Rosenthal, R., C.J. Friedman, C.A. Johnson, K.L. Fode, T.R. Schill,
C.R. White, and L. Vikan-Kline.
1964   "Variables affecting experimenter bias in a group situation."
        Genetic Psychology Monographs 70 (November):271-296.

Rosenthal, R., N. Friedman, and D. Kurland.
1966   "The instruction reading behavior of the experimenter as an
        unintended determinant of experimental results." *Journal of
        Experimental Research and Personality* 1:221-226.

Rosenthal, R. and J. Gaito.
1963   "The interpretation of levels of significance by psychological
        researchers." *Journal of Psychology* 55 (January):33-38.

Rosenthal, R. and J. Gaito.
1964   "Further evidence for the cliff effect in the interpretation of
        levels of significance." *Psychological Reports* 15:570.

Rosenthal, R. and E.S. Halas
1962   "Experimenter effect in the study of invertebrate behavior."
        Psychological Reports 11 (August):251-256.

Rosenthal, R. and L. Jacobson.
1966   "Teachers' expectancies: determinants of pupils' I.Q. gains."
        Psychological Reports 19:115-118.

Rosenthal, R. and L. Jacobson.
1968   *Pygmalion in the Classroom: Teacher Expectation and
        Pupils' Intellectual Development.* New York: Holt, Rinehart
        and Winston.

Rosenthal, R., P. Kohn, P.M. Greenfield, and N. Carota.
1965   "Psychology of the scientist: XIV. Experimenters'
        hypothesis-confirmation and mood as determinants of
        experimental results." *Perceptual and Motor Skills* 20
        (June):1237-1252.

Rosenthal, R., P. Kohn, Patricia M. Greenfield and N. Carota.
1966   "Data desirability, experimenter expectancy, and the results
        of psychological research." *Journal of Personality and Social
        Psychology* 3 (January):20-27.

Rosenthal, R. and R. Lawson.
1964   "A longitudinal study of the effects of experimenter bias on
        the operant learning of laboratory rats." *Journal of Psychi-
        atric Research* 2 (June):61-72.

Rosenthal, R. and G.W. Persinger.
1962   "Let's pretend: subjects' perception of imaginary experi-
        menters." *Perceptual and Motor Skills* 14 (June):407-409.

Rosenthal, R. and G.W. Persinger.
1968   "Subjects' prior experimental experience and experimenters'
        outcome consciousness as modifiers of experimenter expec-
        tancy effects." Unpublished manuscript, Harvard University.

Rosenthal, R., G.W. Persinger, L. Vikan-Kline, and K.L. Fode.
1963a   "The effect of early data returns on data subsequently ob-
        tained by outcome-biased experimenters." *Sociometry*
        26:487-498.

Rosenthal, R., G.W. Persinger, L. Vikan-Kline, and K.L. Fode.
1963b   "The effect of experimenter outcome-bias and subject set on
        awareness in verbal conditioning experiments." *Journal of
        Verbal Learning and Verbal Behavior* 2 (September):
        275-283.

Rosenthal, R., G.W. Persinger, R.C. Mulry, L. Vikan-Kline, and M. Grothe.
1964a "Emphasis on experimental procedure, sex of subjects, and the biasing effects of experimental hypotheses." *Journal of Projective Techniques and Personality Assessment* 28 (December):470-473.

Rosenthal, R., G.W. Persinger, R.C. Mulry, L. Vikan-Kline, and M. Grothe.
1964b "Changes in experimental hypotheses as determinants of experimental results." *Journal of Projective Techniques and Personality Assessment* 28:465-469.

Rosenthal, R., G.W. Persinger, L. Vikan-Kline, and R.C. Mulry.
1963 "The role of the research assistant in the mediation of experimenter bias." *Journal of Personality* 31 (September): 313-335.

Rosnow, R.L. and R. Rosenthal.
1966 "Volunteer subjects and the results of opinion change studies." *Psychological Reports* 19 (December):1183-1187.

Ross, S., A.D. Krugman, S.B. Lyerly, and D.J. Clyde.
1962 "Drugs and placebos: a model design." *Psychological Reports* 10:383-392.

Roth, J.A.
1966 "Hired hand research." *American Sociologist* 1:190-196.

Rubin, Dorothy.
1969 "Halo effect in individual response to an attitude questionnaire." *Perceptual and Motor Skills* 28 (February):258.

Rule, Brendan Gail, and Mark L. Sandilands.
1969 "Test anxiety, confidence, commitment, and conformity." *Journal of Personality* 37 (September):460-467.

Sachs, E.L.
1952 "Intelligence scores as a function of experimentally established social relationships between child and examiner." *Journal of Abnormal and Social Psychology* 47 (April): 354-358.

Sales, S.M.
1966 "Supervisory style and productivity: review and theory." *Personnel Psychology* 19:281-282.

Sampson, E.E., and L.B. Sibley.
1965 "A further examination of the confirmation or nonconfirmation of expectancies and desires." *Journal of Personality and Social Psychology* 2 (July):133-137.

Sanders, R. and S.E. Cleveland.
1953 "The relationship between certain examiner personality

variables and subjects' Rorschach scores." *Journal of Projective Techniques* 17 (March):34-50.

Sapolsky, A.
1960   "Effect of interpersonal relationships upon verbal conditioning." *Journal of Abnormal and Social Psychology* 60 (March):241-246.

Sarason, I.G.
1958   "Interrelationships among individual difference variables, behavior in psychotherapy, and verbal conditioning." *Journal of Abnormal and Social Psychology* 56 (May):339-344.

Sarason, I.G.
1962   "Individual differences, situational variables, and personality research." *Journal of Abnormal and Social Psychology* 65 (December):376-380.

Sarason, I.G.
1965   "The human reinforcer in verbal behavior research." Pp. 231-243 in L. Krasner and L.P. Ullmann (eds.), *Research in Behavior Modifications: New Developments and Implications,* New York: Holt, Rinehart and Winston.

Sarason, I.G. and M.G. Harmatz.
1965   "Test anxiety and experimental conditions." *Journal of Personality and Social Psychology* 1 (May):499-505.

Sarason, I.G. and J.M. Minard.
1963   "Interrelationships among subject, experimenter, and situational variables." *Journal of Abnormal and Social Psychology* 67 (July):87-91.

Sarason, I.G. and G.H. Winkel.
1966   "Individual differences among subjects and experimenters and subject's self-descriptions." *Journal of Personality and Social Psychology* 3 (April):448-457.

Sarason, S.B.
1951   "The psychologist's behavior as an area of research." *Journal of Consulting Psychology* 15 (August):278-280.

Sarbin, T.R.
1950   "Contributions to role-taking theory: I. Hypnotic behavior." *Psychological Review* 57:255-270.

Schachter, S.
1959   *The Psychology of affiliation.* Stanford: Stanford University Press.

Schachter, S. and J.E. Singer.
1962   "Cognitive, social and physiological determinants of emotional state." *Psychological Review* 69:379-399.

Scheflen, A.E.
1964 "The significance of posture in communication systems." *Psychiatry* 27:316-331.

Scheier, I.H.
1959 "To be or not to be a guinea pig: preliminary data on anxiety and the volunteer for experiment." *Psychological Reports* 5 (June):239-240.

Schein, E.H. and W.G. Bennis.
1965 *Personal and Organizational Change Through Group Methods: The Laboratory Approach.* New York: Wiley.

Schubert, D.S.P.
1960 "Volunteering as arousal seeking." Read at American Psychological Association.

Schubert, D.P.
1964 "Arousal seeking as a motivation for volunteering: MMPI scores and central nervous system stimulant use as suggestive of a trait." *Journal of Projective Techniques and Personality Assessment* 28 (September):337-340.

Schulman, Gary I.
1967 "Asch conformity studies: conformity to the experimenter and/or to the group?" *Sociometry* 30(1):26-40.

Schulman, Gary and William Freed.
1970 "The effect of evaluation apprehension and the pretest lie on the verdicability of post-experimental interviews." In progress.

Schulman, Gary I. and W. Freed.
Personal communication. Paper in preparation.

Schultz, D.P.
1967a "Birth order of volunteers for sensory restriction research." *Journal of Social Psychology* 73:71-73.

Schultz, D.P.
1967b "Sensation-seeking and volunteering for sensory deprivation." Paper read at Eastern Psychological Association (April):Boston.

Schultz, D.P.
1967c "The volunteer subject in sensory restriction research." *Journal of Social Psychology* 72:123-124.

Schultz, D.P.
1969 "The human subject in psychological research." *Psychological Bulletin* 72:214-228.

Scott, W.A.
1957 "Attitude change through reward of verbal behavior." *Journal of Abnormal and Social Psychology* 55:72-75.

Scott, W.A.
    1959   "Attitude change by response reinforcement: replication and
            extension." *Sociometry* 22:328-335.

Secord, P.E.
    1968   "On the meaning of the laboratory experiment and its rele-
            vance to human action: a preliminary statement." Reprint:
            ditto.

Segail, M.H., D.T. Campbell, and M.J. Herskovits.
    1966   *The Influence of Culture on Visual Perception.* Indianapolis:
            Bobbs-Merrill.

Severin, F.T. (ed.)
    1965   *Humanistic Viewpoints in Psychology; A Book of Readings.*
            New York: McGraw-Hill.

Sgan, M.L.
    1967   "Social reinforcement, socioeconomic status, and suscepti-
            bility to experimenter influence." *Journal of Personality and
            Social Psychology* 5 (February):202-210.

Shames, M.L. and J.G. Adair.
    1967   "Experimenter-bias as a function of the type and structure
            of the task." Paper presented at the meeting of the Canadian
            Psychological Association (May), Ottawa.

Shapiro, J.L.
    1966   "The effects of sex, instructional set, and the problem of
            awareness in a verbal conditioning paradigm." Unpublished
            master's thesis, Northwestern University.

Sheehan, Peter.
    1969   "E-expectancy and the role of awareness in verbal condi-
            tioning." *Psychological Reports* 24 (February):203-206.

Shepard, H.A.
    1964   "Explorations in observant participation." Pp. 379-394 in
            L.P. Bradford, J.R. Gibb, and K.D. Beane (eds.), *T-group
            Theory and Laboratory Method: Innovation in Re-
            education.* New York: John Wiley and Sons, Inc.

Sherif, M., O.J. Harvey, B.J. White, W.R. Hood, and Carolyn W. Sherif.
    1961   *Intergroup Conflict and Cooperation: The Robbers Cave Ex-
            periment.* Norman, Oklahoma: University Book Exchange,
            Institute of Group Relations.

Sherif, M., and Carolyn W. Sherif.
    1953   *Groups in Harmony and Tension: An Integration of Studies
            on Intergroup Relations.* New York: Harper.

Sherif, Carolyn W., M. Sherif, and R.E. Nebergall.
    1965   *Attitude and Attitude Change: The Social Judgment-
            Involvement Approach.* Philadelphia: Saunders.

Sherman, S.R.
   1967 "Demand characteristics in an experiment on attitude
         change." *Sociometry* 30 (September):246-261.

Shor, R.E.
   1959 "Explorations in hypnosis: a theoretical and experimental
         study." Unpublished doctoral dissertation, Brandeis Univer-
         sity.

Shrinkman, P.G. and C.L. Kornblith.
   1965 "Comment on observer bias in classical conditioning of the
         planarian." *Psychological Reports* 16 (February):56.

Siegman, Aron W.
   1956 "Responses to a personality questionnaire by volunteers and
         nonvolunteers to a Kinsey interview." *Journal of Abnormal
         and Social Psychology* 52 (March):280-281.

Sigall, Harold and Elliot Aronson.
   1969 "Liking for an evaluator as a function of her physical attrac-
         tiveness and nature of the evaluations." *Journal of Experi-
         mental Social Psychology* 5 (January):93-100.

Sigall, H., E. Aronson, and T. Van Hoose.
   1968 "The cooperative subject: myth or reality?" Department of
         Psychology, University of Texas.

Silverman, Irwin, Arthur D. Shulman, and David Wiesenthal.
   1970 "Effects of deceiving and debriefing psychological subjects
         on performance in experiments." *Journal of Personality and
         Social Psychology* 14:203-212.

Silverman, Irwin.
   1964a "In defense of dissonance theory: reply to Chapanis and
         Chapanis." *Psychological Bulletin* 62 (September):205-209.

Silverman, I.
   1964b "Note on the relationship of self-esteem to subject self-
         selection." *Perceptual and Motor Skills* 19 (December):
         769-770.

Silverman, I.
   1966 "The effects of experimenter outcome expectancy on
         latency of word association." Paper presented at the meeting
         of the Eastern Psychological Association (April):New York.

Silverman, I.
   1968 "Role-related behavior of subjects in laboratory studies of
         attitude change." *Journal of Personality and Social
         Psychology* 8 (April):343-348.

Silverman, I. and C. Marcantonio.
   1965 "Demand characteristics versus dissonance reduction as
         determinants of failure-seeking behavior." *Journal of
         Personality and Social Psychology* 2 (December):882-884.

Silverman, I. and C.R. Regula.
  1968   "Evaluation apprehension, demand characteristics, and the
          effects of distraction on personality." *Journal of Social
          Psychology* 75 (August):273-281.

Silverman, Irwin and Arthur D. Shulman.
  1970   "A conceptual model of artifact in attitude change studies."
          Sociometry 33 (March):97-107.

Simon, Herbert A.
  1957   *Models of Man.* New York: Wiley.

Sjoberg, L.
  1968   "When can the subject be trusted not to think?" *The Scan-
          dinavian Journal of Psychology* 9 (4):274-276.

Smart, Reginald G.
  1966   "Subject selection bias in psychological research." *Canadian
          Psychologist* 72 (April):115-121.

Smith, H.L. and H.H. Hyman.
  1950   "The biasing effect of interviewer expectations on survey
          results." *Public Opinion Quarterly* 14 (Fall):491-506.

Snow, Richard E.
  1969   "Unfinished pygmalion." *Contemporary Psychology* 14
          (April):197-199.

Sommer, R. and H. Ross.
  1958   "Social interaction in a geriatrics ward." *International Jour-
          nal of Social Psychiatry* 4:128-133.

Soskin, W.F. and Vera P. John.
  1963   "The study of spontaneous talk." Pp. 228-281 in R.G.
          Barker (ed.), *The Stream of Behavior.* New York: Appleton-
          Century-Crofts.

Spence, K.W.
  1964   "Anxiety (drive) level and performance in eyelid condi-
          tioning." *Psychological Bulletin* 61:129-139.

Spielberger, C.D.
  1962   "The role of awareness in verbal conditioning." Pp. 71-101
          in C.W. Eriksen (ed.), *Behavior and Awareness—A Sympo-
          sium of Research and Interpretation.* Durham, N.C.: Duke
          University Press.

Spielberger, C.D.
  1965   "Theoretical and epistemological issues in verbal condi-
          tioning." Pp. 149-200 in S. Rosenberg (ed.), *Directions in
          Psycholinguistics.* New York: Macmillan.

Spielberger, C.D., A. Berger and K. Howard.
  1963   "Conditioning of verbal behavior as a function of awareness,
          need for social approval, and motivation to receive re-

inforcement." *Journal of Abnormal and Social Psychology* 67 (September):241-246.

Spielberger, C.D., and S.M. Levin.
  1962   "What is learned in verbal conditioning?" *Journal of Verbal Learning and Verbal Behavior* 1:125-132.

Stanton, Frank.
  1939   "Notes on the validity of mail questionnaire returns." *Journal of Applied Psychology* 23 (February):95-104.

Staples, F.R. and R.H. Walters.
  1961   "Anxiety, birth order, and susceptibility to social influence." *Journal of Abnormal and Social Psychology* 62 (May):716-719.

Stare, F., J. Brown, and M.T. Orne.
  1959   "Demand characteristics in sensory deprivation studies." Unpublished seminar paper, Massachusetts Mental Health Center and Harvard University.

Stephens, J.M.
  1936   "The perception of small differences as affected by self-interest." *American Journal of Psychology* 48 (July): 480-484.

Stevenson, H.W.
  1961   "Social reinforcement with children as a function of CA, sex of E, and sex of S." *Journal of Abnormal and Social Psychology* 63 (July):147-154.

Stevenson, H.W.
  1965   "Social reinforcements of children's behavior." Pp. 97-126 in L.P. Lipsett and C.C. Spiker (eds.), *Advances in Child Development and Behavior.* Volume 2. New York: Academic Press.

Stevenson, Harold W. and Sara Allen.
  1964   "Adult performance as a function of sex of experimenter and sex of subject." *Journal of Abnormal and Social Psychology* 68 (February):214-216.

Stoke, S.M. and E.D. West.
  1931   "Sex differences in conversational interests." *Journal of Social Psychology* 2 (February):120-126.

Stollak, G.E.
  1967   "Obedience and deception research." *American Psychologist* 22:678.

Straits, Bruce C. and Paul L. Wuebben.
  1971   "The campus as a data bank: college students' reactions to social scientific experimentation; research implications." Final grant report, Office of Education, Bureau of Research,

U.S. Department of Health, Education, and Welfare. Grant No. OEG-9-70-0011 (057).

Straits, Bruce C., and Paul L. Wuebben.
1973 "College students' reactions to social scientific experimentation." *Sociological Methods and Research* 1:355-386.

Straits, Bruce C., Paul L. Wuebben, and Theophile J. Majka.
1972 "Influences on subjects' perceptions of experimental research situations." *Sociometry* 35 (December):499-518.

Stricker, L.J.
1967 "The true deceiver." *Psychological Bulletin* 68 (July):13-20.

Stricker, L.J., S. Messick, and D.N. Jackson.
1966 "Suspicion of deception in a conformity study." Reprint: mimeo.

Strupp, H.H.
1959 "Toward an analysis of the therapist's contribution to the treatment process." *American Psychologist* 14:336.

Suedfeld, P.
1964 "Birth order of volunteers for sensory deprivation." *Journal of Abnormal and Social Psychology* 68 (February):195-196.

Suchman, E. and B. McCandless.
1940 "Who answers questionnaires?" *Journal of Applied Psychology* 24 (December):758-769.

Symposium.
1947 "Survey on problems of interviewer cheating." *International Journal of Opinion and Attitude Research* 1:93-106.

Taffel, C.
1955 "Anxiety and the conditioning of verbal behavior." *Journal of Abnormal and Social Psychology* 51 (November): 496-501.

Taylor, J.A.
1953 "A personality scale of manifest anxiety." *Journal of Abnormal and Social Psychology* 48:285-290.

Temerlin, M.K.
1963 "On choice and responsibility in a humanistic psychotherapy." *Journal of Humanistic Psychology* 3:35-48.

Thalhofer, Nancy N.
1969 "Experimenter bias in reporting opinion statements." *Psychological Reports* 24 (April):470.

Thibaut, J.W. and H.H. Kelley.
1959 *The Social Psychology of Groups.* New York: Wiley.

Thomas, W.I. and F. Znaniecki.
1918 *The Polish Peasant in Europe and America.* New York: Dover Publications.

Thorndike, E.L.
1932 *The Fundamentals of Learning.* New York: Teachers College, Columbia University.

Tiffany, D.W., J.R. Cowan, and E. Blinn.
1968 "The sample and personality biases of volunteer subjects." Reprint: mimeo.

Timaeus, Ernst, and Helmut E. Lueck.
1968 "Experimenter expectancy and social facilitation: II. Strooptest performance under the condition of audience." *Perceptual and Motor Skills* 27 (October):492-494.

Troffer, S.A. and C.T. Tart.
1964 "Experimenter bias in hypnotist performance." *Science* 145 (September):1330-1331.

Turner, G.C. and J.C. Coleman.
1962 "Examiner influence on Thematic Apperception Test responses." *Journal of Projective Techniques* 26 (December): 478-486.

Ude, Luahna and Roger E. Vogler.
1969 "Internal versus external control of reinforcement and awareness in a conditioning task." *The Journal of Psychology* 73 (September):63-67.

Verplanck, W.S.
1962 "Unaware of where's awareness. Some verbal operants—notates, monents, and notants." Pp. 130-158 in C.W. Eriksen (ed.), *Behavior and Awareness—A Symposium of Research and Interpretation.* Durham, N.C.: Duke University Press.

von Neumann, J.
1958 *The Computer and the Brain.* New Haven: Yale University Press.

Wallach, M.A., N. Kogan and D.J. Bem.
1964 "Diffusion of responsibility and level of risk taking in groups." *Journal of Abnormal and Social Psychology* 68:263-274.

Wallach, M.S. and H.H. Strupp.
1960 "Psychotherapists' clinical judgments and attitudes towards patients." *Journal of Consulting Psychology* 24 (August): 316-323.

Wallin, Paul.
1949 "Volunteer subjects as a source of sampling bias." *American Journal of Sociology* 54 (May):539-544.

Walster, Elaine.
1964 "The temporal sequence of post-decision processes." Pp. 112-128 in L. Festinger (ed.), *Conflict, Decision, and Dissonance.* Stanford, California: Stanford University Press.

Walster, E., E. Berscheid, D. Abrahams, and V. Aronson.
  1967 "Effectiveness of debriefing following deception experiments." *Journal of Personality and Social Psychology* 6 (August):371-380.

Ward, Charles D.
  1964 "A further examination of birth order as a selective factor among volunteer subjects." *Journal of Abnormal and Social Psychology* 69 (September):311-313.

Wartneberg-Ekren, U.
  1962 "The effect of experimenter knowledge of a subject's scholastic standing on the performance of a reasoning task." Unpublished master's thesis, Marquette University.

Watson, Goodwin B.
  1966 *Social Psychology: Issues and Insights.* Philadelphia: Lippincott.

Webb, E.J., D.T. Campbell, R.D. Schwartz, and L. Sechrest.
  1966 *Unobtrusive Measures: Nonreactive Research in the Social Sciences.* Chicago: Rand McNally and Company.

Webster, Murray Jr.
  1969 "Source of evaluations and expectations for performance." *Sociometry* 32 (September):243-258.

Wieck, K.E.
  1964 "Reduction of cognitive dissonance through task enhancement and effort expenditure." *Journal of Abnormal and Social Psychology* 68:533-539.

Weick, K.E.
  1965 "Laboratory experimentation with organizations." Pp. 194-260 in J. March (ed.), *Handbook of Organizations.* Chicago: Rand McNally and Company.

Weick, K.E.
  1966a "Systematic observational methods." In G. Lindzey and E. Aronson (eds.), *Handbook of Social Psychology.* (Revised Edition) Reading, Massachusetts: Addison-Wesley.

Weick, K.E.
  1966b "Task acceptance dilemmas: a site for research on cognition." In S. Feldman (ed.), *Studies of Cognitive Interaction.* New York: Academic.

Weick, K.E.
  1967 "Promise and limitations of laboratory experiments in the development of attitude change theory." Pp. 51-75 in Muzafer Sherif and Carolyn W. Sherif (eds.), *Attitude, Ego-Involvement, and Change.* New York: John Wiley and Sons.

Weiss, L.R.
  1969 "Effects of subject, experimenter, and task variables on com-

pliance with the experimenter's expectation." *Journal of Projective Techniques and Personality Assessment* 33 (June): 247-256.

Wessler, R.L.
1968 "Experimenter expectancy effects in psychomotor performance." *Perceptual and Motor Skills* 26:911-917.

Wessler, R.L. and M.E. Strauss.
1968 "Experimenter expectancy: a failure to replicate." *Psychological Reports* 22:687-688.

White, C.R.
1962 "The effect of induced subject expectations on the experimenter bias situation." Unpublished doctoral dissertation, University of North Dakota.

White, H.A. and D.A. Schumsky.
1972 "Prior information and 'awareness' in verbal conditioning." *Journal of Personality and Social Psychology* 24:162-165.

Whittaker, J.O.
1964 "Parameters of social influence in the autokinetic situation." *Sociometry* 27:88-95.

Wickes, T.A. Jr.
1956 "Examiner influence in a testing situation." *Journal of Consulting Psychology* 20 (February):23-26.

Williams, F. and H. Cantril.
1945 "The use of interviewer rapport as a method of detecting differences between 'public' and 'private' opinion." *Journal of Social Psychology* 22 (November):171-175.

Williams, J. Allen Jr.
1964 "Interviewer-respondent interaction: a study of bias in the information interview." *Sociometry* 27 (September): 338-352.

Williams, J. Allen Jr.
1968 "Interviewer role performance: a further note on bias in the information interview." *Public Opinion Quarterly* 32 (Summer):287-294.

Williams, J.H.
1964 "Conditioning of verbalization: a review." *Psychological Bulletin* 62:383-393.

Wilson, P.R. and J. Patterson.
1965 "Sex differences in volunteering behavior." *Psychological Reports* 16 (June):976.

Winkel, Gary H. and I.G. Sarason.
1964 "Subject, experimenter, and situational variables in research on anxiety." *Journal of Abnormal and Social Psychology* 68 (June):601-608.

Wohlford, Paul and Grad L. Flick.
  1969 "Sex-of-the-rater bias in clinical diagnosis of organic brain damage using the Bender-Gestalt and memory-for-designs tests." *Perceptual and Motor Skills* 29 (August):107-114.

Wolf, A. and J.H. Weiss.
  1965 "Birth order, recruitment conditions, and volunteering preference." *Journal of Personality and Social Psychology* 2 (August):269-273.

Wolfgang, Aaron.
  1967 "Sex differences in abstract ability of volunteers and non-volunteers for concept learning experiments." *Psychological Reports* 21 (October):509-512.

Wolfle, D.
  1960 "Research with human subjects." *Science* 132 (October): 989.

Wrightsman, Lawrence S.
  1966 "Predicting college students' participation in required psychology experiments." *American Psychologist* 21 (August):812-813.

Wuebben, P.L.
  1967 "Honesty of subjects and birth order." *Journal of Personality and Social Psychology* 5 (March):350-352.

Wuebben, P.L.
  1968 "Experimental design, measurement, and human subjects: a neglected problem of control." *Sociometry* 31 (March): 89-101.

Wuebben, P.L.
  1969 "The social context of experiments: subjects' 'illicit' post-experimental communications; methodological implications." Paper presented at the Annual Meeting of the Pacific Sociological Association held in Seattle.

Wuebben, P.L., B.C. Straits, and A. Crowle.
         "Confession of prior knowledge of deceptive experimental procedures as a function of evaluation apprehension and commitment." Paper in preparation.

Wyatt, D.F. and D.T. Campbell.
  1950 "A study of interviewer bias as related to the interviewers' expectations and own opinions." *International Journal of Opinion and Attitude Research* 4:77-83.

Young, Robert K.
  1959 "Digit span as a function of the personality of the experimenter." *American Psychologist* 14 (July):375.

Zajonc, R.B.
  1965 "Social facilitation." *Science* 149:269-274.

Zamansky, H.S. and R.F. Brightbill.
  1965 "Attitude differences of volunteers and nonvolunteers and of susceptible and nonsusceptible hypnotic subjects." *International Journal of Clinical and Experimental Hypnosis* 13:279-290.

Zegers, R.A.
  1968 "Expectancy and the effects of confirmation and disconfirmation." *Journal of Personality and Social Psychology* 9:67-71.

Zimbardo, P.G.
  1959 "Involvement and communication discrepancy as determinants of opinion change." Unpublished doctoral dissertation, Yale University.

Zimmer, Herbert.
  1956 "Validity of extrapolating nonresponse bias from mail questionnaire follow-ups." *Journal of Applied Psychology* 40 (April):117-121.

Zoble, Edward J.
  1968 "Interaction of subject and experimenter expectancy effects in a tone length discrimination task." Unpublished AB thesis, Franklin and Marshall College.

Zoble, Edward J. and Richard S. Lehman.
  1969 "Interaction of subject experimenter expectancy effects in a tone length discrimination task." *Behavioral Science* 14 (September):357-363.

Zuckerman, M., D.P. Schultz and T.R. Hopkins.
  1967 "Sensation seeking and volunteering for sensory deprivation and hypnosis experiments." *Journal of Consulting Psychology* 31 (August):358-363.

References

Chapter 3, "Reconciling Conflicting Results Derived from Experimental and Survey Studies of Attitude Change," Carl I. Hovland.

Berelson, B.R., Lazarsfeld, P.F., and McPhee, W.N. *Voting: A Study of Opinion Formation in a Presidential Campaign.* Chicago: Univer. Chicago Press, 1954.

Cooper, Eunice, and Jahoda, Marie. "The evasion of propaganda: How prejudiced people respond to anti-prejudice propaganda." *J. Psychol.,* 1947, 23, 15-25.

Doob, L.W. *Public opinion and propaganda.* New York: Holt, 1948.

French, J.R.P., Jr. "A formal theory of social power." *Psychol. Rev.,* 1956, 63, 181-194.

Goldberg, S.C. "Three situational determinants of conformity to social norms." *J. Abnorm. Soc. Psychol.,* 1954, 49, 325-329.

Gosnell, H.F. *Getting Out the Vote: An Experiment in the Stimulation of Voting.* Chicago: Univer. Chicago Press, 1927.

Hovland, C.I. "Effects of the mass media of communication." In G. Lindzey (Ed.), *Handbook of Social Psychology.* Vol. II. *Special Fields and Applications.* Cambridge, Mass.: Addison-Wesley, 1954. Pp. 1062-1103.

Hovland, C.I., Harvey, O.J., and Sherif, M. "Assimilation and contrast effects in reactions to communication and attitude change." *J. Abnorm. Soc. Psychol.,* 1957, 55, 244-252.

Hovland, C.I., Janis, I.L., and Kelley, H.H. *Communication and persuasion.* New Haven: Yale Univer. Press, 1953.

Hovland, C.I., Lumsdaine, A.A., and Sheffield, F.D. *Experiments on Mass Communications.* Princeton: Princeton Univer. Press, 1949.

Hovland, C.I., Mandell, W., Campbell, Enid H., Brock, T., Luchins, A.S., Cohen, A.R., McGuire, W.J., Janis, I.L., Feierabend, Rosalind, L., and Anderson, N.H. *The Order of Presentation in Persuasion.* New Haven: Yale Univer. Press, 1957.

Hovland, C.I., and Pritzker, H.A. "Extent of opinion change as a function of amount of change advocated." *J. Abnorm. Soc. Psychol.,* 1957, 54, 257-261.

Hovland, C.I., and Weiss, W. "The influence of source credibility on communication effectiveness." *Publ. Opin. Quart.,* 1951, 15, 635-650.

Janis, I.L., Hovland, C.I., Field, P.B., Linton, Harriett, Graham, Elaine, Cohen, A.R., Rife, D., Abelson, R.P., Lesser, R.S., and King, B.T. *Personality and Persuasibility.* New Haven: Yale Univer. Press, 1959.

Katz, E., and Lazarsfeld, P.F. *Personal Influence.* Glencoe, Ill.: Free Press, 1955.

Kelman, H.C., and Hovland, C.I. "Reinstatement of the communicator in delayed measurement of opinion change." *J. Abnorm. Soc. Psychol.,* 1953, 48, 327-335.

Kendall, Patricia L., and Lazarsfeld, P.F. "Problems of survey analysis." In R.K. Merton and P.F. Lazarsfeld (Eds.), *Continuities in Social Research: Studies in the Scope and Method of "The American Soldier."* Glencoe, Ill.: Free press, 1950. Pp. 133-196.

Klapper, J.T. *The Effects of Mass Media.* New York: Columbia Univer. Bureau of Applied Social Research, 1949. (Mimeo.)

Lazarsfeld, P.F., Berelson, B., and Gaudet, Hazel. *The People's Choice.* New York: Duell, Sloan, and Pearce, 1948.

Lipset, S.M., Lazarsfeld, P.F., Barton, A.H., and Linz, J. "The psychology of voting: An analysis of political behavior." In G. Lindzey (Ed.), *Handbook of Social Psychology.* Vol. II. *Special Fields and Applications.* Cambridge, Mass.: Addison-Wesley, 1954. Pp. 1124-1175.

Maccoby, Eleanor E. "Pitfalls in the analysis of panel data: A research note on some technical aspects of voting." *Amer. J. Sociol.,* 1956, 59, 359-362.

Riecken, H.W. (Chairman) "Narrowing the gap between field studies and laboratory experiments in social psychology: A statement by the summer seminar." *Items Soc. Sci. Res. Council,* 1954, 8, 37-42.

Sherif, M., and Sherif, Carolyn W. *Groups in Harmony and Tension: An Integration of Studies on Intergroup Relations.* New York: Harper, 1953.

Zimbardo, P.G. "Involvement and communication discrepancy as determinants of opinion change." Unpublished doctoral dissertation, Yale University, 1959.

Chapter 4, "Promise and Limitations of Laboratory Experiments in the Development of Attitude Change Theory," Karl E. Weick.

Barker. R.G. (Ed.). *Stream of Behavior.* New York: Appleton-Century-Crofts, 1963.

Barker. R.G., and Gump, P.V. *Big School, Small School.* Stanford, Calif.: Stanford Press, 1964.

Barker, R.G., and Wright, H.F. *Midwest and Its Children.* Evanston, Ill.: Row, Peterson, 1955.

Blake, R.R., and Brehm, J.W. "The use of tape recording to simulate a group atmosphere." *J. Abnorm. Soc. Psychol.,* 1954, 49, 311-313.

Braden, Marcia, and Walster, Elaine. "The effect of anticipated dissonance on pre-decision behavior." In L. Festinger (Ed.), *Conflict, Decision, and Dissonance.* Stanford, Calif.: Stanford Press, 1964, pp. 145-151.

Breer, P.E., and Locke, E.A. *Task Experience as a Source of Attitudes.* Homewood, Ill.: Dorsey, 1965.

Campbell, D.T., "Factors relevant to the validity of experiments in social settings." *Psychol. Bull.,* 1957, 54, 297-312.

Cartwright, D. "The effect of interruption, completion and failure upon the attractiveness of activities." *J. Exp. Psychol.,* 1942, 31, 1-16.

Cook. S.W., and Selltiz, Claire. "A multiple-indicator approach to attitude measurement." *Psychol. Bull.,* 1964, 62, 36-55.

Davis, J. "Study of 163 outstanding communist leaders." *Proc. Amer. Soc. Soc.,* 1930, 24, 42-55.

Ekman, P. "Differential communication of affect by head and body cues." *J. Pers. Soc. Psychol.,* 1965, 2, 726-735.

Festinger, L. "Behavioral support for opinion change." *Publ. Opin. Quart.,* 1964, 28, 404-417.

Festinger, L., and Maccoby, N. "On resistance to persuasive communications." *J. Abnorm. Soc. Psychol.,* 1964, 68, 359-366.

Freedman, J.L. "Long-term behavioral effects of cognitive dissonance." *J. Exp. Soc. Psychol.,* 1965, 1, 145-155.

Freedman, J.L., and Sears, D.O. "Selective exposure." In L. Berkowitz (Ed.), *Advances in Experimental Social Psychology,* 1965, Vol. 2. New York: Academic, pp. 57-97.

Friedman, N. "The psychological experiment as a social interaction." Unpublished doctoral dissertation, Harvard Univ., 1964.

Goldman-Eisler, Frieda. "Speech analysis and mental processes." *Lang. and Speech,* 1958, 1, 59-75.

Hall, E.T. *The Hidden Dimension.* Garden City, New York: Doubleday, 1966.

Hargreaves, W.A., and Starkweather, J.A. "Recognition of speaker identity." *Lang. and Speech,* 1963, 6 (2), 63-67.

Hoffman, L.R., and Maier, N.R.F., "Valence in the adoption of solutions by problem-solving groups: concept, method, and results." *J. Abnorm. Soc. Psychol.,* 1964, 69, 264-271.

Hovland, C.I. "Reconciling conflicting results derived from experimental and survey studies of attitudinal change." *Amer. Psychol.,* 1959, 14, 8-17.

Jones, E.E., and Thibaut, J.W. "Interaction goals as bases of inference in interpersonal perception." In R. Tagiuri and L. Petrullo (Eds.), *Person Perception and Interpersonal Behavior.* Stanford, Calif.: Stanford Press, 1958, pp. 151-178.

Kelman, H.C. "Compliance, identification, and internalization: three processes of attitude change." *J. Confl. Resolut.,* 1958, 2, 51-60.

Krout, M.H. "An experimental attempt to determine the significance of unconsious manual symbolic movements." *J. Gen. Psychol.,* 1954, 51, 121-152.

Leventhal, H., and Niles, Patricia. "A field experiment on fear arousal with data on the validity of questionnaire measures." *J. Pers.,* 1964, 32, 459-479.

McGuire, W.J. "A syllogistic analysis of cognitive relationships." In M.J. Rosenberg and C.I. Hovland (Eds.), *Attitude Organization and Attitude Change.* New Haven: Yale Univ. Press, 1960, pp. 65-111.

McGuire, W.J. "Inducing resistance to persuasion: some contemporary approaches." In L. Berkowitz (Ed.), *Advances in Experimental Social Psychology.* Vol. 1. New York: Academic, 1964, pp. 191-229.

Mahl, G.F. "Disturbances and silences in the patient's speech in psychotherapy." *J. Abrnom. Soc. Psychol.,* 1956, 53, 1-15.

Mausner, B. "The effect of prior reinforcement on the interaction of observer pairs." *J. Abnorm. Soc. Psychol.,* 1954, 49, 65-68.

Merton, R.K. *Social Theory and Social Structure.* (Rev. ed.) Glencoe, Ill.: Free Press, 1957.

Milgram, S., Mann, L., and Harter, Susan. "The lost-letter technique: a tool of social research." *Publ. Opin. Quart.,* 1965, 29, 437-438.

Miller, N. "Defaming and agreeing with the communicator as a function of communication extremity, emotional arousal, and evaluative set." Paper presented at Eastern Psychol. Assn.

Orne, M.T. "On the social psychology of the psychological experiment: with particular reference to demand characteristics and their implications." *Amer. Psychologist,* 1962, 17, 776-783.

Pittenger, R.E., Hockett, C.F., and Danehy, J.J. *The First Five Minutes: A Sample of Microscopic Interview Analysis.* Ithaca, New York: Paul Martineau, 1960.

Schachter, S., and Singer, J.E. "Cognitive, social and physiological determinants of emotional state." *Psychol. Rev.*, 1962, 69, 379-399.

Scheflen, A.E. "The significance of posture in communication systems." *Psychiatry*, 1964, 27, 316-331.

Schein, E.H., and Bennis, W.G. *Personal and Organizational Change Through Group Methods: The Laboratory Approach.* New York: Wiley, 1965.

Severin, F.T. (Ed.). *Humanistic Viewpoints in Psychology.* New York, McGraw-Hill, 1965.

Shepard, H.A. "Explorations in observant participations." In L.P. Bradford, J.R. Gibb, and K.D. Benne (Eds.), *T-Group Theory and Laboratory Method.* New York: Wiley, 1964, pp. 379-394.

Sherif, Carolyn W., Sherif, M., and Nebergall, R.E. *Attitude and Attitude Change: The Social Judgment-Involvement Approach.* Philadelphia: Saunders, 1965.

Sherif, M., Harvey, O.J., White, B.J., Hood, W.R., and Sherif, Carolyn W. *Intergroup Conflict and Cooperation: The Robbers Cave Experiment.* Norman, Okla.: Inst. of Group Relations, 1961.

Sommer, R., and Ross, H. "Social interaction in a geriatric ward." *Int. J. Soc. Psychol.*, 1958, 4, 128-133.

Soskin, W.F., and John, Vera P. "The study of spontaneous talk." In R.G. Barker (Ed.), *The Stream of Behavior.* New York: Appleton-Century-Crofts, 1963, pp. 228-281.

Temerlin, M.K. "On choice and responsibility in a humanistic psychotherapy." *J. Humanistic Psychol.*, 1963, 3, 35-48.

Thibaut, J.W., and Kelley, H.H. *The Social Psychology of Groups.* New York: Wiley, 1959.

Wallach, M.A., Kogan, N., and Bem, D.J. "Diffusion of responsibility and level of risk taking in groups." *J. Abnorm. Soc. Psychol.*, 1964, 68, 263-274.

Walster, Elaine. "The temporal sequence of post-decision processes." In L. Festinger (Ed.), *Conflict, Decision, and Dissonance.* Stanford, Calif.: Stanford Press, 1964, pp. 112-128.

Watson, G. *Social Psychology: Issues and Insights.* Philadelphia: Lippincott, 1966.

Webb, E.J., Campbell, D.T., Schwartz, R.D., and Sechrest, L. *Unobtrusive Measures: Nonreactive Research in the Social Sciences.* Chicago: Rand McNally, 1966.

Weick, K.E. "Reduction of cognitive dissonance through task enhancement and effort expenditure." *J. Abnorm. Soc. Psychol.*, 1964, 68, 533-539.

Weick, K.E. "Systematic observational methods." In G. Lindzey and

E. Aronson (Eds.), *Handbook of Social Psychology.* (Rev. ed.) Reading, Mass.: Addison-Wesley, 1966a.

Weick, K.E. "Task acceptance dilemmas: a site for research on cognition." In S. Feldman (Ed.), *Studies of Cognitive Interaction.* New York: Academic, 1966b.

Whittaker, J.O. "Parameters of social influence in the autokinetic situation." *Sociometry,* 1964, 27, 88-95.

Zajonc, R.B. "Social facilitation." *Science,* 1965, 149, 269-274.

Chapter 6, "A Program for Research on Experiments in Social Psychology," Henry W. Riecken.

Birney, R.C. "The achievement motive and task performance: a replication." *J. Abnorm. Soc. Psychol.,* 1958, 56, 133-135.

Sachs, E.L. "Intelligence scores as a function of experimentally established social relationships between child and examiner." *J. Abnorm. Soc. Psychol.,* 1952, 47, 354-358.

Goffman, E. *The Presentation of Self in Everyday Life.* New York: Doubleday (Anchor), 1959.

Kahn, R.L., and Cannel, C.F. *The Dynamics of Interviewing.* New York: Wiley, 1957.

Cook, Peggy. "Authoritarian or acquiescent: some behavioral differences." *Am. Psychologist,* 1958, 338 (Abstract).

Rosenthal, R. "Note on the fallible E." *Psychol. Rep.,* 1958a, 4, 662.

Rosenthal, R. "Projection, excitement and unconscious experimenter bias." *Am. Psychologist,* 1958b, 13, 345-346 (Abstract).

Orne, M.T. "The nature of hypnosis: artifact and essence." *J. Abnorm. Soc. Psychol.,* 1959, 58, 277-299.

Chapter 7, "Covert Communication in the Psychological Experiment," Robert Rosenthal.

Aronson, E., Carlsmith, J.M., and Darley, J.M. "The effects of expectancy on volunteering for an unpleasant experience." *Journal of Abnormal and Social Psychology,* 1963, 66, 220-224.

Bateson, G., Jackson, D.D., Haley, J., and Weakland, J.H. "Toward a theory of schizophrenia." *Behavioral Science,* 1956, 1, 251-264.

Carlsmith, J.M., and Aronson, E. "Some hedonic consequences of the confirmation and disconfirmation of expectancies." *J. Abnorm. Soc. Psychol.,* 1963, 66, 151-156.

Crowne, D.P., and Marlowe, D. *The Approval Motive.* New York: Wiley, 1964.

Friedman, N. "The psychological experiment as a social interaction." Unpublished doctoral dissertation, Harvard University, 1964.

Gordon, L.V., and Durea, M.A. "The effect of discouragement on the revised Stanford Binet Scale," *J. Genetic Psychol.*, 1948, 73, 201-207.

Harvey, O.J., and Clapp, W.F. "Hope, expectancy, and reactions to the unexpected." *J. Personality Soc. Psychol.*, 1965, 2, 45-52.

Hefferline, R.F. "Learning theory and clinical psychology—An eventual symbiosis?" In A.J. Bachrach (Ed.), *Experimental Foundations of Clinical Psychology.* New York: Basic Books, 1962, pp. 97-138.

Katz, R. "Body language: A study in unintentional communication." Unpublished doctoral dissertation, Harvard University, 1964.

Luft, J. "Interaction and projection." *J. Projective Techniques*, 1953, 17, 489-492.

Mills, T.M. "A sleeper variable in small groups research: The experimenter." *Pac. Soc. Rev.*, 1962, 5, 21-28.

Milmoe, S., Rosenthal, R., Blane, H.T., Chafetz, M.E., and Wolf, I. "The doctor's voice: Postdictor of successful referral of alcoholic patients." *J. Abnorm. Psychol.*, 1967, 72, 78-84.

Mintz, N. "On the psychology of aesthetics and architecture." Unpublished manuscript, Brandeis University, 1957.

Orne, M.T. "On the social psychology of the psychological experiment: With particular reference to demand characteristics and their implications." *Amer. Psychologist*, 1962, 17, 776-783.

Pfungst, O. *Clever Hans (The Horse of Mr. von Osten): A Contribution to Experimental, Animal, and Human Psychology.* (Trans. by C.L. Rahn) New York: Holt, 1911. (Republished: 1965)

Reece, M.M., and Whitman, R.N. "Expressive movements, warmth, and verbal reinforcements." *J. Abnorm. Soc. Psychol.*, 1962, 64, 234-236.

Riecken, H.W. "A program for research on experiments in social psychology." In N.F. Washburne (Ed.), *Decisions, Values and Groups.* Vol. 2. New York: Pergamon Press, 1962, pp. 25-41.

Rinquette, E.L., and Kennedy, T. "An experimental study of the double bind hypothesis." *J. Abnorm. Psychol.*, 1966, 71, 136-141.

Rosenthal, R. "The effect of the experimenter on the results of psychological research." In B.A. Maher (Ed.), *Progress in Experimental Personality Research.* Vol. 1. New York: Academic Press, 1964, pp. 79-114.

Rosenthal, R. *Experimenter Effects in Behavioral Research.* New York: Appleton-Century-Crofts, 1966.

Rosenthal, R., and Jacobson, L. "Teachers' expectancies: Determinants of pupils' IQ gains." *Psychol. Reports*, 1966, 19, 115-118.

Rosenthal, R., Kohn, P., Greenfield, P.M., and Carota, N. "Experimenters' hypothesis-confirmation and mood as determinants of experimental results." *Perceptual and Motor Skills,* 1965, 20, 1237-1252.

Rosenthal, R., Persinger, G.W., Mulry, R.C., Vikan-Kline, L., and Grothe, M. "Changes in experimental hypotheses as determinants of experimental results." *J. Projective Techniques and Personality Assessment,* 1964, 28, 465-469.

Rosenthal, R., Persinger, G.W., Mulry, R.C., Vikan-Kline, L., and Grothe, M. "Emphasis on experimental procedure, sex of subjects, and the biasing effects of experimental hypotheses." *J. Projective Techniques and Personality Assessment,* 1964, 28, 470-473.

Sampson, E.E., and Sibley, L.B. "A further examination of the confirmation or nonconfirmation of expectancies and desires." *J. Person. Soc. Psychol.,* 1965, 2, 133-137.

Sarason, I.G., "The human reinforcer in verbal behavior research." In L. Krasner and L.P. Ullman (Eds.), *Research in Behavior Modifications: New Developments and Implications.* New York: Holt, Rinehart & Winston, 1965, pp. 231-243.

Shapiro, J.L. "The effects of sex, instructional set, and the problem of awareness in a verbal conditioning paradigm." Unpublished master's thesis, Northwestern University, 1966.

Stevenson, H.W. "Social reinforcement of children's behavior." In L.P. Lipsitt and C.C. Spiker (Eds.), *Advances in Child Development and Behavior.* Vol. 2. New York: Academic Press, 1965, pp. 97-126.

Taylor, J.A. "A personality scale of manifest anxiety." *J. Abnorm. Soc. Psychol.,* 1953, 48, 285-290.

Chapter 8, "On the Social Psychology of the Psychological Experiment," Martin T. Orne.

Asch, S.E. *Social Psychology.* New York: Prentice Hall, 1952.

Brunswik, E. *Systematic and Representative Design of Psychological Experiments with Results in Physical and Social Perception.* (Syllabus Series, No. 304) Berkeley: Univer. California Press, 1947.

Damaser, Esther C., Shor, R.E., and Orne, M.T. "Physiological effects during hypnotically-requested emotions." *Int. J. Clin. Exp. Hypn.,* 1963.

Frank, J.D. "Experimental studies of personal pressure and resistance: I. Experimental production of resistance." *J. Gen. Psychol.,* 1944, 30, 23-41.

Orne, M.T. "The demand characteristics of an experimental design and their implications." Paper read at American Psychological Association, Cincinnati, 1959.

Orne, M.T. "The nature of hypnosis: Artifact and essence." *J. Abnorm. Soc. Psychol.*, 1959, 58, 277-299.

Pierce, A.H. "The subconscious again." *J. Phil., Psychol., Scient. Meth.*, 1908, 5, 246-271.

Riecken, H.W. "A program for research on experiments in social psychology." Paper read at Behavioral Sciences Conference, University of New Mexico, 1958.

Rosenthal, R. "On the social psychology of the psychological experiment: With particular reference to experimenter bias." Paper read at American Psychological Association, New York, 1961.

Sarbin, T.R. "Contributions to role-taking theory: I. Hypnotic behavior." *Psychol. Rev.*, 1950, 57, 255-270.

Shor, R.E. "Explorations in hypnosis: A theoretical and experimental study." Unpublished doctoral dissertation, Brandeis University, 1959.

Stare, F., Brown, J., and Orne, M.T. "Demand characteristics in sensory deprivation studies." Unpublished seminar paper, Massachusetts Mental Health Center and Harvard University, 1959.

Chapter 9, "Some Unintended Consequences of Rigorous Research," Chris Argyris.

Argyris, C. "Creating effective relationships in organizations." *Human Organization*, 1958, 17, 34-40.

Argyris, C. *Interpersonal Competence and Organizational Effectiveness.* Homewood, Ill.: Irwin, 1962.

Argyris, C. *Integrating the Individual and the Organization.* New York: Wiley, 1964.

Argyris, C. *Organization and Innovation.* Homewood, Ill.: Irwin, 1965.

Argyris, C. "Interpersonal barriers to decision making." *Harvard Business Review*, 1966, 44(2), 84-97.

Argyris, C. "Today's problems with tomorrow's organizations." *J. Management Studies*, 1967, 4(1), 31-55.

Barron, F. "Some studies of creativity at the Institute of Personality Assessment and Research." In H.A. Steiner (Ed.), *The Creative Organization.* Chicago, University of Chicago Press, 1965.

Bennis, W. *Changing Organizations.* New York: McGraw-Hill, 1966.

Brock, C., and Becker, L.A. "Debriefing and susceptibility to subsequent experimental maniuplation." *J. Exp. Soc. Psychol.*, 1966, 2, 314-323.

Burdick, E. *The Ninth Wave.* New York: Dell, 1957.

Edwards, A.L. "Experiments: Their planning and execution." In G. Lindzey (Ed.), *Handbook of Social Psychology*. Reading, Mass.: Addison-Wesley, 1954.

Friedman, N. *The Social Nature of Psychological Research*. New York: Basic Books, 1967.

Hyman, H.H., Cobb, W.J., Feldman, J.J., Hart, C.W., and Stember, C.H. *Interviewing in Social Research*. Chicago: University of Chicago Press, 1954.

Kelman, H.C. "The problem of deception in social psychological experiments." *Psychol. Bull.*, 1967, 67, 1-11.

Kiesler, C. "Group pressure and conformity." In J. Mills (Ed.), *Advanced Experimental Social Psychology*. New York: Macmillan, in press.

Meehl, P.E. "The creative individual: Why it is hard to identify him." In H.A. Steiner (Ed.), *The Creative Organization*. Chicago, University of Chicago Press, 1965.

Mills, T.M. "A sleeper variable in small groups research: The experimenter." *Pac. Sociol. Rev.*, 1962, 5, 21-28.

Orne, M.T. "On the social psychology of the psychology experiment; with particular reference to demand characteristics and their implications." *Amer. Psychol.*, 1962, 17, 776-783.

Rosenthal, R. "On the social psychology of the psychological experiment: The experimenter's hypotheses as unintended determinants of experimental results." *Amer. Scientist*, 1963, 51, 268-283.

Rosenthal, R. "Experimenter outcome-orientation and the results of the psychological experiment." *Psychol. Bull.*, 1964, 61, 405-412.

Rosenthal, R. *Experimenter Effects in Behavioral Research*. New York: Appleton-Century-Crofts, 1966.

Roth, J.A. "Hired hand research." *Amer. Sociologist*, 1966, 1, 190-196.

Sales, S.M. "Supervisory style and productivity: Review and theory." *Personnel Psychol.*, 1966, 19, 281-282.

von Neumann, J. *The Computer and the Brain*. New Haven: Yale University Press, 1958.

Chapter 10, "Dissemination of Experimental Information by Debriefed Subjects: What is Told to Whom, When," Paul L. Wuebben.

Aronson, E. "Avoidance of inter-subject communication." *Psychol. Reports*, 1966, 19, 238.

Campbell, D.T. "Factors relevant to the validity of experiments in social settings." *Psychol. Bull.*, 1957, 54, 297-312.

Carlson, R. "Where is the person in personality research?" *Psychol. Bull.*, 1971, 75, 203-219.

Denner, B. "Informers and their influence on the handling of illicit information." Paper read at the Midwest Psychological Association, Chicago, 1967.

Golding, S., and Lichtenstein, E. "Confession of awareness and prior knowledge of deception as a function of interview set and approval motivation." *J. Pers. Soc. Psychol.*, 1970, 14, 213-223.

Levy, L. "Awareness, learning and the beneficient subject as expert witness." *J. Pers. Soc. Psychol.*, 1967, 6, 363-370.

Lichtenstein, E. "Admission of prior information about deceptive experimental procedures." Unpublished manuscript, University of Oregon, 1968.

Lichtenstein, E. "Please don't talk to anyone about this experiment: Disclosure of deception by debriefed subjects." *Psychol. Reports*, 1970, 26, 485-486.

Rokeach, M., Zemach, R., and Norrell, G. "The pledge to secrecy: A method to assess violations." Paper read at American Psychological Association, 1966.

Schachter, S. *The Psychology of Affiliation.* Stanford University Press, 1959.

Schulman, G., and Freed, W. "Personal communication." Paper in preparation.

Schultz, D.P. "The human subject in psychological research." *Psychol. Bull.*, 1969, 72, 214-228.

Straits, B.C., and Wuebben, P.L. "College students' reactions to social scientific experimentation." *Sociol. Methods and Research*, 1973, 1, 355-386.

Stricker, L.J. "The true deceiver." *Psychol. Bull.*, 1967, 68, 13-20.

White, H.A., and Schumsky, D.A. "Prior information and awareness in verbal conditioning." *J. Pers. Soc. Psychol.*, 1972, 24, 162-165.

Wuebben, P.L. "Honesty of subjects and birth order." *J. Pers. Soc. Psychol.*, 1967, 5, 350-352.

Wuebben, P.L. "Experimental design, measurement, and human subjects: A neglected problem of control." *Sociometry*, 1968, 31, 89-101.

Wuebben, P.L. "The social context of experiments: Subjects' 'illicit' post-experimental communications; methodological implications." Paper read at Pacific Sociological Association, Seattle, 1969.

Wuebben, P.L., Straits, B.C., and Crowle, A. "Confession of prior knowledge of deceptive experimental procedures as a function of evaluation apprehension and commitment." Paper in preparation.

Chapter 11, "Awareness, Learning, and the Beneficent Subject
as Expert Witness," Leon H. Levy.

Adams, J.K. "Laboratory studies of behavior without awareness."
Psychol. Bull., 1957, 54, 383-405.

Buck, R. "Comments on Buchwald's 'verbal utterances as data." In
H. Feigl and G. Maxwell (eds.), *Current Issues in the Philosophy of
Science.* New York: Holt, Rinehart & Winston, 1961, pp. 468-472.

Campbell, D.T., and Fiske, D.W. "Convergent and discriminant validation by the multitrait-multimethod matrix." *Psychol. Bull.,* 1959,
56, 81-105.

Chronback, L.J., and Meehl, P.E. "Construct validity in psychological
tests." *Psychol. Bull.,* 1955, 52, 281-302.

Dulany, D.E. "Hypotheses and habits in verbal 'operant conditioning'."
J. Abnorm. Soc. Psychol., 1961, 63, 251-263.

Dulany, D.E. "The place of hypotheses and intentions: An analysis of
verbal control in verbal conditioning." In C. Eriksen (Ed.), *Behavior
and Awareness—A Symposium of Research and Interpretation.*
Durham, N.C.: Duke University Press, 1962, pp. 102-129.

Edwards, A.L. *Experimental Design in Psychological Research.* New
York: Rinehart, 1960.

Farber, I.E. "The things people say to themselves." *Amer. Pschol.,*
1963, 18, 185-197.

Garner, W.R., Hake, H.W., and Eriksen, C.W. "Operationism and the
concept of perception." *Psychol. Rev.,* 1956, 63, 149-159.

Krasner, L. "Studies of the conditioning of verbal behavior." *Psychol.
Bull.,* 1958, 55, 148-171.

Krasner, L. "The therapist as a social reinforcement machine." In H.H.
Strupp and L. Luborsky (Eds.), *Research in Psychotherapy.* Vol. 2,
Washington, D.C.: American Psychological Association, 1962, pp.
61-94.

Levin, S.M. "The effects of awareness on verbal conditioning." *J.
Exper. Psychol.,* 1961, 61, 67-75.

Orne, M.T. "On the social psychology of the psychological experiment:
With particular reference to demand characteristics and their implications." *Amer. Psychol.,* 1962, 17, 776-783.

Postman, L., and Sassenrath, J.M. "The automatic action of verbal
rewards and punishments." *J. Gen. Psychol.,* 1961, 65, 109-136.

Spielberger, C.D. "The role of awareness in verbal conditioning." In
C.W. Eriksen (Ed.), *Behavior and Awareness—A Symposium of Research and Interpretation.* Durham, N.C.; Duke University Press,
1962, pp. 71-101.

Spielberger, C.D. "Theoretical and epistemological issues in verbal conditioning." In S. Rosenberg (Ed.), *Directions in Psycholinguistics.* New York: Macmillan, 1965, pp. 149-200.

Spielberger, C.D., and Levin, S.M. "What is learned in verbal conditioning?" *Journal of Verbal Learning and Verbal Behavior,* 1962, 1, 125-132.

Taffel, C. "Anxiety and the conditioning of verbal behavior." *J. Abnorm. Soc. Psychol.,* 1955, 51, 496-501.

Thorndike, E.L. *The Fundamentals of Learning.* New York: Teachers College, 1932.

Verplanck, W.S. "Unaware of where's awareness. Some verbal operants—notates, monents, annotants." In C. W. Eriksen (ed.), *Behavior and awareness—a symposium of research and interpretation.* Durham N.C.: Duke University Press, 1962, pp. 130-158.

Williams, J.H. "Conditioning of verbalization: A review." *Psychol. Bull.,* 1964, 62, 383-393.

Chapter 13, "When Dissonance Fails: On Eliminating Evaluation Apprehension from Attitude Measurement," Milton J. Rosenberg.

Brehm, J.W. "A dissonance analysis of attitude-discrepant behavior." In M.J. Rosenberg, C.I. Hovland, W.J. McGuire, R.P. Abelson, and J.W. Brehm, *Attitude Organization and Change.* New Haven: Yale Univer. Press, 1960, pp. 164-197.

Brehm, J.W., and Cohen, A.R. *Explorations in Cognitive Dissonance.* New York: Wiley, 1962.

Carlson, E.R. "Attitude change and attitude structure." *J. Abnorm. Soc. Psychol.,* 1956, 52, 256-261.

Chapanis, Natalia P., and Chapanis, A.C. "Cognitive dissonance: Five years later." *Psychol. Bull.,* 1964, 61, 1-22.

Cohen, A.R., Brehm, J.W., and Fleming, W.H. "Attitude change and justification for compliance." *J. Abnorm. Soc. Psychol.,* 1958, 56, 276-278.

Crowne, D.P., and Marlowe, D. "A new scale of social desirability independent of psychopathology." *J. Consult. Psychol.,* 1960, 24, 349-354.

Culbertson, F.M. "Modification of an emotionally held attitude through role playing." *J. Abnorm. Soc. Psychol.,* 1957, 54, 230-233.

Edwards, A.L. *The Social Desirability Variable in Personality Assessment and Research.* New York: Dryden Press, 1957.

Festinger, L., and Carlsmith, J.M. "Cognitive consequences of forced compliance." *J. Abnorm. Soc. Psychol.,* 1959, 58, 203-210.

Janis, I.L., and King, B.T. "The influence of role playing on opinion change." *J. Abnorm. Soc. Psychol.,* 1954, 49, 211-218.

Kelman, H.C. "Attitude change as a function of response restriction." *Human Relations*, 1953, 6, 185-214.

Lawrence, D.H., and Festinger, L. *Deterrents and Reinforcement: The Psychology of Insufficient Reward.* Stanford: Stanford Univer. Press, 1962.

Lewin, K. *Dynamic Theory of Personality.* New York: McGraw-Hill, 1935.

Mosteller, F., and Bush, R.R. "Selected quantitative techniques." In G. Lindzey (Ed.), *Handbook of Social Psychology.* Vol. 1. *Theory and Method.* Cambridge, Mass.: Addison-Wesley, 1954, pp. 289-334.

Orne, M.T. "On the social psychology of the psychological experiment: With particular reference to demand characteristics and their implications." *Amer. Psychologist*, 1962, 17, 776-783.

Riecken, H.W. "A program for research on experiments in social psychology." In N.F. Washburne (Ed.), *Decisions, Values and Groups.* Vol. 2. New York: Pergamon Press, 1962, pp. 25-41.

Rosenberg, M.J. "Cognitive structure and attitudinal affect." *J. Abnorm. Soc. Psychol.*, 1956, 53, 367-372.

Rosenberg, M.J. "An analysis of affective-cognitive consistency." In M.J. Rosenberg, C.I. Hovland, W.J. McGuire, R.P. Abelson, and J.W. Brehm, *Attitude Organization and Change.* New Haven: Yale Univer. Press, 1960, pp. 15-64.

Rosenberg, M.J. "A research program on consistency and change in social attitudes." Columbus: Ohio State University, 1961. (Mimeo)

Rosenberg, M.J. "Simulated man and the humanistic criticism." In S.S. Tomkins and S.J. Messick (Eds.), *Computer Simulation of Personality.* New York: Wiley, 1963, pp. 113-124.

Rosenthal, R. "On the social psychology of the psychological experiment: The experimenter's hypothesis as unintended determinant of experimental results." *Amer. Scientist*, 1963, 15, 268-283.

Scott, W.A. "Attitude change through reward of verbal behavior." *J. Abnorm. Soc. Psychol.*, 1957, 55, 72-75.

Scott, W.A. "Attitude change by response reinforcement: Replication and extension." *Sociometry*, 1959, 22, 328-335.

Thomas, W.I., and Znaniecki, F. *The Polish Peasant in Europe and America.* Boston: Badger, 1918. 5 vols.

Index